Eclipse in Mission

Eclipse in Mission

Dispelling the Shadow of Our Idols

Rob Goodwin

RESOURCE *Publications* • Eugene, Oregon

ECLIPSE IN MISSION
Dispelling the Shadow of Our Idols

Copyright © 2012 Rob Goodwin. All rights reserved. Except for brief quotations in critical publications or reviews, no part of this book may be reproduced in any manner without prior written permission from the publisher. Write: Permissions, Wipf and Stock Publishers, 199 W. 8th Ave., Suite 3, Eugene, OR 97401.

Resource Publications
An Imprint of Wipf and Stock Publishers
199 W. 8th Ave., Suite 3
Eugene, OR 97401
www.wipfandstock.com

ISBN 13: 978-4-61097-902-3

Manufactured in the U.S.A.

All scripture quotations, unless otherwise indicated, are taken from the Holy Bible, New International Version®, NIV®. Copyright ©1973, 1978, 1984 by Biblica, Inc.™ Used by permission of Zondervan. All rights reserved worldwide.

To my family, as we journey on together

Contents

Preface ix
Abbreviations xv

    1   Introduction 1

Part I DECONSTRUCTION: Critique of modern mission

    2   Mission in History 17

    3   The Contemporary Practice of Mission 30

    4   Influence of the 'Great Commission' 50

    5   Modernity's Impact 71

    6   Linguistic and Hermeneutical Considerations 101

    7   Simplistic Doctrines 115

    8   Summary and Conclusion to Part I 123

Part II RECONSTRUCTION:
          Ontology—a Right Foundation for Mission

    9   Preliminary Thoughts on 'Ontology' 129

   10   Schleiermacher: The Priority of Being 138

   11   Postliberals: Pointing Us Back to Basics 150

   12   Engaging with the Other 160

   13   The Age-Old Essence of Orthodoxy 184

   14   Ontology in Other Core Aspects of Christian Yhought 205

PART III RESOLUTION & CONCLUSION: Christian Mission

   15   Mission: the Christian Life 223

Bibliography 263

Preface

EVERYONE HAS HEARD ABOUT 'Zimbabwe' and the atrocities of governance perpetrated in that land, but many are unable to comprehend just what it means to have lived under its various regimes, or even to have had to leave 'home' and to exist, now, as displaced people—all somewhere (if we are fortunate enough to be 'out' of there) in the global 'Diaspora'.

However, life 'in' Zimbabwe is the context of this writing, which has happened despite the plight of fellow country-men, women and children who live (yes: even today in the twenty-first century!) still, under merciless oppression, sham and deceit, where law and order do not exist, and where corruption in places of power and administration has become the 'norm'. All of us, at one time or another, have had to get used to doing without, or have had to 'make a plan' (many plans!) in order to get the necessities of life. Being here, in foreign lands, is just one of those necessary steps in the process of survival!

Instead of the 'normal' route of theological development (writing articles, attending conferences, and growing in scholarship), this work has developed whilst sitting (even sleeping) in queues: for petrol, for bread, for money; it has happened alongside farming land, growing chickens, rearing cattle (ok, not in a big way, but in order to help make ends meet). It has been formed in response to the lives and experiences of loved ones, over decades: some killed in cold blood, back in the eighties (a whole community who had given their lives to build relationships in post-war Zimbabwe and to feed the broader rural community); others maimed, raped, murdered, abducted, beaten-up, killed by stress and trauma, and driven from homes—families having been split, marriages shattered, and communities blown throughout the world.

This work has involved studying in the West (for lack of adequate institutions back home) and then contextualising those perspectives back into African thought and reality with its blatant distortions of democracy and the intense, personified evil that dwells in the hearts and lives of so many in our land: its atrocities, tragedies, human rights abuses, tortures, unjust imprisonments, naked fear, ruined lives, and the desperate inhumanities meted out against millions of innocent—not to mention the effects of the AIDS epidemic on everyday society.

It has also benefitted from good times and wonderful things as well: having first-hand witness to intensely heroic braveries, saintly love, golden relationships forged through hardship, quality conversations, people and places; even just the climate, flora and fauna of my home country; conversation and story; courage, endurance and defeat; triumph of good over evil; direct perceptions of Jesus Christ, raised from the dead: alive two millennia later, encountering and leading Christian people by His Spirit, throughout our land.

From out of this context, then, a solid realisation: that all people are evil, not just those who are obviously so. Fault is in all of us, and comes from our own self-love, in the place of God. That's what He Himself has clearly shown the world. So the blame is to be levelled at everyone, to a greater or lesser extent—sadly not just those in political, but also church leadership; and ourselves. We all need to keep putting God first; we are all destitute without the saving love of God and gracious guidance of the Holy Spirit; only in Christ, forgiven in Him—reborn in Him, can we accept each other, and seek to go forward under His forgiving grace.

But against this background, too, an observation—a confession perhaps:

When we read other authors, different aspects of what they say strike us in different ways, which often depend upon where we at ourselves, in our own thinking and in relation to the issues that we are grappling with at the time. I confess openly to having used the authors and works that I have done, here, in this very way—to having picked up on particular aspects of the thought of those mentioned herein, in such a way as to give me vocabulary to express what I have. Unfortunately I cannot allege to having heard them accurately, and I am in no way claiming to represent them either comprehensively or even correctly, though of course I have endeavoured to, despite the blinkers that I wear, and I apologise unconditionally in advance for any occasion where I have not. The context of Western scholarship, I have found, is poles apart from the grassroots 'scholarship' that I have had to engage in, in my own experience; this is just the way things are—these are simply the two sides of the table we happen to sit at—but my hope has been to engage these two worlds proactively in order for each to hear and learn from the other: so that both may be enriched through the 'contemplation' of this work (contemplation', for this is more than just a thesis—it is an appreciation of what God has done and who He is in the world).

So, my prayer is that the use I have made of various scholars or theological positions will in no way have detracted from, or added to their thought. If it has, one reason may be the 'stretch' involved in tackling such a multidisciplinary subject: this work encompasses biblical and systematic theology, exegesis, hermeneutics, linguistics, epistemology and missiology—to name but a few. More significant though, I think, is the different contexts that we inhabit, as I have tried to explain.

Beyond the issue of context, further, there are at least four reasons for proceeding to put this work into print.

First, as mentioned briefly by way of introduction below, I write from an awareness of 'mission' that has developed through my formative years—from a burden which, as expressed in this work, has continued to ring true throughout my years growing up in Africa, through until today.

Second, God seemed to clarify the issue enough for it to be accepted as a thesis for doctoral research some fifteen years ago. 'Answers' were not easy: I felt that I wrestled through my research not just with scholarship but with things of eternity, in order to give adequate expression to them. They should merit listening to.

Third, my propositions here have continued to burn true not just in my own thinking: they have been validated, as it were, by those to whom I have been privileged to teach, and with whom I have been able to rethink this subject matter time and again, back in Zimbabwe. These special people, who are in many ways my 'book', have often encouraged me to publish, and to share my thinking.

More, fourthly, the perspectives gained through this work have been formative and freeing in my own life. I could not even begin to tell the story of what they have involved for me and for my primary source of fellowship, encouragement and growth in Christ—my wife and children (though I have already said enough for you to imagine): the miles, countries and cultures the Lord has taken us through in just one lifetime; the avenues of ministry, pain, and abandonment we have endured through the course of a 'normal' Christian life; yet also the hours and years of belonging in Christ together that we have enjoyed as sojourners in the world through which God has been leading us, day by day and year by year.

For at least these reasons, it seems more than appropriate to share my thoughts with a wider fellowship of believers.

Some may have the impression of this being a dated work, perhaps old-fashioned in a way: a work of the 90s, or even earlier. But the problem being addressed is not a new one, and so older voices (unheard, or misunderstood before now) are as appropriate as when first spoken. More, the solution being proposed is far older than our realisations of any problems: it concerns timeless truths that God has been making known to the world about Himself, not just since the earthly time of Christ, but from the very beginning of bible times. Against this timeframe, words from the 70s, or the 50s or even centuries back are as appropriate to today as when they were first heard.

In all this, the argument I present in what follows is simple yet profound, though I hope not simplistic. But because of its profound simplicity I see it to be a key gospel issue which, like other things of gospel significance, will often be 'seen and seen, yet misunderstood' by most.

So my challenge to all who read (even just introductions and conclusions of) this book is equally simple (and it is a continuing challenge to myself, as much as to all of us): to hear what is trying to be expressed (about a timeless reality and an alternative framework for, and understanding of Christian mission); to rethink the authenticity of our own understandings about God as He has revealed Himself to us undeserving people; to hone relationship with this true and living God in a fresh and genuine way (on our knees and in our hearts before Him to consolidate or renew fellowship with Him) that is critical of our presuppositions, and open to truth that belongs and resides beyond ourselves; having done this, to grapple over and again with the implications of that fellowship with God in appropriate and diverse ways, as our contexts determine.

This said then, my first and forever thanks must go to my family: for their trust and joy in the Lord in following me through often desperately unclear and uncertain ways together. Thanks must also go to all who have taught and nurtured me, and have helped me to keep grasping after truth as only Christ has made it known. Thanks, too, to my publishers: for their willingness to adapt to a work and style more suited to my context, and for their professionalism, expertise and assistance throughout the publishing phase.

But then of course ultimate thanks belong to our loving and living Lord, who has offered life to a dying world at the cost of His own life.

For to this we can attest through it all, and because of this we entrust ourselves to Him for the future: His absolute faithfulness and constant presence and provision, despite ourselves.

My desire is, as these pages are turned, that the good news of Christ's death on our behalf will be heard as I once heard it: echoing through cool hallways of Matobo-hill boulders; that the stories of Jesus and His love will resound again as I once listened to them, in the crackling of dry mukwa-wood fires and stories told and songs sung by those gathered around them in His name; and, most, that a revelatory understanding—such as one would enjoy when sipping that first fresh brew of thirst-quenching tea in the shade of a granite kopje—will saturate the reader as he or she considers what is written here, and as they are confronted anew by the 'old, old' truth that the life of Jesus Christ should be basic to how we go into each day of ours, here on earth: that the 'norms' of our perspectives should be Him, and His way of seeing things and the life and reality of the Kingdom of God that He has welcomed us into by His Holy Spirit, and enabled and taught and nurtured us into by being born again in Him: born from above.

In view of this, my prayer is for things that eclipse a true sending by the Father, Son and Holy Spirit—true mission—to become things of the past: forgotten because of the blinding illumination brought by the full Being of God to all who would put Him on the throne of their lives, instead of themselves.

May all who ponder these pages be refreshed by an encounter with the living Lord, and led by Him in an appropriate outworking of that relationship!

Rob Goodwin
March 2012

Abbreviations

Old Testament Books

Genesis	Ge.
Exodus	Ex.
Leviticus	Le.
Numbers	Nu.
Deuteronomy	De.
Joshua	Js.
Judges	Jdg.
Ruth	Ru.
Samuel 1&2	1Sa./2Sa.
Kings 1&2	1Ki./2Ki.
Chronicles 1&2	1Ch./2Ch.
Ezra	Er.
Nehemiah	Ne.
Esther	Es.
Job	Jb.
Psalms	Ps.
Proverbs	Pr.
Ecclesiastes	Ec.
Song of Songs	SS.
Isaiah	Is.
Jeremiah	Je.
Lamentations	La.
Ezekiel	Ek.
Daniel	Da.
Hosea	Ho.
Joel	Jl.

Amos	Am.
Obadiah	Ob.
Jonah	Jh.
Micah	Mi.
Nahum	Na.
Habakkuk	Hb.
Zephaniah	Zp.
Haggai	Hg.
Zechariah	Zc.
Malachi	Ml.

New Testament Books

Matthew	Mt.
Mark	Mk.
Luke	Lk.
John	Jn.
Acts	Ac.
Romans	Ro.
Corinthians 1&2	1Co./2Co.
Galatians	Ga.
Ephesians	Ep.
Philippians	Php.
Colossians	Co.
Thessalonians 1&2	1Th./2Th.
Timothy 1&2	1Ti./2Ti.
Titus	Ti.
Philemon	Phm.
Hebrews	He.
James	Ja.
Peter 1&2	Pe.
John 1,2&3	1Jn./2Jn./3Jn.
Jude	Jde.
Revelation	Re.

Chapter 1

Introduction

Born and brought up in Africa, the good and bad of mission was as clear and real to us as the sunlight and shadows that breathed life into our African bush.

High times were when missionary friends swept in from out of the dark night smelling of diesel, heat and sweat, with stories of wild animals, flooded rivers, broken down trucks, and tyres punctured by bayonet acacia thorns, but most of all with stories of the sweet gospel of Jesus Christ that had the power to turn hearts away from fear and witchcraft, to a God of love. We would listen to these stories deep into the night, warm tongues of fire licking at scented wood branches in the fireplace, and the warmer-still joy of the work of the Holy Spirit in people's hearts and lives burning fresh in our own.

On the down side, a clash of worlds; different value systems between the missionary and ourselves: their deified cultures; exonerated systems; lavish budgets; exotic treats; forever conferences; unexplainably long home-leaves; preferential treatment; superficial involvement; and yet surprisingly, underneath it all, a confusing discontent and angst, often, over what had been their choice in the first place to have had to 'suffer'!

Of course I am generalising.

But it gives a brief, first-hand feel for the mixed blessing of mission, certainly as experienced by a little African boy (though these perceptions have since then simply been 'coloured in' or matured, rather than changed).

In a way, all that follows is a life-response to both of these very real perspectives of appreciation of, and yet frustration with modern mission.

First, as a tribute, it should rightly be regarded as an expression of gratitude to those who bore the gospel to often hostile soils, including my own heart. Clearly, battles have been fought and won in the heavenlies in the name of mission, and no offense is intended against the warriors who have given up lives and loved ones to its cause. On the contrary: if this is an appropriate place to honour those saints, then in the name of the integrity and truth for which they have stood, and the Person to whom they witnessed, this work is dedicated to their efforts and lives, and to the One for whom they lived and for whom so many have died.

Second though, as an investigation, a deep desire for integrity in the Christian church makes this also a response to the perception that all may not be right in mission(s) despite the vastness and seemingly unquestionable existence of the enterprise.

Important to note: this perception of irresolution in mission is not just a personal one—indeed it is not a new concept at all. It is a phenomenon referred to in a number of different ways using words like 'problem' or 'tension' (tempered to 'creative tension' by some) or even 'crisis'.

Factors Surrounding the Crisis in Christian Mission

Although once (as 'recently' as in 1952, before the Willingen World Missionary Conference) there was consensus on the understanding of mission as evangelism (Moreau 2000a:636), rumbles of dissatisfaction have been audible since then, although they have often been ignored.

Various people expressed this unease concerning mission in the publishing of books whose titles told of their concern. Harvey Conn (1983:3), for example, listed: *Missions: Which Way?* and *Shaken Foundations* (Peter Beyerhaus 1971 and 1972); *Christian Missions and the Judgement of God* (David Paton 1964); *The Unpopular Missionary* (Ralph Dodge 1964); *The Ugly Missionary* (John Carden 1964); *Missionary, Go Home!* (James Scherer 1964); *Missions in a Time of Testing* (R.K. Orchard 1964); *Missions in Crisis* (Arthur Glasser and Eric Fife 1961); and *Missions at the Crossroads* (T. Stanley Soltau 1954).

Peter Hamm (1972: Online) mentioned other titles, like: *Revolution in Missions* (Blaise Levai 1957); *Protestant Crossroads in Missions: the Ecumenical-Conservative Encounter* (Norman A. Horner 1968); *The Missionary Between the Times* (R. Pierce Beaver 1968); *Missionary, Come

Back! (Arden Almquist 1970); and *Missions in Creative Tensions: The Greenlake '71 Compendium* (Vergil Gerber 1971).

The last of these titles reflects a more public, formal representation of the crisis. The 'EFMA-IFMA conference at Green Lake, Wisconsin,' wrote Hamm (*ibid.*), was an occasion 'in which 406 mission executives, missions professors, pastors, and national representatives met to grapple with crucial issues relating to church-mission relations.' A year earlier, in Europe, a document had been published, entitled the *1970 Frankfurt Declaration on the Fundamental Crisis in Christian Mission* (though the nature of the crisis was not adequately represented or responded to in it). In Africa, the following year, John Gatu of Kenya (then General Secretary of the Presbyterian Church in East Africa) made his landmark call for a moratorium on the sending of foreign missionaries (featured in the April 1974 edition of the *International Review of Mission*).

These may appear to be out-of-date references to a dated problem, but not much had changed by the time South African missiologist David Bosch discoursed openly about this crisis by way of introduction to his *Transforming Mission* (1991). His contribution was positive: he proposed there that a 'crisis' should be understood not just in terms of danger but in terms of opportunity. But crisis there still clearly was!

All was still not right with mission!

And not much has changed since then. In fact, even less has been said in response to this crisis in the intervening years.

One reason for this could be that the problem of mission has never been adequately defined. It is always much easier to suggest solutions to perceived problems without properly hearing or determining what that problem is. In view of this, a key principle of 'problem solving' in the field of Business Studies has been formalised: that in order to solve a problem one should first define that problem!

This is exactly what appears not to have happened with this particular problem of 'mission'. The problem was never adequately determined and yet (despite inadequate definition) two major developments were still made in response to the perceived crisis in mission in the second half of last century (so Moreau 2000a:636).

The first of these was the (re)introduction of the concept of *Missio Dei*, at Willingen in 1952, which gave the particular stress that mission was something broader than just the activities of the church. The mission of God, in other words, was taking place outside of the established church and it was important, therefore, not to deny 'secular' work (such as feed-Aid programmes) as a valid part of God's mission.

Second, was the significant dropping of 's' from missions (as evidenced in 1970 by the change of the name of the periodical: *International Review of Missions* [plural] to the *International Review of Mission* [singular]).

Both these developments arose from one essential debate: whether Christian mission was about evangelism or social action or both (*ibid.*:637–8). This debate appears to have been the most significant formal response to the issue of crisis from the time of Willingen. But neither this, nor any other responses to the 'problem' ever arrived, nor even claimed to have arrived at a solution. For example Hamm (1972: Online) wrote that the above-mentioned conference at Green Lake, Wisconsin 'did not [even] pretend to find the solutions to the problems.'

More significant than any responses or posited solutions or developments, is that they themselves appear to have overshadowed the actual problem! The crisis in mission that was identified so long ago has all these years been eclipsed by a pseudo-understanding of what mission is and of what the problem back then was perceived to have been about, and by secondary responses to those perceptions.

In view of this, it is being suggested here that the crisis in question is far greater and deeper than the likes of a mere need for humanitarian awareness and involvement (even a need to deal positively with church/mission relationships), or a need for evangelism. It is being proposed that the crisis in mission has still not yet been adequately defined or (therefore) adequately addressed. This, in turn, has distorted the church's understanding and practice of 'mission' up to this point in its history.

Just a number of issues amongst many others that will remain unmentioned are sufficient to show the multifaceted makeup of this crisis.

Mission's Association with Colonial Expansion

The crisis in mission appears to be linked at least in part to its association with and (at times) apparent participation in colonial expansion in modern times.

A classic illustration of this attitude is the difference between black and white perceptions of mission in South Africa as noted for example by missiologist Willem Saayman. He suggested (1994:17) that a white perception of modern mission is of heroism, self-denial, endurance and sacrifice, in 'bringing light to darkest Africa,' and that a black perception of it, in contrast, is of it having brought not light but a 'jungle of western capitalism' (*ibid.*).

The gospel had come wrapped in the culture of Western individualism.

These contrasting perceptions are a commonly sketched dichotomy as reflected in, for example, Brian Stanley's *The Bible and the Flag* (1990), and Stephen Neill's *Colonialism and Christian Missions* (1966).

The issues of 'guilt' and 'blame' are complex and do need to be addressed. At least in part, here, this can start to be done by examining the authenticity of the meaning and practice of modern mission.

The Problem in Relation to Changing People Groups

Another major contributor to the crisis is that whereas once it was easy to distinguish between 'saved' and 'unsaved' people through simple reference to the people group or geographical region to which certain individuals belonged, those once clear and easy boundaries have in many respects faded through the emergence of the global community.

Boundaries of 'faith' have become difficult things to determine. In the West, for example, expressions of faith have become so liberal as to infuriate bishops of the developing nations in the South. Although the following figures (comparing 2010 with a hundred years earlier, 1910) are arguably optimistic, and although statistics like this are difficult to determine at the best of times, professions of Christianity in Europe have been recorded as having dropped from 95 percent to 80 percent of the total population, and in North America from 96 percent to 81 percent of the same (as tabled by Johnson, Barrett and Crossing 2010:31).

In contrast, professions of faith have increased in the majority of other continents. The most marked of these is Africa, where professions of Christianity are up to 48 percent of the total population from 9 percent just a hundred years earlier (*ibid.*:33).

It is this global shift that prompted missiologist Andrew Walls to comment that Christianity was now a 'predominantly non-Western religion' (1996:xix). It is also almost certainly this same shift which prompted Gatu's moratorium call, and African theologian John Mbiti to comment that 'the spreading of Christianity [in Africa] has now gained its own momentum' (1986:12).

The former 'sending' nations, in contrast, have been experiencing loss of faith and a hardening of heart caused by consumerism, materialism and socio-economic affluence. Christianity is regarded not so much as about truth out there but choice within. 'The autonomous human being is . . . in the center—with total freedom of choice' (Newbigin 1986:15). Theology itself is 'just one of the many choices in an arts or humanities faculty curriculum in secular universities . . . in stark contrast to its origins' (D'Costa 1996:341).

So in terms of the statistics cited here, it appears that the West needs 'missionary' attention because of its lapsing professions of Christianity; and it appears that the Third World needs 'missionary' attention because it still has a smaller percentage professing faith than in Europe. But these are only perceptions insofar as 'mission' is currently and popularly understood in the West—because there are, now, like-minded Christians within individual people groups, globally, who can 'talk' about the Christian faith to their own people and in their own way. As a result, there may not be the same overt need for cross-cultural outreach or expansion that there once was. The issue of 'foreign boundaries' is a far more subtle one, now. And so, because of this, the question of the identity of mission has rightly come to the fore.

Dependency

The Third World fears becoming (or is already often resentful over being) dependent on the sending West for everything.

If, for example, the West is available to come out to a developing country to set up theological colleges (which—run in the Western style—are probably a luxury) and schools and hospitals (which both require trained, paid staff who are near impossible to source), then recipients of Western 'favour' and input end up with little choice but to receive with open arms.

The result, however, is that they are immediately dependent on the West for resources to fuel those Western systems. They become subservient to the West and its initiatives: their mindset, their values, their programmes and, in short, the tune of the pipe that they play which has to be danced to. Thus, 'local' initiatives end up as Western-style projects with (more often than not) Western Board Members directing local affairs in a Western way, from afar.

Back in 1971, Emerito P. Nacpil (then president of the Union Theological Seminary near Manila, Philippines) told a gathering of church leaders and missionaries in Asia that under the conditions that existed at the time, a partnership between Asian and Western churches could 'only be a partnership between the weak and the strong . . . [implying] the continued dependence of the weak upon the strong and the continued dominance of the strong over the weak' (cited by Anderson 1974: Online). Anderson himself (*ibid.*) commented: 'The missionary today . . . is a symbol of the universality of Western imperialism among the rising generations of the Third World. Therefore I believe that the present structure of modern missions is dead. And . . . we ought . . . to eulogize it and then bury it . . . In other words, the most *missionary* service a missionary under the present system can do today in Asia is to go home.'

Similarly, Father Paul Verghese, a former associate General Secretary of the World Council of Churches (also cited in Anderson *ibid.*) wrote this: 'Today it is economic imperialism or neo-colonialism that is the pattern of missions. Relief agencies and mission boards control the younger churches through purse strings. Foreign finances, ideas and personnel still dominate the younger churches and stifle their spontaneous growth . . . So now I say, the mission of the church is the greatest enemy of the gospel.'

In its zeal to be active in mission, the West has created a dependency which has become a deep seated issue and an endemic reality in most receiving churches. As a result, 'The mission of the church is the greatest enemy of the gospel' (*op. cit.*)! These are terrifying words, and they demand a thorough theological, biblical response and investigation into the identity of authentic mission.

Short-Term Missionaries

A more recent expression of the crisis in mission is the phenomenon of the short-term missionary (STM). Anthropologist Brian Howell discussed this in relation to the '1,600,000 adults and young people from the United States [who] travel abroad yearly on short-term mission trips, most for two weeks or less duration' (2009:206). The understanding of 'mission' that has developed as a result is that of 'a kind of sacrificial availability for carrying out an assigned task and a lack of connection to any particular place' (*ibid.*:207). It appears that 'a whole industry has developed to service groups who understand that their faith in Christ is calling them to visit another part of the world' (so Koll 2010:93). It did not matter where or to whom people were going, as long as they were able to meet need, and to serve in their short field trip.

Mission is, for the 'STM-er,' about "'bringing" something to a place where there was some demonstrable lack . . . meeting needs or accomplishing projects, every trip, regardless of destination' (Howell 2009:207). It has become 'a movement from plenty to want, from have to have-not, from wealth to poverty . . . "plight-based ministry"' (*ibid.*). Features of short-term mission include 'the slide show . . . power point presentations' and what Howell (paralleling an uninvolved tourist perspective at a holiday resort) refers to as the 'missionary gaze' (*ibid.*) on a world so diversely other than their own!

Short term mission is about sharing Christ and the gospel, rather than about getting to know the culture or people that is being visited (*ibid.*:208), or about 'listening' (Koll 2010:96). Focus is more on the gifts of the individual STM-er, than on getting to know the people to whom one is being sent; in actual fact, it does not really matter to whom or where one goes (Howell 2009:208–9)!

(Needless to say, these things can never be adequately achieved in the short-term, which defies the very identity and existence of the STM-er!)

And it is about the lower class, the poor, and not the wealthy middle or upper classes (*ibid.*:210). It is about 'false charity'—i.e. that which 'constrains the fearful and subdued, the "rejects of life," to extend their trembling hands . . . [rather than] striving so that these hands . . . be extended less and less in supplication, so that more and more they become human hands which work and, working, transform the world' (Freire in Koll 2010:96).

All is not right with mission! The STM-er syndrome reflects something close to what could quite accurately be labelled 'spiritual consumerism'.

Eligibility

There is another 'symptom' of crisis in mission that has to be mentioned—something which those already involved in mission seem often unaware of: that despite a deep desire to be used in 'God's mission in the church' (for want of a better use of words, at this stage in our enquiry), people often find themselves not good enough to be 'picked for the team'.

They have not been to Bible College; if they have, their results were not the best in the class, or their ideas were not conventional enough; they are too shy; they are not 'suited' to the mission field; their families are too big (five children, instead of max. three!); they are not able to raise adequate financial support; their health is not good enough; they are the wrong gender; and so on. For any of these, and for a multitude of other reasons, those with a 'heart for mission' are often rejected (or should we say, more affirmatively: 'not accepted') by missionary selection committees. Deemed ineligible to be involved, they end up floundering to establish another vocation in the shadow of other successful and better-suited people.

Many saints in today's church are dragged along at the tail end of 'the procession' that Paul writes about (1Co. 4:9). They eat the dust kicked up by the rich, wise, strong, honoured 'kings' that he talks about, whilst they themselves remain plain, poor, foolish, weak, dishonoured, hungry and thirsty, ragged, brutally treated, homeless and, in short, the 'scum of the earth: the refuse of the world' (4:13).

At least they can enjoy sweet fellowship with the apostle Paul; and 'king' David (who for so much of his life was outlawed and pursued by Saul); and Moses (alone on the hills, grazing sheep for a way of life); and so many others: surrounded by enemies on every side, hated without reason, engulfed, worn out, calling for help, scorned and shamed, strangers to their brothers, alienated, hated, heartbroken and helpless (Ps. 69)—something more like the oddly assorted 'cloud of witnesses' of Hebrews 11 whom God used in the past.

This is not a bad place to be (though Christian ministry and missions work often appears, at least, to baulk at such experiences). It is certainly a biblical place to be.

But to understand and accept this, certainly in the context of conferences so expansive and successful as 'Cape Town 2010,' one has to first understand just what a real and powerful 'culture' of mission exists globally and, then (which is a harder task), one has to critique this 'culture' and come to terms with the fact that it may not be the glorious entity that it is generally portrayed as being.

Many books will be written about the successes of 'Cape Town' but probably not as many about its failures. Yet even the famous Edinburgh 1910 had the following realistic assessment made about it (Stanley 2009:17):

> The measure of missionary success enjoyed by Christianity in the century that followed arguably owed rather little to the priorities set and the objective enunciated at Edinburgh. The Christian faith was indeed to be transfigured over the next century, but not in the way or through the mechanism that they imagined. The most effective instrument of that transfiguration would not be western mission agencies or institutions of any kind, but rather a great and sometimes unorthodox miscellany of indigenous pastors, prophets, catechists, and evangelists, men and women who had little or no access to the metropolitan mission headquarters and the wealth of dollars and pounds which kept the missionary society machinery turning; they professed instead to rely on the simple transforming power of the Spirit and the Word.

Despite this, the machinations of mission have ground forward over the century past, and the culture of modern mission that has evolved is even more untouchable.

Mbiti (1986:200) expressed this with poignancy, writing: 'Foreign missionary work is highly structured, organised, and well respected at least in the churches that send missionaries. The missionary is still an "untouchable" person in many church circles, in the sense that he is "special," "distant," serving the church in the most "sacrificial" way since he abandons his supposedly comfortable country and goes to distant and supposedly rough lands. In many ways the missionary is a real "hero" ... and to criticize him is almost an unforgivable sin about which he and his church are very sensitive.'

If traditional mission is restricted to the involvement of only a few, select, elite individuals in the church, then perhaps it is 'mission' that is being propagated instead of the Christian gospel.

Activism

Common to all the problems briefly highlighted above (and to the many others that also contribute towards the present crisis in modern mission) is the problem of activism. North American missiologist Charles Van Engen stated that missiology since the 1960s has 'dealt primarily with the strategy and practice of mission' (1996a:17) and that it has been dominated by a 'busy global activism' (*ibid.*).

Miroslav Volf (at one time, a colleague of Van Engen's at the Fuller Theological Seminary), similarly critiqued this 'pragmatic' missiology (1998:5) as that which 'tends to concentrate on the technique because the primary goal is to increase either the number of converts or the utility of social effects' (*ibid.*).

Examples of this can be seen in modern Pentecostalism, which Andrew Walker (1992:58) suggested has simply 'adopted and adapted from American evangelicalism the methods of commerce and business in order to promote their message.'

And this has been recognised for quite some time. Writing when mission's crisis started to be expressed in the 1950s, C.W. Forman observed the same about strategisation in mission. He wrote (1957:89): 'The world is too full of strategies, and people are too much driven by their own cleverly calculated programmes.'

Although the outworkings of activism mentioned above ('strategy,' 'praxis,' 'technique,' 'programmes' and so on) may be useful in a secular environment of commerce and industry, they are not necessarily indicative of theological or biblical correctness or appropriateness. Not even in relation to the 'practical theology' of mission!

Instead what they do in effect is to sideline mission as a specific task of the church: a specialist activity which does not necessarily pertain to the life of the Christian or corporate church so much as to gifted, particular and specific Christian people or groups.

What is being proposed in this work will become increasingly clear: that through an oversimplification of what mission is, and through an impoverished theology of mission and an overstress on (or, more, a false start point of) praxis, mission has lost its way, having become a primarily sectarian exercise.

It could even be that mission as understood and defined in contemporary missiology is a non-theological, non-doctrinal concept altogether. But to suggest this would be to pre-empt our later findings and conclusions.

For now, the point being made has been reinforced: all is not right in mission; there is a problem, a crisis in modern mission that has still not been adequately defined.

A Way Forward

These words from N.T. Wright's consideration of what it means to live as a people of God (1992b:124) are appropriate to any missiological investigation, not least the one that we are embarking on: 'Worldviews are the basic stuff of human existence, the lens through which the world is seen, the blueprint for how one should live in it, and above all the sense of identity and place which enables human beings to be what they are. To ignore worldviews, either our own, or those of the culture we are studying, would result in extraordinary shallowness.'

One popular way in which missiologists and zealous church planters may read this passage is to see it as reinforcing their now commendable sensitivity towards other cultures (in word, at least, if not in actuality): their enthusiastic work on 'contextualisation' and their efforts to appreciate or at least tolerate other cultures. All this is (admirably) based on an appreciation of our differing worldviews, or just straight 'difference' (Presler 2010) and the self worth of others.

Another way of reading Wright's words—far more relevant for our own enquiry—is to hear their appeal to question one's own worldview: in this case the worldview of the culture of modern mission itself. For a culture of mission does exist in churches today. Whether Catholic, evangelical or ecumenical, mission already means something tangible to the regular churchgoer! It has a long developed 'culture' of its own. Yet it is a culture in crisis (despite whether this has even been recognised or not), so we would do well to heed Wright's warning and to critique the whole worldview of modern mission: its presuppositions and basic assumptions—even 'biblical' ones. By so doing, we would hope to get beyond 'extraordinary shallowness' as we seek definition and solution to the problem in contemporary mission.

Such a critique of the worldview of the culture of mission is essential. Although 'mission' has been such an unquestioned 'part' of the church for so long, the worldview of the culture of modern mission should never just be assumed. The major doctrines of the church were critiqued, formalised and where necessary reformed in the relatively recent history of the church. Yet mission was never formalised in any way. Evolving after that Reformation era, and more as a function of the church than as a formal teaching, it has inconspicuously developed into a culture of its own. Without much official attention, it has developed into a *de facto* doctrine of the church without ever having been subjected to critique in any great depth. All-too-often, it seems, the 'theology' of mission has been glossed over because of the more 'important,' more politically urgent problem (in ecclesial spheres) of making 'it' work or of easing church/'mission' tensions.

It is clearly imperative then, at this stage in the 'history' of Christian mission, to critique, if not to reform 'mission' as has been commonly understood, and the theology of mission upon which related missiological praxis has evolved. Unpleasant and unsettling though this may seem, a rigorous deconstruction of 'mission' does appear to be a necessary start to solving the crisis that exists in Christian mission.

Summary

Through symptoms of crisis, like the guilt and blame laid on colonialism, the increasingly ill-defined people-groups and communities of faith in our modern world, the sapping tendency and risk of dependency in the Third World church, the superficial phenomenon of short-term missions, the exclusivism of missions being practiced by certain elite in the church, and the recognition of an overriding activism in all this and many other expressions of mission, it appears that the crisis surrounding modern mission concerns an issue of identity as opposed to mere pragmatics.

Indeed, this focus on praxis may be the root of its problematic identity: mission being currently grounded not so much in biblical theology as in practical methodology.

For modern mission is neither a theology nor a doctrine (despite whole arrays of attempts made to defend it theologically and biblically) but praxis.

As such, its whole identity may be derived from an inadequate start point.

With this in mind, there is no other way forward than to move into a critique of modern mission (its culture and worldview and identity) and to determine the root of the inadequate start point from which it has evolved.

By so doing, the culture of modern mission in today's church may risk having to be shunned in order to hone the core of truth it seeks to represent, and in order to determine an alternative and more authentically biblical and theological doctrine of mission.

During this critique, or deconstruction of mission in Part 1, an alternative approach to the identity of Christian mission will be identified which should unleash a vibrant mission in the church. The aim of Part II will be to articulate that alternative, more authentic approach to understanding mission not as a modern enterprise but rather as a core aspect of the Christian life.

The extent to which we can re-use the same 'labels' that we have used before has yet to be determined. This issue reflects observations made by David Bosch concerning new paradigms of mission that have become apparent at various stages of the history of the church, and the inevitability of an imminent new paradigm. To this end, mission will often be referred to in inverted commas when talked about, especially in our Part III concluding section, and the authentic mission we are hoping to express better may be referred to simply as Christian mission or the Christian life.

PART I

DECONSTRUCTION:
Critique of Modern Mission

Chapter 2

Mission in History

A FIRST PLACE TO begin critiquing our modern worldview of mission is by looking at the way in which we have read it out of history. There is no way that a comprehensive historical overview can be performed here, but sufficient work has been done on this elsewhere. What is important to highlight, though, is at least some of the features of that history, in order to evaluate them.

Acts of the Apostles and the Early Church

A quick look at mission in Acts starts to unravel the problem of modern mission.

Clearly, a major reason for the expansion of the early church was the spirit-filled natures of those who believed, and a desire to share their faith with others. Eusebius (in Tucker 2004:23) wrote about the many Christians who 'felt their souls inspired by the Holy Word with a passionate desire for perfection . . . leaving their homes [as a result] . . . [and setting out] *to fulfil the work of an evangelist . . .* [so laying] *the foundation of faith among these foreign people*.' Their motivation was a deep desire to see others (beyond themselves and their own people) come to faith: not to a global religion, but to a personal belief in the fact that a man who had been a part of their own human history (the man with whom many of them had rubbed shoulders, and eaten and lived for the past years, and whose gruesome death they had witnessed) was actually God. This had been proved to them by the resurrection which so many of them had also physically witnessed, and could testify to (Paul mentions as many as five hundred people on different occasions who saw the Lord [1Co. 15:6]).

Their motivation stemmed from a personal encounter with the true and living God: from personally witnessing His life, death, and resurrection.

But the expansion of Christianity also happened because of something less appealing, and that is the persecution that effected the majority dispersion of Christian people from out of their comfort zones. Persecution for their belief in, and testimonies about Jesus' deity and resurrection drove believers beyond their own borders into the lives and homes of other people in other places. His prediction in this regard had been clear (Lk. 21:12–13): 'they will lay hands on you and persecute you. They will deliver you to synagogues and prisons and you will be brought before kings and governors and all on account of my name. This will result in your being witnesses to them.' Not a high level of voluntary choice would be involved here: such witness would be unavoidable.

So understandably, neither of these 'strategies' are ever much formally recognised in mission surveys today. Neither the 'fire' of personal conviction, eyewitness or testimony, nor the 'fire' of random sociological dispersion caused by traumatic external events could (or would) ever be 'manufactured' voluntarily. These are not 'strategies' that would ever be organised.

And yet they are core to the Acts of the Apostles!

Strange, then, that neither of these two generators of mission are often highlighted in modern mission's considerations of those Acts (though spiritual zeal would admittedly be condoned).

Modern mission instead sketches the missionary journeys of Paul, and draws pragmatic models from these journeys, even though they were primarily spiritual ones at the time (for example, a Macedonian 'call' being modelled today as something that needs to come out of a local community, rather than being recognised as having come originally in a dream, and by the Spirit). Those journeys are held up as blueprints for true missionary advance, so that people who 'follow in the footsteps of St. Paul', as it were, are felt to be providing commendable continuity with the early church.

The whole identity of modern mission derives from its self-perceived obedience to certain 'missionary' commands, and its assumption that the early church responded to the same: like the Acts 1:8 mandate to witness 'in Jerusalem, and in all Judea and Samaria, and to the ends of the earth'; the mandate from Matthew 28 to 'go and make disciples of all nations . . .'; and so on.

Rarely, though, does it embrace or appropriate a 'methodology' of persecution and dispersion (though in retrospect it might try to make sense of tragic events in this way; and it would also, certainly, advocate a spiritual dimension to any practical missiological efforts).

And very seldom (it may be argued) does the sending missionary church truly prostrate itself before the living God and get to know Him in the way that people knew Jesus as He walked the streets of Jerusalem or the paths of Galilee: living as man, dying in rejection, and rising in mystical, unbelievable though tangible victory.

Instead, the 'enterprise' has become the focus of modern mission, and 'God' is now often just an aspect of its genre and vocabulary.

These and several other problems concerning the way modern mission uses Acts and refers to the early church can be summarised as follows.

First, all-too-often, its own twentieth/twenty-first century missiological programmes and methods are read back into the text. Modern mission sees in Acts and the early church, paradigms and examples of all that it counts to be important: methodology, structure, presentation techniques, street evangelism, church planting and growth, models of 'sodality and modality', 'dialogue' and 'contextualisation', and of course issues of 'call', 'sending' and 'gifting'—to mention but a few. It is so important in our evangelical world to support what we say and do with the bible, that the modern missionary movement has become guilty of not letting the text speak for itself and of imposing, instead, its own models and perceptions of mission onto the pages of Scripture. If people were to stop and listen, it would become evident that very little is actually known about how the gospel spread except in the lives of just a few (Paul, Peter and James, possibly John, but not really many more).

Second, it is not clear who exactly was sent, or why. Yes, Paul and Barnabas were sent—but were they the only ones? And was their 'sent-ness' the result of Paul being an apostle, and Barnabas a co-worker of his? What, then, of the other apostles? In what way was their apostleship or sent-ness (*apostelō*—Greek for 'sent') any different? If it was no different, then why do we not hear about their mission (*missio*—Latin for 'sent') or involvement as we hear of Paul's? Yes, we know a bit about Peter, and James—but what about the others? What did 'mission' involve, or look like for them? How 'effective' were they (or is it even right to be trying to measure 'effectiveness', spiritually)? Perhaps the argument from silence—i.e. recognition of what is not said or talked about—should be stronger than the argument from what is commonly referred to (primarily in the 'mission' and ministry of Paul)?

We know of certain non-apostolic missions: the witness and effective ministries of, for example, Philip the Evangelist, and Stephen. About Philip, however, little is said about the fact that he was a humble table waiter (Ac. 6:2,5); or that he had to flee Jerusalem because of persecution (8:1–5); or that the apostles deemed it necessary to come and authenticate his ministry (8:14–17); or that he settled down in Caesarea (8:40, 21:8) and had four daughters (21:9), and lived a seemingly 'normal', domestic sort of life. And we know little about Stephen, except that he too had been a table waiter (6:2,5); that he was full of the Spirit, and highly articulate; and that he suffered a humiliating trial, false accusations (6:8ff) and finally martyrdom (7:54ff).

Beyond these, and a few others, we actually know very little about 'mission' in Acts or in the early church (as far as we understand 'mission' to be, in our age!). Yet clearly it was not just for the apostles, or even just for other gifted individuals, but many others, not written about in Acts: countless unsung heroes and heroines of the Christian faith.

More people must have been involved in 'mission' in the early church than we tend to recognise or even give credit to, and the implication of this is that more people should be (and hopefully are) involved in authentic mission in the church today than we know about. This in turn again brings into question our definition of the term 'mission', as commonly understood.

A third problem about the way modern mission uses Acts, is the way it assumes an understanding of where 'Jerusalem', 'Judea', 'Samaria' and 'the ends of the earth' are—but that it is not at all clear where, or who 'all nations' are in our age. These names and places may represent spiritual people groups (in relation to Jewish and covenantal revelation); or geographical references; they may be ethnic references; but they are almost certainly shifting goalposts, general references to places where the gospel of God has never been heard: in the forgotten hill-tribes of the world, for example, or (equally) the vastly-expanding pockets of people in our former First World who have no clue about the gospel of Jesus Christ; and they must also, surely, be references (therefore) to the likes of my next door neighbour who has not yet heard or understood the gospel.

There may be no obvious logical or spiritual reason why one people group should receive more or less of our attention than any other. But it is our perceptions of people groups (as outlined above) that will determine different responses in each of us. If 'Jerusalem and Judea (etc.)' is taken as a reference to other lands, then mission will be perceived quite differently from it being taken as a reference to the Bank or the City. Mission in the former instance would become an overtly cross-cultural, cross-national, specialist activity that only a few in the church are equipped for, whilst the latter would involve a more subtle but equally challenging cross-cultural work that the majority of people in the church should be, but are almost certainly just not aware of, or equipped for.

A fourth problem: if twenty-first century mission truly is grounded in a biblical mandate, its claim to continuity with the early church falls away at least on this point, because no such 'biblical mandate' ever existed for 'mission' at that time. Modern mission points to passages like Romans 10:14–15 ('How, then, can they call on the one they have not believed in? And how can they believe in the one of whom they have not heard? And how can they hear without someone preaching to them? And how can they preach unless they are sent?'); Matthew 28:19 ('Therefore go and make disciples of all nations, baptising them . . . and teaching them to obey everything I have commanded you'); John 4:35 ('Open your eyes and look at the fields! They are ripe for harvest'); and John 20:21 ('As the Father sent me, so send I you').

But for the early church there was no 'John 4 or 20', no 'Matthew 28', no 'Romans 10'! Yes, an oral culture would almost certainly have been in existence, but any 'missiological' mandates would have been embedded in the life experience of Jesus as a whole.

At best, biblically, there may have been a foreshadowing of our modern day usage of Isaiah 6:8 ('Then I heard the voice of the Lord saying, "Whom shall I send? And who will go for us?" And I said, "Here am I. Send me!"'). But there is no clear evidence of apostles or others in the early church having based their outreach upon this text or any similar ones.

We have to conclude, then, that what motivated the spread of the gospel in the early church was the tangible reality of Jesus, experienced through personal encounter either with Him or others who lived with

Him and witnessed His resurrection, rather than (as is often the case today) 'biblical mandate'. It was also the result of the less popular impulse of persecution. In general, mission in the early church is not what we assume it was, or what we impose onto the texts, or how we understand them today. The people who 'did' mission then are not necessarily the ones that we traditionally popularise, and the places they were sent to differ from those to which we may be 'sent' today.

This brief look at 'mission' in the early church confirms the problem of identity and definition that we have regarding 'mission'.

Catholic Mission

Expansion of the early church gave way, in effect, to Roman expansion, as Rome became the primary benefactor and protector of the Christian faith. Mission historian Kenneth Scott Latourette called the years from A.D. 500–1500 'The Thousand Years of Uncertainty' (the title of Volume 2 of his *History of the Expansion of Christianity*), during which time the church faced two major struggles. The first of these was against Islam (from A.D. 622 onwards, following Muhammad's flight from Mecca to Medina, and the uniting of the Arab tribes under this new monotheistic religion just ten years later). The second was against the 'barbarians of Europe' (animists, polygamists, savages, and pagans who, once conquered, were often forced to be baptised within a month of the pagan tribe being conquered). Prince Vladimer, for example, after his conversion in the northern, Slavic lands in A.D. 988, forced his followers into the church, as did later rulers in Russia (Stamoolis 2000:442). Such 'growth' is umbrella'd under the term 'missionary' activity, but despite the cathedrals which have survived thousands of years, the authenticity of the 'conversions' for which they stand remains dubious—certainly as being representative of whole ethnic kingdoms.

William Carey (1792:33) commented negatively on this historical missional 'norm' with these words: 'But now popery, especially the compulsive part of it, was risen to such an height, that the usual method of propagating the gospel, or rather what was so called, was to conquer pagan nations by force of arms, and then oblige them to submit to Christianity, after which bishopricks were erected, and persons then sent to instruct the people . . .'

His critique was cutting (*ibid.*:34): 'blind zeal, gross superstition, and infamous cruelties, so marked the appearances of religion all this time, that the professors of Christianity needed conversion, as much as the heathen world.'

Our own perception of the validity of such 'mission' should be equally sceptical.

A similar pattern was followed once Europe had become united (politically and religiously) against the Islamic states, and the same aggression was vented for two further centuries with the outcome of the tragic Crusades (A.D. 1099–1291). It was a time referred to as 'a long act of intolerance in the name of God'—a tragic time which 'poisoned relations between the Eastern Orthodox and Western church and increased Islamic hatred of Christianity' (Clouse 2000:249). It was, too, a shameful time during which the Christian faith was 'perverted by vicious knights and greedy merchants who inflicted terrible suffering on thousands of Muslims, Jews, and Christians.' (*Ibid.*).

From a South American perspective, Samuel Escobar (2003:46) put it this way: 'Probably there has been no point at which missionary action and imperial action have been so closely linked in theory and practice as in the evangelisation of the Americas. The Iberian conquest of the Americas was rightly called by some of its agents "the last of the crusades" . . . For them [the kings of Spain and Portugal] to conquer in the name of Spain and thus to enlarge the reach of the Spanish Empire was synonymous with enlarging the kingdom of God.'

Problematic in all of this, is that even the likes of Francis of Assisi (through whom came the order of Dominican and Franciscan Friars) travelled to Egypt 'on the back' of the Fifth Crusade. The good of individuals such as Francis was undeniable; the Sultan of Egypt, for example, is reported to have said: 'If I meet any more Christians like you I will become one myself' (Stamoolis 2000:442). However, mission was still irreversibly associated with the empirical expansion of Europe, globally, and as a result is left (whether that is acknowledged or not) with an enormous sense of guilt and failure as its heritage.

Problematic too (beyond guilt), was the questionable effectiveness of early mission. Nestorian missionaries, for example, had reached as far east as China in the seventh century, but by A.D. 1000 travelling monks into China were unable to find any trace of Christianity in the Chinese Empire.

Towards the end of these dark centuries, despite the questionable methods and motivations behind mission activity up until then, New Testament attitudes to 'mission' ostensibly started to be (re-?) discovered. Ramon Lull, from the Spanish Island of Majorca, in the thirteenth century, became the first known missionary to develop a theory of mission (though similar propositions had been made earlier, and had just not been formalised as effectively). His three basic tenets were to (1) thoroughly learn the local language; (2) develop instructive literature concerning the Christian faith; (3) carry on a courageous witness among the people even to the point of death. He wrote, once: 'Missionaries will convert the world by preaching but also through the shedding of tears and blood and with great labour, and through a bitter death.' He died of such injuries himself (received whilst preaching to Muslims) and he is now known as one of the greatest missionaries in history (so Neill, in Escobar 2003:45).

But what authenticated Lull's life and work? Was his reading of the New Testament or understanding of church traditions necessarily correct? Did his methodology have any impact other than to get himself killed? Was Islam, or were Moslem people affected positively? Was his argument not just an internal, secular argument? To what extent was it an effective expression of Christian truth—of gospel authenticity?

These questions do need to be answered if Lull is to rightly retain the glowing reputation that he holds, and if modern mission is (as it appears) to incorporate his theory as part of its very identity. We need, in other words, to examine the grounds upon which we can, and already do approach the question of what 'mission' is and what it involves, rather than to just build on apparent (and potentially) internal propositions.

After A.D. 1500 not a lot changed in terms of mission rationale in the Roman Catholic Church. The main development was that with the dawn of the Age of Discovery, the boundaries of the then known world started to be pushed back. And of course this, too, was the time when the established church started to split away from Rome through the emergence of Protestantism.

Only two specifically Roman Catholic developments in mission since then are noteworthy.

The first concerns the articulation of its understanding of the church as a missionary church. This is reflected in Vatican II's significant comment: 'the Church on earth is by its very nature missionary, since, according to the plan of the Father, it has its origin in the mission of the Son and the Holy Spirit . . . It is clear, therefore, that missionary activity flows immediately from the very nature of the Church' ('Ad Gentes Divinitus' in Flannery 1992:814,820,857). Mission thus understood as an aspect of the church rightly roots any missional activity of the church in the very person who gives it its identity: the person of God.

However, a less positive development came about through a further expression of the Catholic Church's Enlightenment experience (or articulation of it) that took place at Vatican II. It happened through a shift towards rationalism (perhaps through an effort to 'satisfy' rationalism), and more specifically through an attempt to point to the biblical-ness of its hitherto only ecclesial or papal statements. Thus its discussion on mission, in particular, became peppered with references to New Testament texts that are more tragic in terms of their appearance of mere proof-texting than were its former autocratic claims to papal and ecclesial authority. The texts have been used in a merely popular and an almost naïve and pre-critical hermeneutical sense. As such, they do not represent any significant validation for the missional exercise of the Roman Catholic Church, either past or present.

The observation that has been made through all of this is that the concept of 'mission'—thus defined and practiced through the era of the pre-Protestant Christian church—was not so much a theology as a theory of praxis: one which was, as noted, developed on the back of colonial or other world power expansions.

Protestant Mission

Protestantism—through its break with Rome—commenced an era that in actual fact was marked by a surprising inactivity as regards mission. Indeed, the Protestant church was criticised by Rome for not getting involved in mission.

The commonly held reason for this is that Protestant energies were being spent on theological self-defence and on developing its own doctrinal and theological positions.

In addition, the trend at that time appeared to be towards hyper-Calvinism where outreach to the non-Christian world was not felt to be an obligation of the Christian. Calvin (1960:1057) had understood the offices of apostle and evangelist as having been temporary. Luther, similarly, had held that none, since the first apostles, had received a general apostolic command, and he had spoken of 'infiltrating and clandestine preachers' as 'apostles of the devil' (1958:393). In the opinion of the Reformers, the 'Great Commission' had been fulfilled through the original apostles, and the church therefore had no commission left for a mission to the world (Thomas 1995:43). To this end, it was only pietists who were ambitious in mission, and Orthodoxy was cool, even hostile towards it. So, for example, a Hamburg preacher, Neumeister, is recorded as saying: '"Go into all the world," the Lord of old did say. But now: "Where God has placed thee, there he would have thee stay"' (Warneck 1979:79).

Thus, whilst the overt reason for the Reformers' lack of mission involvement was that they had no time to develop a theology of mission (in relation to more pressing doctrines that they had to articulate) it could be proposed, instead, that the thought of the Reformers did not necessitate a separate mission theology. Indeed, Calvin and Luther's thought, already highlighted in brief, would suggest that the absence of mission in their thinking was theological and not just an issue of oversight! It appears that they did not deem mission *per se* to even be a valid theological discipline or doctrine worth mentioning. Theirs, then, would tie with our earlier comment made in relation to the early church: that the mission activity of the first Christians was not so much about careful methodology as about a personal response to the gospel and a living faith in the risen Lord.

This may be adequate reason for us to stop 'saying' mission, and 'talking about' mission, and even for us to consider doing away with the traditional concept and models of 'mission' in preference for simply living authentic Christian lives in response to the core truths of the Christian faith (like God, and His life and love in and for us).

But this is again to pre-empt our overall conclusions, proposed in Part III.

Evangelical Mission

Evangelical mission has always sought to associate itself with the early expansion of the Christian faith: the simple spreading of the gospel of Jesus Christ by those who had known him. It would have taken its form from Reformed and Protestant theology in Europe not missiologically, but in terms of looking to identify its origins prior to the Roman Church in the first churches after Christ's resurrection, as attested to biblically. William Carey (a clear representative of evangelical mission) talked about this as a time when nations had 'agreed one after another to cast off the yoke of popery, and to embrace the doctrine of the gospel' (1792:35).

It was only in 1910 (in eventual and apparent response to Carey's call for a world conference for mission, a hundred years earlier) that the first conference for World Mission was held in Edinburgh, Scotland. From this conference, the first strictly evangelical conference was held in 1966 in Berlin, and (subsequently) in Lausanne (1974), Pattaya (1980), Manila (1989) and of course Cape Town (2010).

Berlin, spearheading these evangelical conferences, was reported as being the 'first worldwide gathering of regional evangelists and other leaders in an evangelistic effort' (Henry 1966a:32). It stressed the 'urgent need for a return to evangelistic priorities,' and was significant in bringing together fundamentalism and neo-evangelicalism. It was, thus, marked by reports of people praying 'for tongues of fire . . . [and waiting] for man-made walls to tumble' (Henry 1966b:2). These reports portrayed evangelical mission as somewhat fundamental and pietistic.

Lausanne conferences, under the leadership of John Stott, followed something more of the 'bible-based, Great Commission' approach to mission that had been an aspect of the Berlin Congress. There, Stott had led daily devotions on the theme of the 'Great Commission', expounding various 'Great Commission' passages.

These are all consistent features of evangelical mission: a tendency toward fundamentalism and pietism; gospel-centredness and bibliocentricity, with a particular focus on the motif of the 'Great Commission' (which will be investigated in greater detail, below).

Ecumenical (liberal) Mission

Integral to an ecumenical or liberal mission is an attempt to incorporate all people: to dialogue with people of all persuasions and other faiths.

The 1910 Edinburgh conference has also been viewed as the first ecumenical movement on world mission—but this should be understood narrowly, as neither the Roman Catholic nor the Orthodox Churches were invited. It was a Protestant gathering. Out of it, however, came the three branches of the International Missionary Council (IMC), the Life and Work movement, and the Faith and Order movement—the latter two of which combined in 1948 under the umbrella of the World Council of Churches, and the first of which was also incorporated under an ecumenical umbrella as the Commission for World Mission and Evangelism (CWME)—New Delhi (1961).

The extent of ecumenical mission reaches to the likes of a Liberationist mission which is based overtly on social praxis rather than biblical theology. Its purpose has been to institute social justice over against religious or evangelising programmes.

However, the aims of these ecumenical missions are as limited as 'mission' had been hitherto. They are, amongst other things, to seek ways to express the visible unity of the church; to facilitate common witness of churches in partnership with each other; to express common concern for service, justice, peace and the reconciliation of the world; and to foster spiritual renewal in the church towards unity, worship, mission and service.

It appears that the message of this approach is simply to validate all approaches to faith, and to coordinate their social efforts, rather than to spell out the uniqueness of the person of Christ in response to the inherently sinful state of humanity.

Summary

The problem proposed earlier has been reinforced by this brief survey and critique: the problem of activism and identity in mission. From the beginnings of Christianity, 'mission' has been zealously done but not so keenly thought about, theologically.

In the early church, mission was not necessarily as programmatic or particular as one is led to believe by reading 'mission(s)' out of the New Testament texts. 'Roman' mission tended to exact group confessions in their colonial takeovers. Protestant mission at least was silent on the matter (for the reason proposed here that 'mission' was not felt to be an issue so much as living out a genuine life of faith). Evangelical mission has tended to focus on the praxis of conversion programmes, whilst ecumenical mission's similar focus has been more on the purpose of unity.

In none of these eras was mission 'theology' ever specifically developed, except as a defence of mission as it existed in its then current form, at any one time. It appears that theologies of mission came about primarily to backup what had already been decided upon in pragmatic terms, regardless of what an independent biblical theology of mission would have suggested.

In other words, the crisis of modern mission is that it has derived from, and has (thus) become and/or been propagated as an inherently programmatic activity of the church and a practical theology of the Christian academy. This may well be because it never underwent any significant levels of independent theological scrutiny.

To this end there is a confirmed need to continue a carefully critical assessment of 'mission' in order first to better define the problem surrounding its contemporary identity, and then to formulate a more authentic theology of what it should be.

CHAPTER 3

The Contemporary Practice of Mission

IT IS IMPORTANT NOW to identify and articulate just what mission 'is' in the contemporary world, as reasonably and accurately as possible.

One way to do this is through consideration of certain mission statistics that have been published. (The fact that 'mission statistics' are even being published is in itself a significant statement of presuppositions and perceptions as regards the identity of mission.)

Literature, too, gives an important indication of where mission is at.

But a first obvious place to look is to a seminary where 'mission(s)' has a high profile. For the way in which mission is practiced is largely a by-product of how it is taught (if not in the churches, then formally in seminaries).

A School of World Mission

It would be hard to look beyond the institution which until very recently, 2003 (so Fuller 2010b: Online), included those very words in its name: the Fuller School of World Mission, now called the School of Intercultural Studies, Fuller Theological Seminary.

Yet it is also very hard (for this writer in particular, writing from an African context where it is not natural to critique either authority or the West) to look too long, or to evaluate too hard, an institution or the people associated with it who have excelled and contributed so significantly in mission, and whose names and reputations in the field of theology and mission are in so many ways respected.

The only reason for continuing is, as argued earlier, that such an assessment does need to be done. If there is indeed a crisis in mission then all that is associated with it (as far as one can define or determine what it is) does require an honest and thorough appraisal. More than this: it does make it slightly easier and less personal, though no less relevant, that the seminary chosen is now known by a different name, except by the likes of its Alumni. So we will refer to it here as the Fuller School of World Mission.

Even so, it is important to explain that the following critique and comments are not intended to downplay the achievements of individuals or groups mentioned. It is just that enough other works 'out there' already applaud the institution's positive points, and so for the sake of theological integrity the specific aim of this work is not to linger further on those achievements, but rather to test them.

The respect that has already been given to the school, its founders and present faculty for all that it has accomplished, and the credibility that it has held in the mission academy (Newbigin, 1983:136 referred to it as 'one of today's most influential schools of missiology') would all suggest that it fairly represents contemporary mission. And so this makes it an obvious and important institution to critique briefly.

Features

Certain features have always surrounded the School of World Mission.

First, which is understandable in its cultural context, was the individualism that has always been fabric to the School. George Marsden (1987:2) writing a history on it observed this: 'The most distinctive institutions of American evangelicalism have often been parts of the personal empires of successful evangelists . . . [They have usually been] run autocratically or by an oligarchy . . . [and have been] regarded virtually as private property . . . designed for a purpose, which could be defined by the people in immediate command, with no need to answer to ecclesiastical authority. These institutions were thus extraordinarily shaped by the personalities of the individuals who founded and controlled them. Fuller Seminary was such an institution . . . shaped by the individuals who control it.'

One such strong personality was founder Charles Fuller himself, a radio-evangelist who was experienced in working on his own and who had established his radio ministry 'entirely on a free-enterprise basis' (*ibid.*:17). His individualistic tendencies are further evidenced by the occasion of his splitting from a Presbyterian church to found an independent congregation in 1925 (*ibid.*).

Another significant individual involved in the early life and formation of the School was Donald McGavran. The strength of his individual character is shown by his formation of the Institute for Church Growth in Pasadena, and his insistence that it first be merged with the School of World Mission before he would get involved in the latter. The merger was reflected, tangibly, in the extension to the title of the School that he insisted on: 'the Fuller Institute for Church Growth/School of World Mission' (*ibid.*:238; so too Van Engen 1996b:208).

Equally significant has been the School's focus on specific individuals: its purpose having been to 'provide professional missiological training for career missionaries' (so Wagner 1979:5)—a phenomenon that has, as already noted, led to missionary people being regarded as 'untouchable persons' in the church (so Mbiti, *op. cit.*).

Later, we will critique individualism as a basic feature of the all-too-often celebrated, but in many ways impoverished Enlightenment. Clearly an individually-inspired institution, training individuals (whether they are working in teams or not) to reach individuals, is a markedly Western development. As such, it has also been critiqued by non-Western contexts (and of late even by certain Western contexts) where the value of community is held in high regard. From an African context, for example, Mbiti's oft-quoted dictum of Africa 'I am because we are' offers a valid and powerful evaluation of the Western/ Enlightenment/ Cartesian dictum: 'I think, therefore I am' (which will be looked at again, below).

The results of individualism in mission are striking. If it is only select individuals who are trained to be career missionaries, one is left wondering whether the untrained remainder of the church are less important, less relevant or indeed less adequate as regards mission: whether ordinary Christians are perhaps not good enough, not qualified or spiritual enough to be involved in mission proper.

A second feature of the School has been an apparent triumphalism concerning where mission is at globally. It has perceived global mission to be in its last stages, suggesting as recently as in its 1996–97 catalogue (Fuller 1996:122) that it remains only for the discipling of nations to be done: 'We at the School of World Mission . . . believe that we stand at a critical juncture of the missionary task. Everything in the past 185 years of modern missions has set the stage for a great harvest. Apart from some small ethnic groups in Oceania, Asia, Africa and Latin America, the "discipling of the peoples" (Matthew 28:19) remains to be done.'

Statistics below suggest that Christianity has little to be triumphant about and that mere discipling of the non-Christian two-thirds of the world is certainly not all that remains for the church in mission to do.

Thirdly, a sense of 'mandate' in mission seemed to characterise the School. In 1983 a statement entitled 'The Mission Beyond The Mission' was adopted and is still included as one of its key vision statements (Fuller 2010a: Online). It is organised around the following imperatives (*ibid.*):

> Imperative 1. Go and make disciples.
> Imperative 2. Call the church of Christ to renewal.
> Imperative 3. Work for the moral health of society.
> Imperative 4. Seek peace and justice in the world.
> Imperative 5. Uphold the truth of God's revelation.

Whilst these imperatives may be laudable Christian aims and goals, we suggest later (in particular in relation to the first of these) that to see them as biblical 'mandates' or imperatives is not necessarily correct hermeneutically, exegetically or even in terms of biblical theology.

In addition, our review of the spread of Christianity in the early church and 'mission' in Acts has already pointed out that the spread of Christianity may not be a primary response to hallowed 'mandate' so much as to uncomfortable—indeed traumatic, fatal and completely involuntary—persecution!

We need to hold the 'mandatory' incentive or motive to mission with careful gloves.

Another (fourth) core tenet of the School has been its concept of the 'call' of God to mission. 'Today,' the School has claimed (Fuller 1996:122), 'God calls Christians of every continent and culture to the task of making Jesus Christ known, loved and believed in throughout the world.'

And yet, whilst 'making Jesus Christ known, loved and believed in' is undeniably important, it not just a feature of the Christian life particular to 'today' (as opposed to other days or era's of church history), nor is it necessarily to do with any one specific 'call' (as opposed to mere Christian life).

Debatable too is the 'evidence' of God's call that is cited: *viz.* that God 'grants remarkable responsiveness in many populations' (*ibid.*:122). 'Responsiveness' *per se* does not validate (or necessarily invalidate) a person's work or call. In fact the direct opposite is true: a genuine call—authentic grounds for being in any form of vocation or ministry in any particular place—enables perseverance in that situation especially in the absence of responsiveness, rather than the other way around.

If 'the call of God' is a feature of modern mission, it is extremely tenuous—certainly in relation to the scant presuppositions that tend to be outlined in traditional mission contexts such as the one we are looking at here.

A fifth feature of the School's understanding of mission was its stress on numbers. Growth in numbers (epitomised through McGavran's church growth principles) was assumed as a measure of success in mission, for (apparently): 'propagating his gospel to the ends of the earth by multiplication of believers and churches is the supreme and controlling purpose of the Christian mission to the world' (*ibid.*). Marsden noted Fuller's stress of numerical growth through his observation that the quality and effectiveness of mission has often been measured in terms of 'soul winning' (1987:243).

And yet growth in numbers is not necessarily a valid gauge of genuine spiritual growth or even of conversion. The apostle Paul talked about the sons of God only being revealed sometime in the future (Ro. 8:18) and Jesus talked about a final day of judgement only in the future when the sheep and the goats would be separated (Mt. 25:32).

The grassroots effect of stressing church growth numerically is often that evangelism becomes aggressive (so Harrison 1984:75) and 'worldly', rather than necessarily 'successful'.

One final feature of the School was its presupposition of 'co-mission' (Fuller 1996:122): that we are 'co-mission workers with God'. And yet it is hard, if not impossible to trace the biblical roots of this concept. Certainly the concept of being 'co-workers' with God is mentioned (by Paul in particular in many places [e.g. Ro. 16:3,9] and Jesus Himself, calling on people to ask God to send out workers [e.g. Mt. 9:38]) but the concept of co-mission is never mentioned. The likes of Verkuyl (1978:6) have offered that 'God calls for participants and volunteers in his mission,' but the grounds upon which he proposes this are more from the paradigm of modern mission than rigorous exegetical or biblical argument.

And so, again, it appears that the concept has been imposed not just on Scripture but also on God. 'Co-mission' may be an interpretative concept that simply assumes, and is assumed from traditional mission.

These founding principles can all be easily traced into contemporary representations of mission, but each one of them may simply have derived from common practice and modern assumptions of what it is.

This very tradition itself may be the cause of a mission which is in crisis.

Faculty

Three prominent faculty members of the School caricature (if nothing else) where mission is at in the academy.

Donald McGavran

Donald McGavran has already been mentioned for his role in founding the Institute for Church Growth in Pasadena at the late age of sixty-one (Yates 1994:215), but the significance of this was his renown as founder of the Church Growth Movement as a whole (Wagner 1981:105).

McGavran's understanding of mission would have grown out of praxis, in view of facts such as that he had been born to missionary parents, was drawn through the Student Volunteer Movement (SVM) into committed discipleship and missionary service (so Yates 1994:215) and that he served for over thirty years in India as a third generation missionary. After this he moved into the field of the theory of group conversions (McGavran 1986:53). Arising out of this highly functional context, his concept of mission as simply 'carrying out God's unswerving purpose' (McGavran 1984:8) was grounded not in theological rigor so much as missiological presupposition.

His missiology appears to have derived more from praxis and tradition than exegesis of any kind. Although once he did dedicate a chapter of a significant of book of his to the subject of the 'Great Commission' (Matthew 28:19), the chapter was written by someone else (Everett Harrison, then-Professor Emeritus of New Testament at the Fuller Theological Seminary [McGavran 1984:20–30]). McGavran admitted that he himself was unqualified for that purpose (*ibid.*).

Important for McGavran was his priority of evangelism over social concern. The evangelistic mandate, as opposed to the cultural one was in his view primary (Wagner 1981:200). Whilst social action may be a legitimate programme for the church it was not so for mission itself (McGavran 1972a:16).

This, in turn, played into his empirical ecclesiology and almost statistical and restrictive soteriology. For McGavran was 'a great proponent of soul winning. Winning converts was [in his view] what missions was all about' (Marsden 1987:243). Classical mission, he insisted (1972a:16), was about winning souls. His first basic principle of church growth supported this view (McGavran 1984:169): that church growth should be seen as 'a chief and irreplaceable goal of Christian mission.' The same is seen in the following observation about McGavran: 'Mission, mission education, and missiology were [for him] all seen through the lens of church growth principles that were to foster the numerically verifiable growth of churches' (Van Engen 1996b:216).

A major problem with this numerical approach is that it appears to have overlooked the real essence of church. Numbers cannot necessarily verify how a church has grown in real terms, because numbers do not represent what a church really is, as discussed further, below.

Through all this, a type of elitism appears to ingrain McGavran's thought, for the professional or career missionary is in his view almost distinct from all other Christian people in the church. They are the ones he sees as the real doers of mission (1972b:188), and this function in turn occurs through '... not the church ... not the denomination ... [but] an agency of the denomination.' This sense of elitism is also seen in the similar distinction that he makes between 'ministers and practising Christians ... [the] executives of the hundreds of missionary societies; and missionaries who go overseas as special messengers of God's grace' (1984:5).

In the same manner he prioritises world-evangelisation over local-evangelisation: the former being only for those specifically equipped and trained for that task. For in his view, 'carrying on God's total purpose necessitates the provision of a distinct task force for each great task. These specialised task forces must be recruited, trained, funded, and kept at work' (*ibid.*:8).

This emphasis results in more than just a superior category of Christian: it tends towards a high activism in mission as 'an *enterprise*' (McGavran 1970:34) and as a task, or series of tasks (McGavran 1984:11–16).

It is no surprise then that McGavran has been referred to as something more of a 'technician of church growth' (Marsden 1987:242) than a missiologist, one whose arguments appear all-too-often to be 'buttressed by statistics of doubtful validity, questionable exegesis of the

New Testament evidence and . . . impatience with alternative views to his own' (Yates 1994:216).

Together with the brief critique of the features of the School of World Mission just done, these comments about McGavran and his work (despite the risk of having been oversimplified) do cast a valid question mark over the missiology that is taught both in the big schools of world mission and as filtered down into our churches.

C. Peter Wagner

Similar subtle, though real criticisms can be levelled at another former faculty member of the School: C. Peter Wagner. Through his studies under McGavran at both the Fuller Theological Seminary (Lindsell in Wagner 1971:9) and the School of World Mission itself (Wagner 1979:5), Wagner confessed to having emerged a 'fond disciple' of his (*ibid.*). Wagner later became one of the faculty and for a time an associate and colleague of McGavran's, later succeeding him as Professor of Church Growth (*ibid.*:206,217).

As can be expected from such a close association between the two, Wagner's thought is problematic in ways similar to that of McGavran's.

For one, he had an effectively anthropocentric understanding of salvation as a personal response to the gospel. Although a hint of broad-mindedness may be reflected by his question 'Just what *does* it mean to be saved?' (1981:130), Wagner shows the narrowness of his approach by answering with another question (*ibid.*): 'What does it mean to repent and be converted?' Salvation, for Wagner, was repentance and conversion: a simple, cognitive response of assent to the gospel. Admittedly he did recognise that salvation involved a life of obeying Jesus 'as Lord' (*ibid.*:136), but it was still primarily about a person's response to God (*ibid.*:145).

Whilst this is not the place to argue a soteriological alternative (this will be done later) it is important to pre-empt that discussion by pointing out two things here: first, that salvation should look not simply to a past, personal decision so much as to a past, salvific and substitutionary act of Christ on the cross; second, that the dynamics of salvation are not just about the past, but about both the present and the future as well. For example, Paul writes about those of 'us who *are being* saved' (1Co. 1:18—italics added). Just to confess 'Jesus as Lord' (*ibid.*:4) and to 'openly and consciously declare' him to be Lord (*ibid.*:5) may be simply about doing things Wagner's way. It may be more about adopting an evangelical lifestyle (McDonald 1996) than undergoing a real and total change of heart.

This suggests a weak eschatology: an inadequate discussion of the end times and the fact that a saved life involves continuation of relationship with God beyond the grave and into eternity (not to mention any dimension of realised eschatology in the here and now).

All this also indicates a weak christology: that although repentance does involve a 'turning from and turning to . . . the center [of] Jesus Christ' (Wagner 1981:138,159), Wagner's perception and articulation of 'Christ' has not been a feature of his writing. Because of this, perhaps, the 'centre' he talks of (albeit under the title 'Christ') could be little more than the focus of a person's own personal spirituality or churchmanship.

Another problem with Wagner's theology is his understanding of the church. He confessed to talk not about 'ecclesiology as such . . . [but] about the ecclesiology found in the Church Growth movement' (so Van Engen 1981:47). This movement would see 'harvest' (the mark of 'numerical church growth') to be a supreme mark of the true church (*ibid.*:509). The church was, for Wagner (*ibid.*:510), 'uniquely the People of God, gathered in Him . . . in order to be sent by him into the world with a special task and a special proclamation.' Evidence of the true church would be its 'yearning for numerical growth' (*ibid.*:511) and (he suggests) one may even need to bypass certain churches for the purpose of results (*ibid.*)!

Wagner's stress was very much on individuals as opposed to the corporate, and he clearly segregated the career missionary away from the average person in the pew. Mission for Wagner was a specialist task—one in which only a few, elite individuals could be engaged. Because of this, he wrote that although 'every Christian is a witness . . . not every Christian is a missionary. The missionary gift involves a special kind of witness' (Wagner 1971:75). He proposed that 'a missionary is a person who engages in a structured rather than a casual witnessing situation and who is sent to his ministry rather than called to it' (*ibid.*:77). That 'everyone is a missionary' he held to be a 'highly inaccurate' statement, writing: 'This is an overly sentimental use of the word missionary . . . the pastry chef could be called a faithful Christian worker or an effective witness for Christ, but please, not a missionary' (*ibid.*:84).

Lesslie Newbigin (1979:310) critiqued Wagner on this point, suggesting that it is wrong to talk of the institutionalisation of a 'double standard, one for the "nominal" Christian, and the other for an elite group who have made the "second-level" decision.' All Christians should be involved in Christian mission!

Of even deeper significance is that Wagner's statements appeared to derive from little more than his own thinking. For example, Wagner offers minimal, even evasive rationale for mankind's involvement in mission in the first place, writing: 'For reasons we have not been informed of, God has chosen to use human beings to accomplish His evangelistic purposes in the world' (1971:15). And then confusion, perhaps even inconsistency arises when he admits elsewhere that 'the Spirit does not need human help [and that] to need assistance is an absurd possibility for omnipotence' (*ibid.*:26)! Yet Wagner goes on to observe that 'In His divine wisdom, the Spirit has decreed a measure of human responsibility; and it is left for us to accept this fact, not to question it' (*ibid.*).

If Wagner had shown the source of his opinion it might have been easier to weigh his contribution, but it appears to have come simply from his own speculation. Howard Peskett (1996:482) summed it up well in a review of Wagner's *The Acts of the Holy Spirit*, writing: '[Wagner's] speculations on one page tend to escalate into assumptions on the next ... [and] we see in [his] books, not a picture of [for example] Luke and his work, but of Wagner's mirrored face.'

Another theological critique must of course speak to Wagner's pneumatology—the field through which he gained reputation (especially in places like Africa) from his dealings with 'territorial spirits' and the 'supernatural' (these being just two of his own oft-used phrases as reflected in article titles of his like 'Supernatural Power in World Missions' and 'Territorial Spirits and World Missions'). His approach can be illustrated by the fact that he co-taught 'Signs, Wonders, and Church Growth' at the School of World Mission with the faith-healer John Wimber (Marsden 1987:292). The course involved '"practical sessions" in which signs and wonders, including actual healings, were performed in class' (*ibid.*). However as already noted, Wagner's statements do seem to come from his own assumptions, like: 'Christians would be wise to exorcise their homes from demons, especially if they had travelled to pagan temples in foreign lands where the demons might have attached themselves to persons or luggage' (*ibid.*:294, citing an article by Wagner entitled 'Can Demons Harm Christians? *Christian Life*. May 1985. 76).

All of this highlights a weak hermeneutic. Admittedly Wagner does recognise the importance of being 'faithful to the Scriptures' (1981:150) and he also affirms (*ibid.*:153) that 'the ultimate bedrock of all theologizing is God's holy Word, the Bible.' He even points out (concerning a specific hypothesis of demon possession) that there is 'little value in this hypothesis, unless we can find some biblical warrants for it' (1989:280).

And yet finding a 'biblical warrant' *per se* does not guarantee an idea, and Wagner's use of the bible does tend towards a proof-texting of his own thought. His understanding of adequate bible study, for example, is determined simply by the 'mature common sense' that goes into it (1971:16); his definition of mission (simply 'making disciples') derives directly from a narrow and mandatory interpretation of Matthew 28:19 (1972:218) as discussed below; even non-biblical paradigms of thought are cited when it suits Wagner, like his recommendation of a *Reader's Digest* article by James Michener as a suitable model for all mission strategists (1971:29–30).

These criticisms of a world professor in mission are intended not to downplay positive contributions that Wagner may have made in his career, but simply to tease out aspects of the illusive problem ingraining modern mission. These are—we would suggest as a result—a weak soteriology, christology, ecclesiology, pneumatology, hermeneutic and/or 'biblical' argument.

Charles Van Engen

A critique of the Fuller School of World Mission would not be complete without reference—however brief that may be—to a more recent faculty member and leading missiologist at the School, Charles Van Engen. His missiological contributions have been significant and broad but just one example of his thought will be looked at here.

Van Engen argued at one point (1996b:208) that missiological education involved 'a delicate balance between specialization and integration in a three-arena approach to missiology' (those three 'arenas' being text, context and community, or bible, world and church [*ibid.*:219]). The 'delicate balance' that he identified would be determined in relation to what he termed 'a specific integrating idea that would serve as a hub around which one may approach a re-reading of Scripture' (*ibid*.:223).

Because of the importance this proposed 'hub' one might expect it to be a key doctrine of the church; or perhaps the person of Jesus Christ himself; or the leading of the Holy Spirit as one prays through Scripture as hermeneutical key. Van Engen does, admittedly, acknowledge (*ibid*.:223) that all possible integrative themes should 'be held together in terms of their proximity to Jesus Christ, the head of the body, the church.' He even acknowledges that Christ is, Himself, the centre (*ibid*.:225). More: he states that 'we are trying to avoid bringing our own agendas to the Scriptures and superimposing them on Scripture' (*ibid*.:223).

However, the 'hub' that he had identified turns out to be little more than the 'church growth agenda of Donald McGavran' (*ibid*.:222). This it is 'that forms the raison d'être of the ICG/SWM [Institute for Church Growth/School of World Mission]' (*ibid*.). His overriding stress is clear (*ibid*.): 'For the ICG/SWM, in faithfulness to its founder and to its raison d'être, this integrating theme is church growth.' And it is the role of the theologian of mission to 'articulate and to "guard" the center'—this 'center' of church growth (*ibid*.:224).

The core hermeneutic of the School, thus, appears (at least as identified in these three all-too-brief examples) to continue to be the principal of church growth—even, perhaps, to the point of seeing mission itself epitomised by this concept (Van Engen 1981:3).

This may be valid to the extent to which church is viewed in ontological wholeness, as discussed further on. This criticism may also be difficult to understand in view of Van Engen's appeal to 'Scripture' and condemnation of proof-texting and seeing the bible simply as a source of commands for mission (1993:29). And yet he does bring his own hermeneutic, and his very concept of mission does appear to have been formed before coming to the bible.

In contrast to this, the role of the missiologist should not be to simply 'articulate and "guard" the center' (as proposed) so much as to ensure the authenticity of the centre that it is guarding. It is the identity of that 'center', as well as the presupposition of 'mission' itself which is being brought into question here.

This, together with all that has been gleaned from looking at contemporary mission teaching thus far, suggests that questionable hermeneutics and a debatable worldview (insofar as unquestioned Enlightenment principles so ingrain the way mission is taught and thought about) are strong components of the crisis in mission that we are addressing.

These issues will have to be investigated, but two other areas need looking at in our attempt to understand where contemporary mission is at and what modern mission 'is', before we do this.

Some Statistics

A key feature of modern mission is its reference to, and use of statistics (as shown already) or numbers.

At the dawn of the nineteenth century the Baptist missionary William Carey, stopping off in Cape Town (*en route* to India) to refresh and restock like all other travellers of his day, was confronted by the number of other denominations and people already doing exactly what he was doing. He called for a more united missionary effort by all mission agencies and denominations, and a combining of resources.

Approximately one hundred and fifty years after this appeal, Olan Hendrix (1966:227) expressed a similar opinion. Referring to the *August 31, 1965 Statistical Report of the Interdenominational Foreign Mission Association* (IFMA) he observed: 'IFMA includes forty-seven missions with 8,413 missionaries and home staff members.' This called, in his opinion, for a merger of societies within IFMA. His overriding perception was this: 'There are simply too many foreign mission organizations. We may lack missionaries, preaching, and conversions, but there are too many separate missionary groups' (*ibid.*).

His observation was of a vast but fragmented number of people (and groups) doing a fragmented number of things for God, using a huge amount of resources, but without being necessarily effective (*ibid.*).

Some forty years later the same ineffectiveness of contemporary mission is being reflected in statistics published annually in the *International Bulletin of Missionary Research* (IBMR). Originally published by David Barrett as annual statistics on global mission, a few notable statistics from the new 'Status of Global Mission' format are summarised for 2010 in TABLE 1, below.

TABLE 1
Summary of Statistics on Global Mission
(figures taken from Johnson, Barrett and Crossings 2010:36)

	AD 1900 A	mid-2000 B	mid-2010 C	incr/(decr) 1900-2010 C–A	last 110 years %age incr/(decr)	incr/(decr) 2000-2010 C–B	last 10 years ave. new/week
World population (million)	1,620		6,907				
Foreign Mission Sending Agencies	600	4,000	4,700	4,100	683%	700	1
Christian Service Agencies	1,500	23,000	28,000	26,500	1,767%	5,000	10
Foreign Missionaries	62,000	420,000	400,000	338,000	545%	(20,000)	(38)
National Christian Workers	2.1 mill		12 mill	10 mill	471%	1.1 mill	2,115
Income of global foreign missions			US$29bill!				
Cost effectiveness (cost per baptism!)			US$588mill!				
World Christians (million)			2,292				
World Christians as % of world pop.	34.4%		33.2%				(1.3%)!

These statistics are startling:

1. Between the years 1900 and 2010, the world population has increased from 1.6 to almost 7 billion people.
2. There has, however, been more than just a corresponding growth in foreign mission sending agencies during this time: it has been a 683 percent increase from 600 (in the year 1900) to 4,700 (in 2010)!
3. This represents an average growth, over the last ten years, of more than one new foreign mission sending agency being formed every week!

A similarly impressive growth has been in the number of Christian service agencies:

1. a growth from 1,500 to 28,000 over 110 years
2. over the last ten years alone, this has constituted an average growth of almost ten new agencies every week!

Related to this is the growth in foreign mission personnel:

1. an increase from 62,000 at the turn of the century to 420,000 a century later
2. this constituted an average increase of fifty nine new foreign missionaries per week over those one hundred years!
3. interestingly, though, there has been a negative growth (a decrease of 2000 foreign missionaries/year, or thirty eight/week) over the last ten years
4. this decrease, however, is countered by the huge increase in short-term missionaries sent overseas, as already discussed (something like 1.6 million from the USA alone, each year).

This growth in national Christian workers as opposed to foreign mission workers is shown in the increase in those national Christian workers during this period:

1. from 2.1 million to 12 million, over 110 years
2. or, put another way, an average addition 2,115 workers per week over the last ten years!

What a tremendous growth in personnel and enterprise!

As to the effect of such missionary praxis, however, the irony of these otherwise impressive and encouraging figures is that the number of Christians as a percentage of the world population has actually decreased from 34.4 percent in 1900 to 33.2 percent in 2010 (*ibid.*)—a decrease against the world population as significant as 1.3 percent!

The conclusion that we can draw from these figures is poignant and challenging: that despite all the financial input involved in Christian work over the last century (an estimated global 'income'—should this be 'expenditure'?!—for foreign missions of US$29billion/annum and an average 'cost' of US$588,000 for every baptism [*ibid.*]) and despite all the strategising in world mission that has taken place, Christianity is still a mere third of the world population (and falling). This relative drop in World Christianity is in spite of a century of unparalleled effort and use of resources!

By way of an analysis of similar figures in 1997, David Barrett acknowledged the dismal observations that we have been forced to make. He commented poignantly: that despite the significant level of Christian activity in present times (e.g. through the distribution of approximately 1.8 billion bibles per annum), 'other *Christians* including ourselves . . . are the focus of 97 percent of all Christian ministry in the world' (1997:24—italics added)! The United Bible Society made this assessment: 'We are doing a better job in reaching out to Christians than we are to non-Christians. Most of our effort is therefore to the people who have been reached by the gospel *already!*' (*ibid.*).

Admittedly, only total figures are being commented on here, rather than internal movements particular to different people groups. In chapter 1, for example, it was noted that African professions of faith increased from 9 percent to 48 percent over the last hundred years, whilst European professions decreased from 95 percent to 80 percent over the same period of time (*op. cit.*). In addition, it is not clear what proportion of growth occurs because of 'Great Commission' activity, or as a result of the fire of the gospel itself spreading through virgin forest.

It does appear, though, that despite a remarkable expenditure of resources, activity is largely directed towards the church itself.

So what should be done?

Barrett's proposal was for a more strategic deployment of mission forces in non-Christian people-groups (an obvious solution to which his research is bound to point).

But as we outwork our current thesis of the need for critique of our 'own' mission structures and norms, it is important to be wary of Barrett's presuppositions: his theology and the framework of mission within which he is working.

One significant presupposition relates to his understanding of mission as a fulfilment of the 'Great Commission' mandate (in the usual 'Great Commission' texts). This is evidenced by the inclusion in his statistics of the category 'Great Commission Christians (active)' (which has been continued in, and is reflected in the *statistic line 26* in Johnson *et al.* 2010:36) by which he means 'active church members who take Christ's Great Commission seriously' (Barrett 1994:24). The significance of this category, for Barrett, is shown by the way he commented positively on the way 'Great Commission Christians' had increased from 50 million to 759 million in relation to a tripling of the world population and world Christians, and a total of 2 billion Christians in the world in 1997 (1997:25).

The validity of this 'Great Commission' presupposition as basic to a right identity of mission will be investigated, below. This has to be done, because apart from simply striving to do 'it' better (i.e. to better obey the 'Great Commission' and increase the fruit of one's labour), the most obvious way forward is to reconsider the validity of modern mission's current perspective on the 'Great Commission' and to start recognising, and working out the implications of one's 'captivity to outmoded paradigms,' as suggested by Engle and Dyreness (2000:79). In their view, 'methods and plans' about mission have for too long seemed to 'drive programs more than do biblical principles' (*ibid.*:20). In other words: 'pragmatics have replaced theological reflection and biblical obedience' (*ibid.*:21).

Pragmatism does appear to be the overriding focus of mission 'thinking'.

One final observation needs to be made about Barrett's statistic that 'Great Commission' Christians make up a third of the Christian population. If this is the case, we need to ask ourselves what the other two-thirds of Christian people are doing, and why and how mission can be regarded so separately from their normal Christian lives, and whether this is right.

This issue will be addressed in final conclusion, Part III.

Mission Literature

Where better to gain a fair representation of contemporary mission than through a review of mission literature. This could include mission journals or periodicals, missiological books or (to ensure maximum coverage) book reviews and abstracts.

At least three missiological journals were recently identified as key (Liston 2010:215): *Missiology*, the *International Bulletin of Missionary Research* (*IBMR*), and *Missionalia*. But two further periodicals can be included to make up a 'big five' of mission journals, so broadening the spectrum of what may safely be considered representative of contemporary mission: the World Council of Churches' quarterly *International Review of Mission* (*IRM*) with its ecumenical approach and, occupying a more conservative position: the *Evangelical Missionary Quarterly* (*EMQ*).

An examination of these 'big five' has been conducted for the sample year of 1996 (though an examination of any one year would produce the same comprehensive result).

The overriding observation made was the almost absolute praxeological point of view from which all articles (reviews and abstracts) had been written—in other words, the approach of getting mission done, and activism in the church.

There were hints of an alternative 'start point': not in mission needing to be done, but in God and His purposes being sought. For reasons which will be explained, this may be termed an 'ontological' approach.

In the *Evangelical Missionary Quarterly*, for example, Niringiye (1996:60–68) pointed out that 'the supreme arguments for missions are not found in any specific words . . . [but] in the very being and character of God.' In *Missiology*, Noll (1996:47–64) highlighted that the core of God's own mission is the person of Jesus Christ, and a restored relationship with Him, and that it is independent of the missionary enterprise. Camps (1996:33–36), in the *International Bulletin of Missionary Research*, called for a new theology of the Logos (as the one who has been active among us from the very beginning of creation and who will be until the end of time). *Missionalia* published an article by Hastings (1996:16) in which he suggested that 'mission means, in the last analysis, an out flowing of loving activity to replace isolation and division by shared friendship, lies by truth, impoverishment by the kind of material affluence which is not prodigal or corrupt.' He highlighted the problematic concept of the specialist missionary, acknowledging that 'the "full-time missionary" is, almost by definition, an over-committed person, prone to a one-sided fanaticism' (*ibid.*).

However, the perspective of all these examples was still of 'mission' as something undertaken by a select few only, and as something which is distinct from the normal Christian life. No articles, reviews or abstracts examined in that sample year of 1996 proposed anything significant about what may be regarded as the overshadowed ontological dimension.

Research done by Liston on the three key periodicals mentioned above highlighted a similar domination of praxis in mission. Amongst other things he noted these: a prevalence of articles written on the organisation of missions (2010:216); that the majority people group conducting missiological research today are mainly Western, and male (*ibid.*:217); and (*ibid.*:218) that 'the vast majority (77 percent) of missiological research had . . . no clear theological focus and perspective'—except for 'reaching out with the love of Jesus.'

All this underlines a clearly praxeological basis of modern mission, and an immediate need for a careful examination and critique of any theological foundations that it may have. If there is only tenuous theological substance to contemporary mission, then the practice itself and the common understanding of what it is may be at least inadequate, if not altogether wrong.

More than this, though, it stresses the need for a right approach to, and understanding of Christian mission to be developed: not from the presupposition of praxis and activity, so much as from a position which is conspicuous by its almost total absence in mission literature: the eclipsed dimension of ontology.

Analysis and Conclusion: Definition of the Problem

Mission in the contemporary world is predominantly marked by features of individualism, triumphalism, mandate, call, consciousness of numbers and 'confessions' of the faith and an overall 'co-mission' with God. It is often associated with romanticism, self-sacrifice, going to foreign lands, crossing of cultures and strong personalities. It is impossible not to associate contemporary mission with Enlightenment principles, anthropocentricity, poor (or at least narrow, self-authenticating) theology and simplistic hermeneutics and exegesis, especially in relation to the 'Great Commission' passage. Weighed on the scale of its own statistics, it has not seen a growth in Christianity (in comparison with growth in world population) over the last century, despite a massive use of financial and personnel resources.

In view of the survey of the contemporary practice of mission performed in this chapter, it is safe to conclude that contemporary mission has in the main evolved out of, and is continuing within a paradigm of praxis. Mission arises, often, from something more of a desire to do and to be effective in, than from a comprehensive theological start point.

As such, contemporary mission is not necessarily complete or accurate, for it may be simply the product of various activities in the church, and the practice of the church itself, that has determined the model and meaning of 'mission' as we understand it today, rather than a reliable biblical theology.

The reason for pragmatics being so dominant in the church is not clear at this stage. But for the purposes of defining the problem in modern mission it is important, now, to pursue a few strands of 'suspicion' that have been raised thus far: first, that modern mission has been influenced by a pragmatic reading of the 'Great Commission'; second, that the identity of modern mission has been impacted by the basic principles of the Enlightenment; third (thus), that mission in modernity has been approached from the dominant perspective of praxis, rather than from the overshadowed dimension of ontology; fourth, that modern pragmatism has evolved out of the simplistic hermeneutic and exegesis surrounding the concept and current practice of modern mission; and fifth, too, that it is undergirded by inadequate doctrinal substance.

CHAPTER 4

Influence of the 'Great Commission'

MODERN MISSION HAS ARGUABLY been constructed on the massive 'pragmatic rock' of the 'Great Commission'.

Two major expressions of this 'rock' need to be looked at: first, the way in which the 'mandate' of the 'Great Commission' to 'Go!' (Mt. 28:19) has come to be interpreted in contemporary mission and, second, the way in which it has been modelled or outworked historically especially by the influential 'father of modern mission' (Gonzalez 1985:306,307), William Carey.

If this 'rock' proves to be solid and trustworthy we will need to look elsewhere for a solution to the problem of the identity of mission. If it turns out to be something more sand-like, however, then this 'sandy rock' of the 'Great Commission' may be a significant part of the crisis in mission that we are investigating.

How the 'Great Commission' has been Interpreted Biblically

The importance of the 'Great Commission' as rationale for the movement of modern mission is undeniable.

Its prominence was reflected by the question posed by Warneck (reputedly the father of modern missiology [so Yates 1994:4 and Conn 1983:6]): 'Why do we do mission work? The shortest and most popular answer is: because Jesus Christ has commanded it.' (1897:91 cited in Boer 1961:26). Boer's own opinion is that the authority for witness in the early church 'cannot have been any other one than the Great Commission' (*ibid*.:184–5). Hudson Taylor's oft-cited words ingrain traditional mission logic: 'The Great Commission is not an option to be considered; it is a command to be obeyed.'

The 'Great Commission' undergirded key conferences over the last hundred years or so.

It was core to the key World Missionary Conference in Edinburgh, 1910, which was a clear coming together of groups who shared the purpose of giving 'the gospel to the world' (Anderson 2000:1029).

A telling observation of the two world missionary conferences in the 1950s is this: 'The questions of Willingen and Ghana—Why mission? What is mission?—were not even asked in Edinburgh. Everybody still knew exactly what mission was' (so Bosch 1980:3): mission was, at that time, the 'Great Commission'.

It was also foundational to subsequent conferences like the Berlin Congress (1966), which was outspokenly to 'refocus the twentieth-century Church's sight on the great commission of Jesus Christ' (Henry 1966c:3). The closing statement of that Congress proposed (so Henry and Mooneyham 1967:5) that the task of all believers was 'to proclaim to all people the good news of salvation through his atoning death and resurrection; to invite them to discipleship through repentance and faith; to baptize them into the fellowship of his Church; and to teach them all his words'—a strong echo from Matthew 28:19. Of particular note at that Congress was John Stott's already mentioned daily devotions on the 'Great Commission' where, when he focused on Matthew 28:16-20, he looked at 19-20a in particular.

The same 'Great Commission' stress on mission can be seen in the ethos of organisations and activities that grew out of the Berlin Congress, like the mission sodality or classical mission agency. As organisations standing distinct from the established church, sodalities are essentially rooted in the pragmatic concept of the Great Commission 'mandate' or 'going out'. The Church Mission Society for example, in which Lesslie Newbigin was an ordained missionary from 1956, was (in his words) a 'perfect example of the true sodality' (1979:305).

In his first year as Director of the Commission on World Mission and Evangelism of the World Council of Churches, Emilio Castro wrote of the 'total missionary task of the church' and of the 'international missionary task' (1973:141)—sentiments that (through their mandatory and global totalitarian natures) come directly from the concept of the 'Great Commission'.

Evangelically, John Stott was core to the drawing up of the Lausanne Covenant (which was foundational even to the Cape Town 2010 conference), this being: 'to obey Christ's commission to proclaim it to all mankind and to make disciples of every nation' (Lausanne Covenant 2010: Online).

All these developments are in a way summarised in David Barrett's concept of the science of missiometrics which 'studies missions in ways that are empirical, quantitative and metrical' (Barrett 1995:154) and which points to the '6 billion human beings grouped in 13,000 ethno-linguistic peoples, speaking over 10,000 languages' and the 'huge lists . . . vast computer memory and prodigious processing power' that is needed to monitor it all (*ibid.*:160). And missiometrics is, in Barrett's view, nothing less than a tool 'to assist the church in obeying its Lord's commands' (*ibid.*).

Each of the fields examined above (history and practice) reflects an apparent obedience to the 'mandate' of the 'Great Commission' and a dominant sense of activism in the face of global unbelief.

Matthew 28 Versus Any Other 'Great Commission Text'

Beyond the issue of the importance of the 'Great Commission' is the importance of Matthew 28 in particular.

As noted, Matthew 28:16–20 is not the only biblical rendering of the 'Great Commission'. However, why 28:16–20 in particular should be looked at is because of its prime positioning in Matthew's Gospel and thus in the New Testament as a whole.

David Bosch sketched the importance of this text (1991:5–57): it has not always enjoyed such repute in biblical scholarship (as recently as 1908, Adolf von Harnack even considered whether these words were a later addition to the Gospel! [1962:242 in Bosch 1991:56]). It was only in the 1940s that Michel and Lohmeyer pioneered detailed exegetical work on the passage. And it was only in 1977 that Meier offered this definitive conclusion about Matthew 28:16–20: 'The one thing scholars are agreed upon is the pivotal nature of these verses' (1977:407 in Bosch 1991:57).

Now this conclusion is well held. Gerhard Friedrich (in Bosch *ibid.*) listed various opinions which gave consensus to this passage as 'the theological program of Matthew' (J. Blank), 'a summary of the entire gospel of Matthew' (G. Bornkamm), 'the most important concern of the Gospel' (H. Kosmala), 'the "climax" of the gospel' (U. Luck), 'a sort of culmination of everything said up to this point' (P. Nepper-Christensen), 'a "manifesto"' (G. Otto), and 'a "table of contents" of the gospel' (G. Schille), with Friedrich himself describing it as 'the crowning culmination at the end of his gospel' (*ibid.*).

Peter Cotterell observed the same: that this passage is the peak or 'high-point' of Matthew's Gospel (1990:95). And Bosch (1991:57) concluded in this way: 'Today scholars agree that the entire gospel points to these final verses: all the threads woven into the fabric of Matthew, from chapter 1 onward, draw together here.'

If Matthew 28:16–20 had been a mere addendum to the writing of Matthew, it would not hold the weight that it does as a pivotal section of that Gospel. However, because no other record of the 'Great Commission' is contained in such a prominent passage of Scripture, Matthew 28:16–20 has been deemed to be of critical significance to the present discussion.

The way in which this passage has been interpreted will play into our understanding of how the 'Great Commission' as a whole has been interpreted.

Textual Considerations

Claims to Matthew 28:16–20 as mandate for mission admittedly arise out of significant criteria: for example, the fronted verb 'go', in 28:19, to which the rest of the command is related by a series of subordinate verbs (i.e. 'making disciples', 'baptising' and 'teaching'); the significance of the new universal faith for 'all nations' not just the Jews; the authority of the risen Lord behind the mandate (through his encounter with the eleven on a mountain top [which is a setting for revelation in Matthew], his powerful appearance [which provoked awe and worship, v.17] and his declaration ['all authority has been given to me . . .'] which is reminiscent of the Son of Man text in Daniel 7:14 [so Senior and Stuhlmueller 1983:251–252]).

'Use' of the Text

However beyond just the text, the concept of the 'Great Commission' has come to include things like a person's 'call' (McGavran 1986:53, as discussed), the romantic tradition of mission, elitism, triumphalism and the overall activism of mission. The 'Great Commission' has become more of a conceptual point of reference than a necessarily textual one: an umbrella under which anything done in the name of mission(s) will find shade.

So it includes more than it should because of its textual simplicity, but it also excludes more than it should, for the same reason: all of the texts on which the 'Great Commission' concept is based are usually treated out of context, as shown below, thus omitting a whole breadth of possible meaning, because of a favourite one.

For example, an appeal to Matthew 28 as basis for the 'Great Commission' is at best a reference to just Matthew 28:19–20a, but generally no more. This overlooks any significance of the Matthew 28 pericope discussed earlier which in this case is not being seen or heard as a whole but rather as a verse-and-a-half in isolation.

Bosch (1991:341) had grave concerns about this very issue, as expressed in these words: 'The Great Commission . . . is usually couched in a most simplistic form of biblical literalism and proof-texting, with hardly any attempt at understanding the commission from within the context in which it appears in Scripture.'

Clearly, a detailed examination of the pericope as a whole is required.

Structure of the Text—an Illegitimate Basis for Authority

In line with popular thinking, New Testament scholar Martin Dibelius designated verses 18–20 of the pericope in question 'a missionary command' (1971 in Meier 1977:417).

But Meier's right response was this: 'Is "missionary command," which strictly speaking refers only to 19–20a, an adequate description of the whole of 18–20, to say nothing of 16–20? For reasons which will become clear . . . we think not. It focuses on only one element, and does not adequately designate the whole' (1977:417).

There has been a simple oversight of the broader context and implications of Matthew 28:16–20. This all echoes earlier discussion on the crisis of mission which was suggested to have been eclipsed by mere responses and proposed solutions to that crisis. The whole of Matthew 28:16–20 has been effectively eclipsed by verses 19–20a, which would explain why this oversight has in turn led to a continued failure to locate the core of authentic mission.

Once identified, that core would bridge our contemporary paradigm of missiological thought and action with the necessary new one Bosch anticipated.

Thus again it appears that the text itself does need to be examined in detail.

How this will be done is a more difficult question, especially in view of Meier's rather negative conclusion that 'no form-critical category yet proposed fits Matt. 28:16–20' (1977:424). The pericope is 'so idiosyncratic,' he suggests here, 'that it defies the labels of form criticism.'

It is not within the scope of this work to pursue this argument, but Meier's conclusion begs an alternative method for, or approach to analysing this passage.

Because of this, a linguistic analysis of the text will be attempted.

Linguistic Analysis of the 'Great Commission'

The oversight of two particular linguistic elements—'peak' and 'resolution'—bring into question the authority for mission so commonly attributed to this pericope.

Cotterell and Turner note that the determination of the peak of a discourse is paramount to a correct understanding of the whole (1989:245). Linguists Longacre and Levinsohn (1978:105) suggest further that two peaks may exist in narrative writing: the first, denoted by 'peak', marks the 'deep structure confrontation (climax),' and the second, 'peak^1', marks the 'deep structure denouement.'

In view of certain standard linguistic phenomena of peaking in narrative structure, shown below, it can be argued that the peak of Matthew 28:16–20 is represented by v.18 ('then Jesus came to them'), and only its secondary peak (peak^1) by the following verse, v.19 ('therefore go!').

This would suggest the climax of the discourse to be the person and presence of the risen Christ rather than the commission that He gives to those on the mountain (whether to others, in later ages or not, is debatable).

But in order to grasp the significance of this suggestion we need first to look at the linguistic phenomena that support it.

'Peak' as Person

The main, confrontational peak clearly appears to begin and build up from the start of the pericope, v.16 (Cotterell notes the significant lack of peaking before this point [1990:89]). This is due to the standard features of peaking discussed in, for example, Cotterell and Turner (1989:246), Longacre (1983:25–38) and Longacre and Levinsohn (1978:109).

By following certain guidelines outlined by these linguists, the following features of peaking can be identified in v.16 of our passage:

1. the gathering of participants (the eleven disciples),
2. the change of location (to a mountain, in Galilee),
3. the possible rhetorical underlining with regard to the importance of the place (that Jesus, Himself, had wanted them to go there),
4. the heightened vividness, through tense shift (from the present of 'this very day,' v.15, to the past of v.16),
5. the change of pace (of the pericope as a whole), vv.16–20 taking the space of only five verses to sum up the whole of the Gospel as well as pointing the reader towards the future end of the age, and
6. a change of vantage point (from that of the women, soldiers and Jews, to that of the disciples).

And yet the following verse (v.17) delays the peak again. This is also evidenced by standard linguistic features, but this time features of a 'delay' in reaching a peak, in particular the relatively mediocre 'strength' of words used in v.17 in contrast to v.18, such as:

1. reference to 'when' (v.17), which is subordinate to the 'then' of v.18,
2. the fact that they only *saw* Him (v.17), in contrast to His actual *coming* to them in the following verse,
3. use of the pronoun 'him' (who they saw, in v.17) as opposed to *Jesus Himself* in v.18, and the emphasis that this proper noun ('Jesus') actually adds,
4. the observation concerning doubt (v.17) indicating that all was not yet right; only *some* were able to worship Jesus.

In other words, there is a definite absence of the resolution that was anticipated in v.16, and so our attention is pointed beyond v.16, and now even beyond v.17, to the following verse.

And sure enough v.18 does appear to climax the pericope with the following resolution being brought to the weaker/wanting statements of vv.16&17, through these features:

1. *'then'* (addressing the doubt of v. 17),
2. *'Jesus'* (the *person—proper noun*—being in focus instead of just 'him' in v.17),
3. the fact that Jesus actually *'came to them'* (he was not simply seen and worshipped and/or doubted) but presenced Himself with them. The 'gathering of participants' is completed by the introduction of the key figure of the narrative, Jesus Himself, here.
4. More than this, though, is the reassurance of Jesus' word, *spoken to them, and with them*. As commented by Gundry (1982:594): 'Neither the appearance of Jesus removes doubt . . . nor does proof of Jesus' corporeality remove doubt . . . Rather, it is Jesus' word that quiets all doubt even though that word does not take up the question of doubt.'

Beyond the resolution and peaking features just noted, the content of Jesus' speech itself adds additional elements of peaking to v.18:

1. rhetorical underlining (concerning the extent of his authority: not just in heaven, but on earth as well, or *vice versa*),
2. re-emphasis of the key participant in the narrative through use of personal pronoun 'me' ('Jesus . . . "me"'),
3. heightened vividness, through both

    (a) a shift in tense from past ('they *saw*' and 'he *came*') to perfect past ('all authority *has been* given to me'), but also through

    (b) a shift in person from Jesus to the One who had given Him authority. The sense that this gives is one of equality between Jesus and that Other (a sentiment that is clearly supported by relating Revelation 1 with Daniel 7, where Jesus [the one who was dead and is now alive] in the former, is overtly described there in language used of the Ancient of Days in the latter). Thus, significantly, we have an added feature of peaking in this verse:

4. a further shift of vantage point (from the person of Jesus who is already, and humanly known to the listening disciples, to this otherness of heaven itself and the One bestower of authority in heaven and on earth).

Thus, there is strong linguistic evidence for regarding v.18, and the person of the risen Christ and Cosmic Lord—equal with, and one with God—as the climax of the discourse and Gospel as a whole.

'Resolution' as Other

Behind this very clear peak, verses 19–20a (the 'commission') fall into second place, and should be regarded not as the actual peak but as the secondary peak (peak¹). This will have obvious implications for the traditional interpretation made of this 'passage' (or rather these diminished verses). But more of that later!

Longacre and Levinsohn explain this secondary peak (peak¹) as a 'decisive event which loosens up the story and makes resolution possible' (1978:105).

This would suggest that the 'commission' is not so much a peak as a resolution or response. In relation to the person of Jesus, the 'commission' is a mere practical outworking of the significance of His presence in the lives of those who have encountered Him, and been encountered by Him.

It is the peak (Jesus, from the vantage point of heaven and otherness) which (or Who) is the point of focus and priority in this pericope. Only in relation to that encounter and person do the implications of the risen Lord's presence and the event of His life, death, resurrection and inauguration in authority start to be unpacked as a result of denouement (or secondary peak: peak¹) in ways that will be relevant for the disciples' lives on earth, as they look towards the future.

In Longacre's words, the projected denouement (in our case, the 'commission') 'takes us up to a certain point, the events aren't over yet, but the author, in effect, tells us: this is how things of this sort customarily proceed and this will be no doubt the end of the whole matter' (1983:13).

And this is certainly the sense that we get in verses 19–20a: things are clearly not over yet. Benjamin Hubbard (1974:71) noted an open-endedness to the Gospel, caused by the absence of the element of 'conclusion' which is normally a part of commissioning passages in Old Testament parallels.

This open-endedness occurs as a result of the final words of the pericope which refer to 'the very end of the age' and which predict an ultimate end-time closure. It emphasises the lapse in time that has now even become our own reality in the twenty-first century as we too process this cosmic appearance and join in anticipation of the 'end of the age'.

However, because of who it is that the peak brings into focus, the significance of this amazing event in which we all share (to a greater or lesser extent) is not about what we have been included in, or what we may be getting engaged in practically but rather about Jesus, the divine authority, who has promised to presence Himself with us ceaselessly in life.

God of heaven and of earth, the One who has absolute authority over life and creation, and who is made known to us and given to the fallen world in Jesus Christ, will be (as He is even today, 2000 years later) with His people all the way.

This is the backbone of this pericope and indeed the whole of Matthew's Gospel and the Christian gospel itself.

Yes, the importance of verses 19–20a should not be overlooked, nor should the many (not invalid) reasons for understanding this verse as the climax of the passage be understated, for example: (1) the 'go' that reintroduces the disciples, and gathers, again, the participants; (2) the concentration of participles that heightens the vividness of the verse (e.g. to baptize and to teach); (3) the new shift of vantage point from heaven to earth that again takes place; and (4) the change of pace from the poised state of watching, waiting, worshipping, doubting, and even being addressed by the risen Lord, to the emphatic 'go' which suddenly breaks into the discourse.

However there is, still, an overriding stress on the otherness and absoluteness of Jesus, here, emphasised further (beyond what we have noted already) by reference to the 'Father, Son and Holy Spirit' and by the total dependence that is anticipated of His people upon what Jesus Himself had commanded in the past (i.e. 'teaching them to obey everything I have commanded you').

Re-emphasis of the important presence of God comes in other ways as well. In v.20b, for example, it is shown through Jesus' intimate words: '*I* am with you always'—again alluding to the future, but emphasising His presence in the present. And 20c ('to the very end of the age') could be regarded as the *finis* of the pericope and Gospel, the 'formulaic ending' (like 'they lived happily ever after,' [so Longacre and Levinsohn 1978:104])—but it is not a statement in isolation: it is a repetition of what we have seen already concerning the continued presence of God with His people (v.18 'Jesus came to them,' and 20b 'I am with you always'). It is about His presence: the presence of the Jesus of history, yes, but now also risen and equated with the fullness of the Living God Himself, with us 'always, to the very end of the age.'

The profundity and importance of this concept is stressed by the *inclusio* that it forms with Matthew 1:1 (concerning 'the genealogy of Jesus Christ, Son of David') and, more overtly, 1:23 ('Emmanuel, God with us'). Leon Morris (1992:749), commenting on Matthew, recognises this *inclusio*, writing: 'This Gospel opened with the assurance that in the coming of Jesus, God was with his people (1:23), and it closes with the promise that the very presence of Jesus Christ will never be lacking to his faithful follower.' Douglas Hare also recognised the *inclusio* but traced it meaningfully further back than the start of the Gospel to that great theme in the Hebrew Scriptures 'I am with you', writing (1993:335): '"I am with you" is a formula ascribed to God in the Old Testament . . . The attribution of the formula to the risen Jesus reminds us at the conclusion of the Gospel that Jesus is still Emmanuel, "God with us"' (*ibid.*). And Forman (1957:57–59) reflected the importance of the *inclusio* when in answer to the question 'What is the foundation of world unity?' he suggested that it is none less that the personal love of God: 'God with us.'

Resolution of this Matthean pericope, thus, resides not in the 'Great Commission' as mandate, but in the profound significance of the reality of the 'gift' and ongoing presence of God.

Assessment

Of significance for our critique of modern mission as we come to the end of this section, then, is that the 'Great Commission' is not the primary focus of Matthew's last five verses but simply the unpacking of that focus—the resolution of the peak.

The peak and emphasis of Matthew 28:16–20 as the crown of the Gospel is not on the doing of mission but on the reality out of which any relevant action will derive: the presence and being of God, in Jesus Christ.

The 'command/instruction/mandate' (or however one wants to refer to it) to 'Go!' is a mere response to the presence of One who was dead, but who is now alive.

More than this: that promise of the presence of God is all the more wonderful because of the way it is a promise for all people, not just the 'few' who audibly first heard those words, but for the generations of others who have and who will hear of the promise of the presence of God through to 'the very end of the age,' and who will enjoy that presence. Just as 'going' was a denouement of that personal peak then, so too it will be a resolution of the peak now: an effect of Christ's resurrected, glorified life in the lives of all believers in our own world, and through into future ages as well. It will be a mere consequence of the presence of God with all who acknowledge Him, until the Last Day.

Understanding Matthew 28:19–20a in this way gives it a context and a meaning far beyond mere mandate. And it does not seem appropriate to give contemporary renderings of the 'Great Commission' the weight that they currently hold in mission rationale and identity today. As a result, 'mission' that derives out of such a pragmatic interpretation of the 'Great Commission' may actually be a false concept, or at least seriously distorted or, at best, should be understood simply and more correctly as that which is derived only in relation to an encounter with the risen and ever-living Lord.

The priority being recognised here missiologically is not the mandate, or the Commission, but the person of God. Thus what is being suggested is that from a right ontology—in other words from an encounter with, and a living relationship with God, Who is with us always—a relevant praxis will happen by simple way of response.

The 'Great Commission' Modelled in History

It was proposed earlier that there are two major ways of approaching the massive 'pragmatic rock' of the 'Great Commission' upon which modern mission has been constructed. The first of these was the way in which the 'mandate' of the 'Great Commission' has come to be interpreted biblically.

It remains now to look at the second: the way in which it has been modelled in history, in particular by William Carey.

The pivotal influence of the 'Great Commission' on modern mission has already been noted. But it is only a recent influence. Johannes van den Berg (1956:165) argued that although by the end of the nineteenth century 'Mt. 28:18–20 had completely superseded other verses from Scripture as the principal "mission text"', in the early part of the century it was 'never the one and only motive, dominant in isolation; it always occurred within a special context' (*ibid.*). Although by the end of that century, mission thinking and incentive was 'unequivocally on obedience' (Bosch 1991:341), at the beginning of the century the 'Great Commission' was never an 'overruling stimulus' for mission activity (van den Berg 1956:177). It was 'always connected with other motives' (*ibid.*) such as the millennial hope of puritan believers (as argued by Murray 1971:95). Charles Chaney (1976:259) dated the influence of Matthew's 'Great Commission' to as early as 1810, and other testimonies of its influence are known marginally before that time. Robert Morrison (1792–1834) and Adoniram Judson (1788–1850), for example, 'explicitly stated that it was primarily because of obedience to Christ's command that they had gone to the mission field' (so Boer 1961:26.)

In relation to these dates, Boer reasonably argues (*ibid.*:27) that impetus for the 'Great Commission' influence in modern mission stemmed from William Carey's 1792 publication: *An Enquiry into the Obligations of Christians to Use Means for the Conversion of the Heathens*. This opinion is held by many, like Van Engen (1996a:4,37), Stanley (1990) and Payne (1993:309) who date the modern era of missionary expansion from 1792.

Commenting on Carey's publication, Boer wrote: 'Once the eyes of the Church were opened to her missionary duty, the command of Christ around which Carey had so effectively centered his appeal became the basis on which the missionary witness of the Church was consciously built' (1961:24–25).

Historically, then, it appears that the 'Great Commission' was indeed articulated in a significantly influential way by William Carey. His *Enquiry* came to be regarded as 'the major biblical motive for Protestant missions for more than a century' (Thomas 1995:64) and even as 'the manifesto of the modern mission movement' (Boer 1961:22) and 'the charter of modern mission with its argument, review, survey and programme' (Kahn 1976:218 in Smith 1993:293).

It is therefore necessary to critique this influential writing and historic model.

Reaction Against Contemporary Attitudes

Carey's *Enquiry* was, in part, a reaction to prevailing (Reformed) attitudes toward mission.

Yes, Augustine of Hippo's argument (some fifteen centuries earlier) had largely paralleled his own (so Thomas 1995:16–19). And just a few hundred years before Carey, Anabaptist theologian Balthasar Hubmaier had argued, like him, that 'the Lord's commission to preach and baptise was as compelling today as when first spoken' (*ibid.*:35). Even Adrian Saravia—a younger contemporary of Calvin—had argued that the apostles' fulfilment of the 'Great Commission' would have been limited, and that it therefore applied to the whole church in subsequent times (*ibid.*:41–43). Others, like the German nobleman Justinianus von Welz (1621–68), had even appealed for student-volunteers to preach the gospel in non-Christian areas (so Boer 1961:21).

However, the dominant attitude towards mission (and Matthew 28 in particular) was still one of distance and irrelevance: that the Lord would usher in His kingdom in His time. For Calvin (as mentioned already, in brief), the offices of apostle and evangelist had not been 'established in the church as permanent ones' (1960:1057), but the Lord had raised them up 'at the beginning of his Kingdom, and now and again revive[d] them as the need of the times demand[ed]' (*ibid.*:1056). About 'evangelists' in particular he wrote: 'I call this office "extraordinary" because in duly constituted churches it has no place' (*ibid.*:1057). More permanent was the task of the pastor which, although similar to that of the apostle, was limited to its own church, or parish (*ibid.* paras. 4 and 5). The same was advocated by Luther and, thus, Lutheran orthodoxy.

This background of Reformation and post-Reformation thought is reflected by way of introduction to Carey's pamphlet (1792:8): 'It seems as if many thought the commission was sufficiently put in execution by what the apostles and others have done; that we have enough to do to attend to the salvation of our own countrymen; and that, if God intends the salvation of the heathen, he will some way or other bring them to the gospel, or the gospel to them.'

The pamphlet continues (*ibid.*): 'There seems also to be an opinion existing in the minds of some, that because the apostles were extraordinary officers and have no proper successors, and because many things which were right for them to do would be unwarrantable for us, therefore it may not be immediately binding on us to execute the commission, though it was so upon them.'

Carey's approach was a counter-argument. It may even be that it was 'a reaction to a long held theological misconception' (so Boer 1961:72). In short, it suggested that the fate of those who do not hear the gospel in any person's age is the responsibility of the Christian church.

His appeal was persuasive, but the validity of what he proposed depends largely upon the biblical basis for his *Enquiry* and on the soundness of his theological argument.

Biblical Basis for the Enquiry

We have already noted the importance of the 'Great Commission' to modern mission. And certainly the 'Great Commission' concept—the concept of mandate, and reaching the nations—was motivational for Carey. These are words that he used (1792:5) which strongly allude to the 'Great Commission': 'When he had laid down his life, and taken it up again, he sent forth his disciples to preach the good tidings to every creature.' Again (*ibid*.:11), showing that the basis of his argument is the 'Great Commission' mandate or command, he wrote: 'When a command exists nothing can be necessary to render it binding but a removal of those obstacles which render obedience impossible, and these are removed already.' Reference to the 'Great Commission' is also implicit in the title of his pamphlet, through use of the word 'obligation' (as mentioned by van den Berg 1956:164).

And yet no 'Great Commission' text has either been cited or exegeted. The concept has merely been appealed to. The closest Carey does get to a textual backing of his 'Great Commission' rationale is a citation of Romans 10:14–15 ('. . . how can they preach unless they are sent' [1792:1]), and this has been done almost simply by way of a cover design (certainly no exegesis or further reference to any text has been made in his treaty). But the context of that passage, like Romans 10:8 for example (which is in turn citing Deuteronomy 30:11–14), highlights so much more than mere pragmatism: 'Now what I am commanding you today is not too difficult for you or beyond your reach. It is not up in heaven, so that you have to ask, "Who will ascend into heaven to get it and proclaim it to us so we may obey it?" Nor is it beyond the sea, so that you have to ask, "Who will cross the sea to get it and proclaim it to us so we may obey it?" No, the word is very near you; it is in your mouth and in your heart . . .'

A reference to Romans 10 which does not pick up on the living dynamic of a relationship with God promised through the old covenant and accessible through the new covenant, and made known to us through the living Word, sounds a louder note by its omission than by its inclusion.

So it would appear that Carey's argument is not so much an appeal to a biblical text as to an assumed 'biblical' concept (the 'Great Commission').

What motivated Carey's appeal to mission, and his theological argument, now need to be established.

Carey's Theological Argument and Motives for Mission

The first sentence of Carey's introduction reads: 'As our blessed Lord has required us to pray that his kingdom may come, and his will be done on earth as it is in heaven, *it becomes us* not only to express our desires of that event by words, *but to use every lawful method* to spread the knowledge of his name' (1792:3—italics added). From making mention of the Lord's requirement for us to pray, Carey then mentions two things: first, negatively, we should not just verbalise desire; second, positively, we should use every lawful method available to us to bring about what we desire.

It appears from this brief sentence that prayer, as a concept and spiritual discipline, is little more than an 'expression of desire' (although admittedly it may coincide with an assumption of what the Lord may want). Motive for prayer is that the 'blessed Lord has required' it, and the essence of prayer, it seems, is 'to express our desires.' Carey's argument, however, is based on an implication that prayer by itself is an ineffectual basis for growth of the Kingdom of God and the things of God. Yet this is unfounded, biblically, and is certainly not explained biblically or theologically in his pamphlet.

Neither is the basis for his 'argument' up to this point reason or logic: its nuance is something more like 'honour' or 'principle'—an assumed 'right' way forward: a 'defy me if you dare!' sort of argument.

This tension between prayer (commanded and inadequate) and action (not commanded but necessary, in Carey's opinion) is referred to again towards the end of Carey's *Enquiry* (1792:81) where he reiterates his perception that prayer alone is inadequate: 'We must not be contented . . . with praying, without exerting ourselves in the use of means for the obtaining of those things we pray for.'

In calling for action beyond mere prayer, however, he appears to be overlooking the whole essence of what prayer is in its acknowledgement of absolute dependence on God for the giving of results, despite what we ourselves are, or are not able to do (so 1Co. 3:7 for example: 'neither he who plants nor he who waters is anything, but only God, who makes things grow').

The difficulty with this pamphlet is that no suitable substantiation for Carey's view is ever given. Neither is any suitable argument put forward suggesting why activity is necessary in addition to prayer. His only argument is that 'were the children of light, but as wise in their generation as the children of this world, they would stretch every nerve to gain so glorious a prize, nor ever imagine that it was to be obtained in any other way' (1792:81).

This introduces a major criticism: that Carey's argumentation and logic is purely secular and humanistic. In contrast to this, the standards required by God of His children (the children of light) are not necessarily or ideally taken from the example of 'children of the world'.

More though, this allusion to the bible by Carey is not consistent with the context of the passage to which he is referring (assuming we have correctly determined the biblical source of that argument!). For example, his appeal to 'stretch every nerve to gain so glorious a prize' could refer to Philippians 3:14 ('I press on towards the goal to win the prize'). In this case, it should be argued that the Philippian context is to do with spiritual perseverance in the church, not soul-winning outside of it! Alternatively, Carey could be alluding to First Corinthians 9:24b ('run in such a way as to get the prize') which is, admittedly, written after v.19 which reads: 'I make myself a slave to everyone, to win as many as possible.' But v.24b broadens the context to being about the spiritual life (or lack of—which would lead to disqualification for the prize [9:27] that is being talked about here), not activism or number-counting evangelism. It is about submission of one's whole person, in purity, to the Lord.

Again: no valid reason has been given why prayer, *per se*, is not adequate, or why '*it becomes us . . . to use every lawful method* to spread the knowledge of his name' (*op. cit.*). This appears to be more of a cultural obligation and argument than a biblical or theological one.

Carey's second possible motivation for mission is his appeal to 'the feelings of humanity' as a 'conscientious activity' (1792:3). This is what he has written:

> In order to this [spreading his name by every lawful means], it is necessary that we should become, in some measure acquainted with the religious state of the world; and as this is an object we should be prompted to pursue, not only by the gospel of our Redeemer, *but even by the feelings of humanity,* so an *inclination to conscientious activity* therein would form one of the strongest proofs that we are the subjects of grace, and partakers of that spirit of universal benevolence and genuine philanthropy, which appears so eminent in the character of God himself. (Italics added.)

Here his motive (beyond 'the gospel of our Redeemer') could again be understood as humanistic rather than necessarily theological or spiritual. He argues that one's mere 'feelings of humanity'—solidarity for another part of the human race—should motivate one to get 'acquainted with the religious state of the world.' It may be that his argument is based on a sort of 'love your neighbour as yourself' rationale which in itself is obviously valid, though not possible without rebirth (i.e. not achievable simply through charitable intentions, or 'inclination to conscientious activity').

But 'conscientious activity' and 'feelings of humanity' are just humanistic sentiments, and not in themselves viable bases for a spiritually distinctive mission movement or era, or ecclesial activity.

A third motivation may be seen in Carey's appeal to the successes of the Moravian Brethren (which showed the 'removal of obstacles' [*op. cit.*] to obedience). Popularised by John Wesley's association with them *en route* to America and back, the Moravians were clearly already engaged in travel to distant lands (here mentioned: Abyssinia, Greenland and Labrador [1792:11]) to carry the gospel at the time of Carey's writing. So the motivation that Carey cites from their example is their practical success, and by so doing he is fuelling a sort of spiritual competitiveness.

A fourth and similar motivation was the example and successes not of the Moravians, this time, but of the 'English traders' (*ibid.*:11–12): 'Or have not English traders, for the sake of gain, surmounted all those things which have generally been counted insurmountable obstacles in the way of preaching the gospel? Witness the trade to Persia, the East-Indies, China, and Greenland, yea even the accursed Slave-Trade on the coasts of Africa. Men can insinuate themselves into the favour of the most barbarous clans, and uncultivated tribes, for the sake of gain.'

Carey's point was simply this: the traders had gone out into the lands of heathen people for the sake of gain—why should obstacles that they had overcome in the process deter ministers confronting those same obstacles, and overcoming them for the sake of the gospel? How much more than these self-centred traders, he argued, should the people of God be reaching out to unsaved, heathen people?

Towards the end of his *Enquiry* Carey appealed, again, to the motivation of the trading company: 'When a trading company have obtained their charter they usually go to its utmost limits; and their stocks, their ships, their officers, and men are so chosen, and regulated, as to be likely to answer their purpose' (*ibid.*:81).

One is struck here, however, by the secular, almost political (or at least socio-economic) nature of his argument. A comment by Bosch reflects this criticism (1991:330): 'Carey took his analogy neither from Scripture nor from theological tradition, but from the contemporary commercial world.'

A fifth argument of his, which comprised the main section of his document (1792:14–37), was Carey's appeal to the comprehensiveness and success of human agency by which the Christian faith had been spread during the expansion of the early church and the then known world despite problems that had been faced. His observation (*ibid.*:28) was that 'the Acts of the Apostles informs us of the success of the word in the primitive times; and [that] history informs us of its being preached about this time, in many other places.' He continued (*ibid.*:30): 'The labours of the ministers of the gospel, in this early period, were so remarkably blessed of God, that the last-mentioned writer [Irenaeus] observed, in a letter to Scapula, that if he began a persecution the city of Carthage itself must be decimated thereby. Yea, and so abundant were they in the three first centuries, that ten years constant and almost universal persecution under Diocletian, could neither root out the Christians, nor prejudice their cause.'

But the basis of his argument (beyond past success) is not clear, and whether 'success' *per se* is a valid rationale for mission is highly questionable.

Mission is often 'unsuccessful'—humanly—and it is at such a point that a true and valid motivation for mission is really needed beyond the criteria of 'success' and simply that 'it' worked in the past (as already dealt with in relation to the concept of 'responsiveness' earlier).

Assessment

Throughout his *Enquiry*, Carey's rationale for mission appears to be commercial and humanistic, rather than necessarily spiritual.

This is common in missiology. Pomerville (1985:129), for example, seemed to portray mission as the 'given' and God as the 'variable' through his discussion of what he considered to be 'a key issue in missiological debate: *how God is active in mission today*' (italics added). This is a dichotomy (albeit not a conscious one) that stresses the inherently secular nature of modern mission and shows an almost condescending attitude towards the place of God's involvement in humanity's mission work.

In view of this, Payne's observation is understandable: 'He who reads the *Enquiry* to-day is struck, first of all, by its sober matter-of-factness and its modernity' (1993:311). Bosch (1991:330) similarly observed 'something businesslike, something distinctly modern' about mission at this time and Nicholls (1993:370) articulated the tenuous simplicity of Carey's writing: 'Carey's hermeneutical principles were literalistic and uncomplicated. He took literally the commands of Jesus and expected God to fulfil his promises. The Bible was his sole means of knowing the truth of God and the way of salvation. An example of his proof text method was his use of the Great Commission of Matthew 28:18–20 in his pioneering booklet.'

Such literalism has already been mentioned and (as discussed) appears to have led to a poorly based, largely rhetorical piece of writing. To this extent, Carey's pamphlet and resulting influence should arguably be treated with less of the awed respect that it is currently given. Certainly the humanistic secularism of his argument (and resultant shape and understanding of mission) should be discarded.

But then we would be left wondering what remains of the modern missionary movement, with its 'charter' or 'manifesto' of William Carey's *Enquiry*.

Summary

Through this critique of how the 'Great Commission' has been modelled in history through the 'father of modern mission' (*op. cit.*), together with the findings of our earlier examination of Matthew 28:16–20 and the way in which that biblical 'Great Commission' passage has been interpreted functionally, this investigation into the 'pragmatic rock' of the 'Great Commission' has confirmed our earlier suspicions: that it is a more sand-like foundation for mission than is commonly assumed. It has also indicated that the dynamic of ontology in mission has been lost—'eclipsed' behind the functionalism of modern mission and its programmes.

Before that paradigm on 'ontology' is further defined and explored, the reasons for high praxis in modern mission still need to be determined.

This will be done by looking at the influence of the Enlightenment, but also at the effect of simplistic linguistics and hermeneutical approaches to 'mission' texts.

CHAPTER 5

Modernity's Impact

IT IS NOT SURPRISING that mission today has been so influenced by the Enlightenment.

Bosch (1991:274, 344) observed that 'The entire modern missionary enterprise is, to a very real extent, a child of the Enlightenment... [The] entire Western missionary movement of the past three centuries [has] emerged from the matrix of the Enlightenment.' Saayman (1996:47) followed this up with the comment: 'Bosch is quite correct in treating the influence of the Enlightenment on the Protestant missionary paradigm in a separate chapter; the tremendous influence of the Enlightenment on Western society as a whole, and on church and mission specifically, certainly warrants this decision.' In a more general sense, Hulme and Jordanova (1990:4) said it like this: 'The major issues of our intellectual life today are still implicated, for better or worse, in the shadows cast by the multifaceted enterprise of the Enlightenment project.'

The influence of the Enlightenment on contemporary mission in particular can be shown in part by outlining the dates of that era in relation to the dates to which modern mission can so easily be traced.

Chronological Outline

A narrow definition might date the era of Enlightenment from the mid-eighteenth century. Commonly recognised Enlightenment thinkers would include Lessing (1729–1781) and Kant (1724–1804), but they would also include earlier d'Alembert (1714–80), Diderot (1713–84), Rousseau (1712–78), Voltaire (1694–1778) and Montesquieu (1689–1755) with even the earliest thinkers including Leibniz (1646–1716) and the English writers Newton (1642–1717) and Locke (1632–1704).

Yet recognition of a still earlier period of Enlightenment is reflected in this comment: 'In England at least, attitudes generally attributed to the Enlightenment were widespread in the late sixteenth century' (Hampson 1968:15).

Indeed, the dawn of the Enlightenment has been traced to as early as the fourteenth century through the collapse of the medieval worldview. From that time onwards, new ways of thinking were indisputably pioneered by the likes of Copernicus (1473–1543), Bacon (1561–1626) and Galilei (1564–1642) whose challenge to the then dominant ecclesial worldview effected events of world significance like the Renaissance and the Protestant Reformation.

Bridging early and late, Paul Hazard (in Hulme and Jordanova 1990:4) argued for the beginning of the 'Enlightenment proper' in the seventeenth century and drew attention to 'the Enlightenment of the way of thinking introduced by Descartes' whose *Discourse on Method* was published in 1637. Certainly by the middle of the eighteenth century 'there was a profound and widely shared feeling among thinking people in western Europe that a new age had come, and that its essential nature was "Enlightenment"' (Newbigin 1986:23).

This eighteenth century was 'commonly referred to by the enlighteners as *their* century . . . [T]he German term *Aufklärung* was common by the 1780s—although its translation as "Enlightenment" only came into English usage in the nineteenth century' (Hulme and Jordanova 1990:4).

It is against this context of Enlightenment that William Carey and his 1792 *Enquiry* (written towards the end of this Enlighteners' century) emerged, and so it would be impossible to deny the influence of the era on the modern missionary movement. The *Enquiry* has actually even been referred to as one of those missionary writings 'worthy of consideration as Enlightenment texts' (*ibid.*). Further, although Great Commission renderings of Matthew 28:19–20a were developed at an even later date than Carey's *Enquiry*, as shown above, they were also clearly established against the background of the Enlightenment.

What 'Modernity' Is

Because of this, it is necessary here to critique the basic tenets of that hugely significant era. By so doing, it should become possible to distinguish 'mission' as a biblical theology (to the extent to which that does exist), from the wrappings of modernity that have almost certainly shaped what 'mission' is in our day.

Reason not Faith

Enlightenment was at root about human affairs being guided by 'rationality rather than by faith, superstition, or revelation' (Outram 1995:3). It was fuelled by 'a belief in the power of human reason to change society and liberate the individual from the restraints of custom or arbitrary authority' (*ibid.*). For d'Alembert (1751) the Enlightenment was about 'intensifying that "light of reason" first lit in Greece, but "rekindled" again in the fourteenth century after almost a millennium of darkness' (Hulme and Jordanova 1990:1, citing Diderot). Cassirer (1979:5) put it this way: 'When the eighteenth century wants to characterize [its] power in a single word, it calls it "reason" . . . [which] becomes the unifying and central point of this century, expressing all that it longs and strives for, and all that it achieves.'

All people were given hope as a result, because reason (being a natural thing) was available to the believer as well as the non-believer: it was something 'independent of the norms of tradition or presupposition' (Bosch 1991:264). Condorcet's oft-quoted verse (in Outram 1995:1) reflected the dreams of the age: 'The time will come when the sun will shine only on free men who have no master but their reason.'

Understandably, reason has often been equated with science. The Enlightenment was 'the age which venerated reason and science as man's highest faculty' (Cassirer 1979:xi). Newbigin (1986:23–4) argued that a central and fundamental element of the Enlightenment was the 'vision of the nature of reality opened up by science.'

And yet the irony of that 'vision' is that science itself, and the natural order, turned out to be Enlightenment's only reality: it was only 'nature—the sum total of what exists—[that was] the really real' (*ibid.*:25).

A complete reinterpretation of 'nature' had come about. Whereas medieval thought explained change and movement in the world of nature in terms of purpose, the Enlightenment explained such changes in terms of cause and effect (*ibid.*). The former teleological (purpose-driven) framework was replaced more by mere analysis and observation. 'The real world disclosed by the work of science was [now viewed as] one governed not by purpose but by natural laws of cause and effect' (*ibid.*:24). Questions about 'why?' came to be replaced by questions about 'how?' which in turn bred more technical, non-personal approaches to knowledge and understanding, and nature itself.

In this way, rationalism affected the whole of public life. In fact Habermas argued that through the Enlightenment a 'public realm' had been created for the discussion and transformation of opinions—or what is now called 'public opinion' (Outram 1995:11). D'Alembert spoke of the progression and totality involved in human knowledge (*ibid.*), and Kant (stressing the political aspect of this new thought in particular) argued that Enlightenment thinking could only be fully realised in the public sphere (*ibid.*).

But individual thinking in the private realm was also bolstered. Kant's '*dare to know*' or '*have the courage to know*' (*sapere aude*) influenced European culture from that day to the present not just in a public sphere but also in a private and individual way. It implied 'that the individual [had] the potential and therefore also the right freely to exercise his reason in the search for reality' (so Newbigin 1992:25).

This was well represented by Enlightenment thinkers, for example through Descartes' dictum '*cogito, ergo sum*' ('I think—therefore I am') the human mind came to be viewed as the basic point of departure for all knowing (Bosch 1991:264). Kant's important essay of 1784 defined Enlightenment as 'man's emergence from self-incurred immaturity' (Kant, in Hulme and Jordanova 1990:1) by 'the use of his own reason, undistorted by prejudice and without the guidance of others' (Kant, in Outram 1995:2).

In other words, the Enlightenment was about 'man's conquest of the inability to use one's own understanding without another's guidance' (Kant, in Miller 1987:42).

Although intimately concerned with scientific viability on a public scale, reason had also become a fundamentally personal and individualistic concept. It was to do with self-realisation, and tied in with notions such as maturity, understanding, freedom and autonomy of the individual as a reaction against religious domination (in some cases even oppression), and even against a 'reverence for antiquity' (Bacon, in Hill 1965:69).

The aspect of individualism will be considered again separately, but for now, and in spite of the apparent 'freedom' that Enlightenment brought, it is important to critique 'reason' as a major tenet of modernity.

Wisdom Rather than Reason

The first point to make is that human reason does not equate with wisdom as a goal of mature Christianity.

The substance of the latter is indicated in various ways, like in the prophetic declaration in Isaiah (55:8): 'For my thoughts are not your thoughts, neither are your ways my ways'; or the apostle Paul's observations (in 1Co. 1:27) that 'God chose the foolish things of the world to shame the wise; God chose the weak things of the world to shame the strong' and so on; or these words of his (1Co. 2:6,7,10): 'We . . . speak a message of wisdom among the mature, but not the wisdom of this age or of the rulers of this age, who are coming to nothing. No, we speak of God's secret wisdom, a wisdom that has been hidden and that God destined for our glory before time began . . . but [which] God has revealed . . . to us by his Spirit.'

Beyond this, Wisdom personified may be equated with the person of God through its association with Jesus Christ. Wisdom was seen in Intertestamental times as a person, and that person has since been associated with Jesus Christ. Wisdom speaks in Ben Sirach (Ecclesiasticus 51:23–27) saying: 'Come to me, you who need instruction, and lodge in my house of learning . . . Bind your neck to the yoke, be ready to accept discipline . . . See for yourselves how little were my labours compared with the great peace I have found.' And Jesus appears to have taken this mantle upon Himself by making a parallel appeal (recorded in Mt. 11:28–30): 'Come to me, all you who are weary and burdened, and I will give you rest. Take my yoke upon you and learn from me, for I am gentle and humble in heart, and you will find rest for your souls. For my yoke is easy and my burden is light.'

Paul writes of 'Jesus Christ, who has become for us wisdom from God—that is, our righteousness, holiness and redemption' (1Co. 1:30), showing 'wisdom' to be far more profound than mere reason through the right-standing and new relationship with God that it makes possible.

The point is that Wisdom, made known in Jesus Christ (who was there with the Father at the foundation of the world [Pr.8]), and equated with Jesus Christ in a very real sense, is what (or, rather, the one Who) discipled Christian people should pursue instead of reason—not just in churchmanship and things spiritual, but in the everyday routines of life and in their expectations regarding society and the world beyond themselves.

The dynamics of Christian 'wisdom' are so different from Enlightenment's 'reason'. In contrast to the 'freedom' promised by Enlightenment, Christianity involves 'slavery' to Christ: it binds a person to the authority of an Other (Another) and even to tradition (albeit not to superstition). And yet the irony and miracle of the Christian life is that although a believer becomes a 'slave' to Christ, he or she does gain a type of freedom; instead of being faced by a master of tyranny, slavery to Christ involves adoption into, and belonging in the eternal family of God, as a child of God and heir together with Jesus Christ of an eternal inheritance of vast proportions (Ep. 1). This is what 'freedom' is for the believer; for 'if the Son sets you free you will be free indeed' (Jn. 8:36).

Modernity's rationalism rightly went beyond medieval superstition, but wrongly constructed false alternatives instead of articulating right belief and faith. Hence postmodernity's critique was that modernity appeared unable to exist 'without a shattering of belief and without a discovery of the "lack of reality" of reality, together with the invention of other realities' (Lyotard 1984:77): those new 'realities' that it invented were themselves often groundless, empty and void.

As a result, postmodernity sifts on through a nihilistic fog of meaninglessness. In its hopelessness, however, almost by way of an argument from silence, it seems to 'sense' the inevitable existence of one controlling, absolute Reality. A prolific postmodern novelist Douglas Coupland (1994:359) once put it this way: 'My secret is that I need God.'

So just as postmodernity begs for and (by so doing) appears to acknowledge the reality of an ultimate and authentic Other beyond the multiplicity of empty traditions and fake 'realities' offered by our age, our own missional thinking needs to look beyond simplistic, 'rote' traditions and mechanics of 'modern mission'. Beyond even mere 'confessions' of 'faith' it needs to engage with the reality that should be source to all that it stands for.

The significance of all this for ourselves is that the 'end product' of 'mission' determined through the 'process' of wisdom would be so different from the 'end product' determined by means of mere rationalism. It would be a 'product' of true freedom accessed (oddly) by first undergoing a voluntary death to self, and submitting oneself in slavery to another.

This is not the way of human rationalism (and thus, often, of guilt and obligation), but of divine wisdom (in a biblical, spiritual sense); it involves a Person: Wisdom (personified in Christ); and it demands, first, a living relationship with that Person—a relationship with God.

Reason by itself is an inadequate means of accessing the full reality of God and His cosmic order and purposes, because He is a Person—Who exists beyond our sinful selves—Who is to be known and encountered.

With this in mind, whereas 'reason' may legitimate, and seek to propagate any number of competing truths or 'realities' (such as liberal or erroneous theologies, activities or churchmanship), the one overriding and authentic Reality will first need to be submitted to (through full confession of one's own state of sin), known, and then very carefully and accurately expressed and witnessed to.

Christianity's articulation of such a Reality will have to be faithful to God's own expression of Himself through bringing into being the historic nation Israel and its Messiah (although He was unrecognised by most of its people at the time: 'eclipsed' behind Scripture and Tradition of His day): Jesus the Christ, of Nazareth.

In this way Christianity, in continuity with what God has pointed out over thousands of years of salvation history, will point beyond its own perception of reality to the reality of the very being of God and His world-order in relation to whom true reality is offered and may be experienced though Jesus Christ. For it is in relation to Him only that people 'may have life, and have it to the full' (Jn. 10:10)!

Concerning mission, then, it is of primary importance to gain wisdom about the purposes of God for the world, for the church and for believers individually in their walks with Him. In relation to the One True Reality it is essential not simply to 'obey' or religiously propagate Christian 'tradition' or ecclesial teaching just for the sake of it, but to first establish the authenticity upon which such traditions or teachings can validly be continued.

In our present case, authentication of the basis upon which the very concept of mission is understood and appropriated in changing world scenarios is required, through Christ as Wisdom.

The Process of Reason

Another critique of reason (which in turn supports 'wisdom' as a more authentic framework for determining truth and meaning) is that reason is not just about a clinical application of lifeless information. Reason involves a process which can often only come about over time.

This aspect of the 'process' of reason was recognised by Enlightenment thinkers: Mendelssohn (1729–86) regarding Enlightenment as a process of education in the use of reason (Outram 1995:1–2) and Kant, similarly, seeing Enlightenment as an 'emergence' (cited in Hulme and Jordanova 1990:1) or as a 'conquest' (cited in Miller 1987:42). Kant wrote: 'If it is now asked whether we live at present in an Enlightened age, the answer is: No, but we do live in an age of Enlightenment' (cited in Outram 1995:2). Enlightenment was 'still to be pursued and brought to completion' (*ibid.*:11).

This is the purpose of us having engaged with *post*-modernity (however briefly), as it is almost certainly trying to pursue goals of Enlightenment that had not been attained in modernity. And reason-as-a-process is attested to by postmodernity's view of itself not as 'modernism at its end but in [a constant] nascent state' (Lyotard 1984:79). We are children of modernity—we have no choice in that. However, we can and must 'move beyond the part of it that betrayed us' (Wells 1992:63).

Put another way, reason *per se* is not an end in itself; rather, it should always be 'moving beyond', assessing new variables and criteria which were not in evidence earlier and responding appropriately to them. Reason alone can rarely propose a final solution to a problem or a given situation.

This certainly equates to our earlier observation that right rationalism is not just a cerebral procedure but that it involves wisdom from above and a relationship with the living God. Right missiology is not just a reasoned response to the gospel or to doctrinal or ecclesial or global circumstances: it is the result of, and involves an ongoing wrestling with God about His purposes in particular situations.

What this will involve for us, then, is a scrutiny of the models or patterns or systems of modern mission that may have appeared 'reasonable' in the past, and an assessment not only of whether they were indeed correct in past definition, but whether they are 'reasonable' and/or appropriate still in our world today.

This should involve a critique not only of the effectiveness of mission hitherto, but also of the correctness of the concept and identity of mission as currently practiced, as in fact we are doing here in Part I. Further, where a crisis of identity is perceived (as is currently the case) it is important to work towards a more durable concept of what mission is, and a more accurate practical expression or outworking of it. This is the purpose of Part II.

And in view of what has just been discussed (in relation to the first point: testing the authenticity of current concepts of mission), this second point (working out a more accurate concept of mission) should not be approached simply through a process of worldly thinking and rationalism, but rather from a viewpoint of 'wisdom' and with the help of the Holy Spirit, as taught in the Christian faith.

Reason's Limits

This raises a third point of critique: that reason needs limits that are not normally given to it.

Kant, amongst others, warned against thinking without limits (Outram 1995:2). Mendelssohn argued, similarly, that reason itself required limitations if social, religious and political order were not to dissolve into chaos (*ibid.*:1–2). This need for control over the consequences of rationalism is poignantly evidenced in the complexity surrounding contemporary ethical debates such as abortion, euthanasia and cloning.

Thus 'reason', whilst being a reasonable enough concept, requires limitations that it cannot and does not provide itself.

Wisdom, in contrast, provides inherent controls that in our specific instance would ensure a much more 'reasonable' or 'right' understanding of what mission is.

Some of these controls or 'limits' have already been suggested, and will be further discussed, and could include various things: church doctrine; community understanding and consensus (or the critical and interpretive community of believers [so Fowler 1985:14], including other church fellowships not just one's own); the control or 'limit' of good and faithful exegesis; (put another way) faithfulness to the Word, or (as suggested later) 'actual texts' (Iser 1974:xi) or 'stable texts' (Thiselton 1992:517); not least, and a distinctive feature of New Testament living: personal guidance by the divine teacher and counsellor sent by Christ, the Holy Spirit (the reality of whose presence and ministry is attested to over and again in e.g. Johannine and Pauline teaching).

All this is of profound practical significance. Mission determined along the lines of wisdom rather than mere reason should be controlled by the limitations outlined briefly here, and more. In this way, any finances, efforts and lives invested in mission are less likely to be dedicated to a 'mission' where God and His purposes have been unknowingly eclipsed!

A Shift from God to Self

This is exactly what happened in and through the Enlightenment: God came to be eclipsed behind the individual self. This second characteristic of Enlightenment thought involved the usurping of the place of God by a person's own self, and the creation of an antithesis between the two. In the words of Bellah *et al.* (1985:80): 'The notion of an unencumbered self is derived not only from psychotherapy, but much more fundamentally from modern philosophy, from Descartes, Locke and Hume.'

Origins

This particular shift came about through the complete inversion of cosmology that took place in the Enlightenment (Bosch 1991:263). In medieval times there had been little room for doubt (Cassirer 1979:39): God was at the 'top' over the church, the king and nobles, people, animals, plants and objects (Bosch 1991:263). However, in the new cosmology of modernity, 'the vision of reality that had supported the rational consciousness of man for a thousand years' (Carré in Hill 1965:8) began to fade. Mankind now took centre-stage and everything else (or at least the place and importance of everything else) came to be determined by and in relation to the individual.

'God' was now pushed to the periphery of human life and came to be considered as an optional extra (for 'me' to decide the relevance of— or not). Through the age of science 'God was eliminated from society's validation structure' (Bosch 1991:263) and people discovered that they could ignore not only the church, but God without anything happening to them (*ibid.*). Just as in the sixteenth century Copernicus and Kepler showed that 'far from being the stable centre of the cosmos, planet earth revolved around a sun and was itself only one of many planetary systems' (Outram 1995:40), people came to believe that God was not necessarily the centre of reality, but rather oneself.

So it was that writers on the Enlightenment era all wrote about 'an absolute decline in religious belief, or a radical shift in its meaning and context' (*ibid.*:32).

For writer/philosopher William Godwin, for example, 'it seemed clear that, whatever the obstacles, man must somehow pursue his own destiny through his own energies and his own genius' (Miller 1987:48).

Vovelle, through his histories of the French Revolution, showed the Enlightenment's attempts in France in particular to stamp out Christian belief there, and to produce new forms of 'rational' or 'natural' religion (Outram 1995: 32).

For Hegel, the Enlightenment was an 'uncompleted project for intellectual and spiritual freedom' (*ibid.*: 33) which ended up undermining the place of faith through destroying 'a crucial aspect of man's self-knowledge, its relation to the absolute and spiritual' (*ibid.*).

But it was primarily through Descartes' already mentioned dictum *cogito ergo sum* that the self came to be popularly expressed as a first principle of knowledge in place of God. He argued for the authority of reason because it 'exists whole and complete *in each of us*' (in Hulme and Jordanova 1990:187—italics added). Descartes testified how in 1619 he had resolved never to accept anything as true if he himself did not have evident knowledge of its truth. His resolution (1912:15) had been simple: 'Never to accept anything for true which I did not clearly know to be such; that is to say, carefully to avoid precipitancy and prejudice, and to comprise nothing more in my judgement than what was presented to my mind so clearly and distinctly as to exclude all ground of doubt.'

'Each of us', 'me/myself/I' and personal attestation to truth had become a first point of reference in the place of God and His own revelation of ultimate truth.

Not a Conscious Movement Against God

The irony is that this 'development' from God to self had not come about through an overtly conscious movement against God. Yes, the Enlightenment freed people to use their minds in establishing and assessing truth, but it did often still acknowledge, and was still concerned with truth in relation to 'a reality that transcends the human mind' (O'Neil 1990:189).

Neither Bacon's empiricism nor Descartes' rationalism had in any way been intended to depose or undermine the Christian faith (Bosch 1991:263). Bacon, for example, had operated 'completely within a Puritan paradigm and presumed a complete harmony between science and the Christian faith' (*ibid.*). Descartes had not specifically intended to depose a tacit acceptance of God's existence and role; he was clear that 'all the things which we clearly and distinctly conceive are true, is only because all that we possess is derived from him' (Descartes 1912:31). As noted, he had simply argued for the authority of reason.

Rationalism was not even regarded as being everything, or as an absolute 'gauge': the need for 'a complete, God's eye view of reality' (O'Neil 1990:189) was still appreciated. In *Principles of Philosophy* Descartes wrote: 'Above all we will observe as an infallible rule that what God has revealed is incomparably more certain than all the rest' (cited in Hampson 1968:19).

Locke tried to argue for the reasonableness of Christianity, although in doing so he admittedly risked 'erecting human reason itself as the focus of a new religion' (Outram 1995:45, referring to Locke's *The Reasonableness of Christianity* of 1695). Newton had recognised the place of God in the ordering and creation of the universe—especially regarding the need for the direct intervention of God in combating decay (Hampson 1968:77). Even d'Alembert's explanation of the conservation of motion without the intervention of God was not intended to nullify God's existence (*ibid.*:90).

'God' and Perfection

Despite all this, any 'God'-talk from this point on was primarily to do with perfectionism, and to do with what natural science or creation hinted at or 'allowed'. The concept of 'God' was on the whole still held to be 'reasonable', but often only in relation to the concept of perfection of reason: in terms of a sort of moral or ethical or even spacial Puritanism or balance.

Although Descartes' ontological argument for the existence of God had been based on reason and the self, for example, it was perfection and ultimate being that he attributed to God, as reflected in the following observation: '[T]he idea of a nature more perfect than myself... [must have] been placed in me by a nature which was in reality more perfect than mine... that is to say, in a single word, which was God' (*ibid.*:28).

'God' had lost any specific identity, and even the existence of God had come to be argued from, or at least viewed in relation to this arbitrary concept of 'perfection'. It was an argument from below: God was a mere explanation of the source of perfection. For example, Descartes considered it 'at least as certain that God, who is Perfect Being, is, or exists, as any demonstration of geometry can be' (*ibid.*:30).

This is almost certainly the way in which the likes of Samuel Taylor Coleridge viewed God. For him, 'the attainment of the "point of possible perfection" seemed "a process of such infinite Complexity, that in deep-felt humility I resign it to that Being . . . 'Who shaketh the Earth out of her place and the pillars thereof tremble"' ' (Miller 1987:48).

At an opposite extreme, 'God' occupied the 'gap', or areas of imperfection or disaster which even insurance companies of today can relate to, and refer to under the blanket term: 'Acts of God'!

Only in relation to perfectionism (or disaster), then, where one's own 'vocabulary' and comprehension had run dry, did reference to 'God' remain. And this is where it appears to have settled, even through into our present day. It is a reference to 'God' that does not involve an acknowledgement of personal sin, or the holiness of God, or God's independent being beyond ourselves and our own small worlds, and the need for the redemption of all mankind in and through the course of daily life.

'God' in Creation

A major reason for equating God with perfection is that 'God' had come to be considered and 'known' not through His own self-revelation but (if at all) more through creation.

This move constituted a 'first step along the road to science becoming an entirely distinct form of intellectual endeavour, [and] of its gradual separation from the "first order" questions dominant in theology, the "Queen of Sciences"' (Outram 1995:53). In other words, self and my perception of the world around me had indeed started to usurp the place of God.

Through Newton (who was considered to be the father of modern cosmology [*ibid.*:131]), Copernicus's alternative system of truth was given expression: truth was seen to be revealed not so much in 'God's word, but in his work; it is not based on the testimony of Scripture or tradition but is visible to us at all times' (Cassirer 1979:43). Because Nature was still held to be the authoritative and lawful system instituted by God (Hulme and Jordanova 1990:10), it was felt that reality and God Himself could be most accurately comprehended through it.

In this way, knowledge and understanding of what God had taken pains to reveal about Himself through His Judeo-Christian involvement with mankind started to erode.

For even Newton's work provided no guarantee that the First Cause of the universe necessarily resembled the God of the Old and New Testaments (Outram 1995:5). His concept of God was attained simply from below, from a human perception of God through the 'work' of Nature. The existence and character of God was argued not on the basis of His own self-revelation but through the capacity of humankind to be conscious of Him.

Voltaire was Newton's prime theological interpreter (Hampson 1968:79). However he only made reference to Newton to support his own Deism (Outram 1995:40)—his 'belief that little or nothing could be known about the creator except the fact of his existence as a precondition for that of the workings of the natural laws governing the cosmos' (*ibid.*:35).

As much as Voltaire 'used' Newton to his own ends, it was equally possible to ignore Newton's 'Supreme Being' (*op. cit.*) with apparent lack of effect. D'Holbach, for example, interpreted Newton in a totally materialistic sense, denying any sort of divine purpose or master plan. 'The whole cannot have an object, for outside itself there is nothing towards which it can tend' (d'Holbach [1770] in Hampson 1968:94).

The likes of David Hume were also sceptical about the idea of God as a first cause in cosmology. Hume pointed out that 'the existence of the order of nature, or of the laws of the cosmos did not necessarily betray anything about the nature of its creator, or indeed that there had been a creator at all' (Outram 1995:41). Hume even rejected the concept of providential order as the product of an 'anthropomorphic imagination' (Hampson 1968:120), saying that it is impossible to 'reason from the character of the natural order . . . to the character of the Deity' (Outram 1995:54). He made the valid assertion that 'the history of religion showed it to be based on superstitious fear' (Hampson 1968:121).

This would accord well with Salvation History. For in it, God had deemed it necessary to reveal Himself to humanity which, despite having certain superstitions and myths about a god, or gods 'out there', was lost in its sin and totally ignorant about the true and living God, its own creator.

To Hume's credit, then, he effectively (though perhaps unknowingly) protected the image of God as Other who had revealed Himself to a fallen creation.

However, the result of his work (in the era of which he was just one voice) was an increased, general cynicism toward the concept or possible existence of God.

Impoverished 'Theology'

Indeed the whole of this lapse from talk of 'God' to points of mere perfectionism and/or natural science or creation resulted in a bland emptiness.

Against this, Locke admitted that natural philosophy could never explain 'first principles'—i.e. the causes of causes (Outram 1995:53). However his views on the nature of perception, namely that the 'autonomous character of reflection' gave the mind certain 'characteristics of the Christian soul' were challenged by Condillac who saw, instead, that 'the mind . . . was merely an agglomeration of ideas which were themselves sense-impressions' (Hampson 1968:113).

Clearly, Enlightenment sentiment 'beyond' rationalism was still bound to the self and to one's own personality.

Kant, primarily through his 1781 *Critique of Pure Reason,* is said also to have 'undermined traditional metaphysics and by default the whole thrust of theology as revelation' (Walker 1996:49). Through Kant's work (*ibid.*): 'the Christian narrative was left with the anthropological and historical Jesus in the phenomenal world . . . [whilst] the eternal Son . . . was left adrift in the noumenal sphere . . . unable to get back to earth [with this result:] . . . Not only was Jesus as the God-man separated into two halves, but the whole mythical and epic dimensions of the story were lost. God was no longer allowed to be God, to be sovereign . . . He could not enter the material world from beyond or outside.'

Because of his relentless critique of rational theology, Kant was even accused of killing God (Hulme and Jordanova 1990:188)!

In His place, the Enlightenment had (in Hegel's words) been producing an image of man 'which emphasised human autonomy and self-sufficiency' (in Outram 1995:33).

The result of this stress upon man and a lapse of consciousness of God was disastrous. Writing in the aftermath of the world wars and the Holocaust, Adorno and Horkheimer observed that mankind 'instead of entering into a truly human condition is sinking into a new kind of barbarism' (cited in Outram 1995:8).

Clearly, faith could not adequately be assessed by rationality or from below—from creation and the natural order—for 'once man became an end in himself . . . once he lost religious aspiration, then he becomes [*sic*] trapped in his own solipsism, unable to judge himself aright, or to form non-utilitarian ties to other human beings' (*ibid.*).

Theology itself had become a totally unattainable goal.

Fake Faith

A final observation that should be made in this section, however, concerns the pendulum swing back to 'faith' that happened after the Enlightenment. Before that time, superstitious faith had been rampant, and the Enlightenment dealt with this (positively in many ways) through cold rationalism.

But that is exactly where it left people: cold and empty. Although radical Enlightenment had seen 'in the unenlightened world nothing but error, superstition, darkness and barbarism' (Im Hof 1994:270), the light of the Enlightenment itself became a 'harsh, chilly light' which sought '"with mathematical conformity to dismiss all that [was] miraculous and mysterious"' (*ibid.*, citing German poet Novalis). It lacked profundity and 'spent itself in barren criticism or shallow moralizing that failed to fertilize the dormant powers of the soul' (*ibid.*). In the 1740s, Edward Young wrote not about 'bright days filled with activity, but nights that enshrined the mystery of nature, the sublimity of the divine, love, death and immortality. This was not the triumphant champions of Enlightenment speaking, but a suffering generation' (*ibid.*:271).

With reason had come scepticism, for it had highlighted an emptiness that existed in the heart of Man.

And so people turned to 'faith' again.

There were certain positive expressions of this faith: a faith which was often undergirded by reason. Wesley claimed (*ibid.*:52) that 'to renounce reason is to renounce religion, that reason and religion go hand in hand'—and because of this he was considered to be 'an Enlightenment thinker . . . an empiricist' (*ibid.*). But beyond rationalism, evangelicalism in the Christian church also sought a heart experience and certainty about the way forward, spiritually. The evangelical awakenings of the 1730s and 1740s on both sides of the Atlantic could both be attributed to the fact that 'they felt it in their hearts' (Noll and Bebbington 1994:34).

On the whole, though, spirituality and 'faith' arose primarily because of what it could do for one's self, rather than because of a fear of God. This is illustrated in the non-Christian arena where the parallel 'development' in things spiritual had been taking place in the 1770s and 1780s through a 'revived interest in occultism, alchemy and magic' (Im Hof 1994:270). It was said at that time: "'Drive out magic, and it will come back at the gallop'" (*ibid.*). A peaking of that same trend is evidenced by simply browsing the shelves in any library or bookshop in the West, today.

The Roman Catholic Church had predicted this of the Enlightenment: that it had been a 'modern heresy' which would in turn be 'countered by a return to blind faith and an acceptance of authority' (so Hampson 1968:282). Whether there has been an 'acceptance of authority' or not remains to be questioned (though may be evident in a high legalism in democratic countries) and the extent to which it was 'blind' was also particular to different people and teaching that they sat under. But there certainly was a return to 'faith' of sorts.

By the end of the eighteenth century, a certain balance does appear to have been reached—people being capable of reading both Voltaire's scathing satires and Young's *Night Thoughts*: 'the former with lucid intelligence, the latter with sentimental abandon' (*ibid.*:272).

However, this return to 'faith' was primarily for the purpose of appeasing one's own spiritual desires and for the pursuit of perfection. If people seemed to be grasping beyond 'self' again, it was only in order, ultimately, to affirm themselves.

And this is the environment we find ourselves in today. Christianity thrives amongst a world of fake faiths that exist out there; it exists (like those other 'faiths') largely just to make us feel good rather than because it is a genuine expression of the living God whom it represents, or a genuine relationship with Him. It is often a 'faith' in relation to 'god' of 'perfection' and (although not necessarily so) of creation: not the true and living God revealed in Judeo-Christian history.

Implications for Mission

All that has been discussed here has direct implications for our understanding of mission and our determination of what it is.

Wrong Focus on Self

In the first place, Christian people are not exempt from—indeed: they are clearly susceptible to—a desire for self-determined significance and a self-driven impetus into getting things done in life, even if they do appear to be the 'things of God'.

Just because things are being carried on 'in the name of' God or the church does not necessarily mean that missionary projects are of Him. Often missionary action derives from own, personal impulses, aims and goals. They are often products of the self, and not of God.

It is this very tendency which causes James to observe in his Epistle that temptation comes not just from the evil one, but often from our 'own evil desires' (Ja. 1:13–15). As discussed in a later chapter, self-centredness is not just a symptom of the Enlightenment: it is the heart of sin.

And the apostle Paul writes consistently against 'selfish ambition', setting it into lists of Godless behaviour (2Co. 12:20; Ga. 5:20), and warning the likes of the Philippians to do nothing out of 'selfish ambition' (Php. 2:3). James also decries selfish ambition (Ja. 3:14,16).

Relevant for our own purposes, here, Paul condemns Christian workers for these attitudes: so for example he writes in Philippians (1:17) of those 'who preach Christ out of selfish ambition.'

A correct alternative to 'selfish ambition' is the ambition to 'lead a quiet life' (1Th. 4:11), which is not a popular mission sentiment! Indeed, selfish ambition has pervaded our current thinking, and the call to lead a quiet life often runs almost contrary to mission teaching. For against the background of the Enlightenment shift from God to self outlined above, it follows that what Paul and James warned the church against in New Testament times will have far more easily permeated the church today. Self-centredness has now been 'formally' accepted as a commonplace aspect or 'doctrine' of our age, and will pass even more unnoticed than it did in the early church.

It is essential to hear this point, and the Christian church would do well to err on the side of caution and assume that 'mission' is almost certainly going to be self- rather than God-centred in its expression and motivation: seeded in the heart of self-centred Man, and promoting the goals and purpose of that same self-centred Man, albeit under a 'Christian' guise.

We should then heed this caution in order to correct the culture of mission that has been developed over the years of Enlightenment and its aftermath, and to seek first God's own purposes for what 'mission' is to be.

Mission from Below

In the same way, self-centredness in mission's message does need to be addressed.

Because of the meaninglessness of life introduced by the Enlightenment through the dearth of the Divine, it is essential to question not only our motives for mission, but also the message of mission which is held out by the church.

Mission should not be 'done' simply to build up a person in his or her sense of self-worth, relevance or even vocation. For personal Christian identity comes simply through one's standing before Christ; importance or worth comes from acceptance by the Father and belonging in the family of God; fulfilment comes through the life of Christ in us, and by living in Him.

As regards the message of mission: it should not be one that simply apes the world and its offers of materialism (the lure of the Prosperity Gospel has been increasingly identified and addressed as a major issue in today's church) or even social welfare (Jesus clearly warned His disciples about keeping gospel priorities when He said: 'the poor you will always have with you' [Mt. 26:11 and parallels]). The message of mission and the Christian faith is about a different life: a life and a 'kingdom' that has been transformed and renewed. It is about the Kingdom of God ('behold: the kingdom of God is at hand' [Mk. 1:14]) and a relationship that is now possible between fallen, forgiven Man, and the King of Kings.

The good news we should be 'offering' or holding out to people is not that of a prosperous life, but of a transformed life.

The relevance of this for Christian mission may be hard for some to hear. Although our Christian intentions may have been genuine, our missional formulations and activities may have simply arisen from our own self-made perceptions of who God is and what He wants, instead of from the real being of God, in essence and in truth.

God from Below

Another error that the church today should be careful to avoid in the wake of the Enlighteners, then, is that of determining who 'god' is and what 'he' wants of us, from below.

The identity and character and purposes of God should be argued not from the natural world but should be described and known in the way that God has revealed Himself through Judeo-Christian history.

Often today's (even 'Christian') 'god' is determined in relation to the 'spiritual' lives and characters of people in the church, more in relation to who they are and what they are feeling than through authentic revealed truths of the established church and a right-reading of Scripture.

The Enlightenment itself has indicated the inadequacy of this approach and the limitations of modernity's theological arguments from below. The form, nature and being of God as speculated over or inferred simply from creation is inadequate in relation to age-old revelations about who He is.

Paul's observation to the Romans (1:25) was an appropriate warning on exactly this point: 'They exchanged the truth of God for a lie, and worshipped and served created things rather than the Creator.'

We ourselves must establish with crystal clarity that our 'god' and the resulting 'doctrines' which we formulate and follow and attempt to propagate are not mere products of 'anthropomorphic imagination' (so Hume in Hampson, *op. cit.*).

Pseudo-Christianity and Pseudo-Mission

In brief summary, and in view of the 'fake faiths out there' that were highlighted earlier, we would do well to be heavily suspicious not just of the 'faith' which we are attempting to propagate as Christian missionaries, but of our own personal faith. We should also be aware that 'mission' itself may be something (like that false faith) which may just have emerged from our own perceptions of Christian obligation and reality.

This may have two main implications for our investigation into the roots of modern mission.

First, good Christian intent may often have undergirded all missional action and formulation. However, those programmes that have developed may not have been of God in essence and in truth—they may have been just products of our own self-made perceptions and concepts of who God is and what He wants. In view of mankind's tendency towards Deism and religiosity (in the absence of a right focus on the true and living God) this danger is a high probability. We need to step back beyond our 'deistic' formulations of mission and to consider the purposes of God Himself.

How this is done, secondly, is a question of critical importance. Will we just go back to the bible, and read our standard mission texts out of it, and think our modernistic rational thoughts in relation to it . . . or will we consider the real being of God: that ultimate Being and Other who has addressed us from beyond ourselves in history? The first is easy to do (quicker, more satisfying, and may appear to yield more tangible results). Much harder is the second: being prepared to wait all one's life, and not to necessarily 'achieve' much for God, as one waits on Him.

One's own programmes, goals, dreams and visions (despite being well grounded in 'religiosity' and sincerity of heart) are worth nothing. We should seek only God's purposes in our world, and be obedient to them. In particular we must be prepared 'to jettison the missionary idea and ideal,' in Bosch's words (1991:344), if those ideas and ideals are man-made; man-centred. We may even need to be prepared to do without the term 'mission' in our thinking—if that is a man-made and/or man-distorted term. By overriding the term 'mission,' for a time, we may be able to start again: to perceive and learn of God what His purpose is in the church and in the world, and to find out whether 'mission' even exists in His vocabulary and designs for us, and if so what it means.

A Further Shift from Community to the Individual

A third closely related and central characteristic of Enlightenment beyond reason and the shift from God to self is the 'radical individualism' (Hulme and Jordanova 1990:12) that ensued because of it. Bosch (1991:267) noted that although the 'community took priority over the individual' during the Middle Ages, Enlightened people came to be regarded as 'emancipated, autonomous individuals.'

Descartes embodied individualism in his very methodology. For example, he determined never to accept anything as true without any evidence of its truth: to include nothing in his judgements than that which 'presented itself so clearly and distinctly' (1912:15) that he personally would have no occasion to doubt it. He decided to accept 'nothing as true unless he himself had a clear and distinct perception of its veracity'

(Hampson 1968:28). In his own words he was 'forced to become [his] own guide' (in Hulme and Jordanova 1990:18). His solitary independence is graphically illustrated by the account of the whereabouts in which his first principle came about: through his recorded isolation and meditations from inside an 'oven' or 'stove' (so Brown 1990:179)—probably a kind of stove-heated oven room where he had presumably crept to keep warm and to do all his thinking, alone!

But individualism was also strongly reflected in the literature that developed over that time: for example (as suggested by Hulme and Jordanova 1990:12) in the autobiographical subject of 'Rousseau's *Confessions* . . . [Defoe's fictional] *Robinson Crusoe* alone and fearful on his Caribbean island, Emile "alone in the midst of human society", the "wild boy" studied by Itard and Victor Frankenstein at work in his corpse strewn laboratory.' America also invented 'the most mythic individual hero, the cowboy, who again and again saves a society he can never completely fit into' (Bellah *et al.* 1985:145).

Reflected by changes in society, the thought of John Locke had enormous influence in America through his argumentation for individual rights: that 'the individual is prior to society' and that society itself only comes into existence through the 'voluntary contract of individuals trying to maximize their own self-interest' (*ibid.*:143). So influential was this thought that it is understood to have at least in part caused the American Revolution of the late eighteenth century.

Sociologically, it fuelled the development of ideologies such as capitalism and Marxism, both of which derived from 'the Enlightenment vision of human beings as autonomous individuals with innate and equal rights to pursue self-chosen ends to the limit of their powers' (Newbigin 1986:118).

The impact of this individualism affected Christianity as well. Bosch (1991:273) noted the 'rampant individualism which soon pervaded Protestantism in particular,' and that before long 'the church became peripheral, since each individual not only had the right but also the ability to know God's revealed will. And because individuals were liberated and independent, they could make their own decisions about what they believed.'

Failure and Inadequate Responses

It was not long, however, before the romanticised place given to the individual began to fade. By the nineteenth century, literature like Mary Shelley's *Frankenstein* showed the bankruptcy of taking the egoistic mastery of nature too far (Hulme and Jordanova 1990:12). Earlier in the century Europeans had 'seen Napoleon's failed attempts to master vast territories and construct empires' (*ibid.*). They were 'frightened of chaos and revolution, and sceptical of the power of reason to bring the necessary degree of coherence to human society. There was a widespread loss of confidence in Enlightenment traditions' (*ibid.*).

Various responses of dissatisfaction to individualism were made. Feuerbach, for example, contended against Kant and Fichte making self-consciousness the basis of all truth. He argued that self-consciousness is 'the basis of individuality, and the individual and all that is proper to it is the most transitory of realities' (Massey 1976:369). Interestingly, his critique extended to Christianity which he regarded in a similar light 'as the religion of the pure self and of the Spirit as one Person.'

Self had become the centre of reality and truth: it was 'the sole center of attention and effort' (*ibid.*:370–372).

As an alternative he suggested 'thinking [(*Denken*)]' to be the 'absolute essence, the unifying and universal basis of all individuals'—but not thinking which 'asserted the primacy of the I, of the self' (*ibid.*:360–370).

Kant himself had also expressed the poverty of the ideal of pure individualism through (amongst other things) his repudiation of an individualistic interpretation of autonomy (i.e. of free, unrestrained, self-sufficient independence). He had argued (O'Neil 1990:195) that 'a solitary individual cannot expect to escape "immaturity" and achieve autonomy, [although] "a people" may do so.' Enlightenment was, for him (*ibid.*), 'autonomy in thinking among an entire public.'

In France, in the 1820s, disciples of de Saint-Simon were similarly active in their critique of Enlightenment's 'glorification of the individual [and] their horror of social atomization and anarchy, as well as their desire for an organic, stable, hierarchically organized, harmonious social order' (Lukes 1973:6). With their systematisation of '*individualisme*' they portrayed the negative aspects of individualism but introduced, instead, a people- or me-centred 'ideological force which served as a

Protestant ethic for the expanding capitalism of the Catholic countries in nineteenth-century Europe' (*ibid.*).

More recently, Amitai Etzioni represented an American move towards communitarianism, and observed the West to be in a 'cold season of excessive individualism' (1995:x). He argued that 'neither human existence nor individual liberty can be sustained for long outside the interdependent and overlapping communities to which all of us belong' (*ibid.*:253). Society was in his view 'a place in which individual rights are vigilantly maintained, while the seedbeds of civic virtue are patiently nurtured' (*ibid.*:267).

Although this sounds credible for what it is affirming, Etzioni's thesis still appears to have been driven ultimately by self interest. Encouragements for people to get involved in the community are simply in order for them to 'achieve their self-interests or because they feel an affinity [of personal preference] with certain others' (Bellah *et al.* 1985:167).

And so, despite these reactions to 'individualism' indicating inherent problems with that ideal, propositions given as an alternative (like communitarianism) have been equally inadequate, primarily because they are still based on an ultimate concern for self, and one's own wants and needs in life.

In Affirmation of the Individual

Concern for, and appreciation of the individual is not necessarily a negative thing, involving a Christopher Lasch-type 'culture of narcissism'—an intention to 'do my own thing' come what may (as discussed by Mouw 1982:454). Indeed, Western individualism has even been regarded as 'radically and generously conceived . . . socially creative, critical and cohesive' (Drury 1991:332).

For the Enlightenment did bring out positive understandings of the individual as well as negative ones. For example, there is a place, biblically, to affirm oneself: God has loved us, and died for us—therefore we are of worth to Him.

So, the gospel does affirm the self and does allow self-love, but only because of God's first love for us, and death on our behalf. As expressed in the Thomistic teaching: 'proper self-love consists in love for the self "in God"' (Pope 1991:387). God should be the centre of authentic self-love. Because Christ died on our behalf, we owe our lives to Him: we are

His slaves (as mentioned above). And yet, because of His mercy, He has given us life, and freedom to live in the family of God.

Bosch (1991:267) noted that an 'emphasis on the individual [has been] discernible in Western theology at least since the time of Augustine.' There has always been a right and biblical expression of the 'self' and/or the 'individual': never as 'emancipated and autonomous but . . . first and foremost, as standing in a relationship to God and the church.'

Dietrich Bonhoeffer challenged the concepts of individualism and human freedom in the twentieth century West, saying that man was truly free only in relation to God and to others. 'Freedom as an inherent possession or right of the isolated individual was therefore alien to him . . . Freedom for Bonhoeffer could only mean freedom in relationship' (so Clements 1986:20,23). Clements, commenting on Bonhoeffer's thought, wrote this: 'We still talk . . . a great deal about the value of the individual and his or her freedom . . . and surprisingly little about Jesus Christ who freely gave up all these things *pro nobis* [for us]' (*ibid.*:24).

Moltmann (1981:14) put it this way: 'The foundation of true self-knowledge is to be found in God.' Volf (1996:70) similarly articulated this essence of the authentic individual self, writing: 'The center of the self—a center that is both inside and outside—is the story of Jesus Christ, which has become the story of the self. More precisely, the center is Jesus Christ crucified and resurrected who has become part and parcel of the very structure of the self.'

The individual also has value because 'the individual case reveals the social as nothing else can' (*ibid.*:332). 'Tragedy is individual' (*ibid.*), but when individual experience finds expression, a real community consciousness is often represented (though of course this may not always be the case). For example the 'I' of the negro-slave represented the cries of the broader community of which it was just a part; and the 'me' of evangelicalism portrayed in Wesley's Hymn ('Died he for me . . .? how can it be/ that thou my God shouldst die for me?') was a similar expression of the community of Christian faith that an individual represented (Mouw 1982:455).

And yes, individualism was even given expression by the Reformation, whose concern was the state of the individual in relation to God (Clements 1986:17). But where no limits or controls were imposed, the church became a mere reflection of an Enlightenment community: little more than a composition of its individual parts; 'nothing more than an aggregate of individuals' (so Lindsay, cited in Lukes 1973:40).

At root, the church had 'ceased to point to God, or to the future: instead it [was] pointing towards itself' (*ibid.*).

Ultimately, then, the individual and self only has value in and through a living relationship with God. Individualism as an Enlightenment concept could never reflect the authentic 'personhood' of Christianity.

Some Effects on Mission

Despite even communitarianism's efforts, the 'individual self' (a term used by Feuerbach, as noted in Massey 1976:369) remains the prime sociological incentive and value system in the West.

As such, it (perhaps even unconsciously) ingrains Christian approaches to mission.

Bebbington (1989:3) highlighted two characteristics of modern evangelicalism: '*conversionism*, the belief that lives need to be changed; [and] *activism*, the expression of the gospel in effort.' He noted (*ibid.*:42) that if overseas missions were to remain 'a permanent expression of the energy that characterised the Evangelical movement . . .' the gospel would simply be 'being remoulded by the spirit of the age' (*ibid.*:104).

His observation and warning is that Christian mission is so little different from any other secular mission or mission statement of our day.

What makes Christian mission unique and of God needs to be crystallised so that it can become distinctive and effective in the church and world. In contrast to 'conversionism', we should be seeking a change of heart and soul in people who we are approaching with the gospel, not just confessions; in the place of mere 'activism', God and His purposes and efforts and designs for life should be being sought and adhered to. This may involve a life of waiting, or prayer—not doing! Or it may involve just living a 'normal' life as a Christian, at peace with God and where He has placed us in the world: doing what He has given our hands to do, to His glory.

So, Christian people should be wary about individualism in mission and in their expressions of faith. Although the 'community' of the church may appear to be being served in 'mission', the 'work' being done may simply be to boost the morale, or to unpack the vision of particular individuals or church groups. Such individuals should first and foremost be in a personal and a living relationship with God, but also with other Christians who are themselves also in fellowship with a broader body of Christian faith.

In terms of who the gospel is being presented to, the church further needs to guard against targeting elite individuals. Instead, it should have the spiritual wellbeing of all people at heart. Its love and outreach should be for all people, especially the 'least likely', rather than just those who may benefit the church.

These people themselves should not be seen as mere individuals, but part of a people group and community which itself needs a change of heart towards God.

Beyond this, the basic doctrines and worldviews propagated in Christian mission need to be scrutinised concerning whether the 'gospel' is simply affirming the individual or speaking of the inherent sinfulness in all people: whether it is teaching of the need for death of the 'old' life in Jesus Christ or merely 'selling' the gospel for its consumerist benefits.

Post-Modernity's Outlook

Beyond the traps and pitfalls of the Enlightenment itself, Lyotard (1984:81–82) laments the subtle return in late Enlightenment or post-modern thinking to the bondage of thought that existed before the age of Enlightenment:

> The nineteenth and twentieth centuries have given us as much terror as we can take. We have paid a high enough price for the nostalgia of the whole and the one, for the reconciliation of the concept and the sensible, of the transparent and the communicable experience. Under the general demand for slackening and for appeasement, we can hear the mutterings of the desire for a return of terror, for the realization of the fantasy to seize reality. The answer is: Let us wage a war on totality; let us be witnesses to the unpresentable; let us activate the differences and save the honor of the name.

Before the Enlightenment, medieval thought was all-encompassing. One world system dominated others (for example the 'fantasy' of one particular ruler or king—or the church or state, or usually both). Whatever it was, the individual was clearly subject to one, higher order.

The period of Enlightenment changed this by ushering in an age which effectively liberated the individual, giving him or her wings to fly on to unknown limits of freedom. It gave absolute respect to each person's perspective, creativity and self-worth.

But what Lyotard warns against in this modern age is a lapse into 'one . . . fantasy' becoming our total reality again: a self-determined fantasy itself becoming a dominating totalitarianism that may override individuality and personhood. He points out that our most recent two centuries have 'paid a high enough price for the nostalgia of the whole and the one' through people seeking *one* system to live by: *one* method to propagate and follow in the place of the diversity that unique personhood can blossom into (in our case: under Christ). A quest for such a singular system may arise from fear over what may come out of an apparent chaotic and confusing (often assumed-to-be conflicting) individualism, but is more likely to be the result of a totalitarian move towards control. The 'whole' or singular systems of Nazism, for example, or of Communism or Apartheid have been tried out in an attempt to order reality and to contain it, and make it easier to govern, and to control. And the results have been devastating.

What Lyotard has warned against, then, is a uniformity or oneness that may standardise the life out of us! This would, in his words *(op. cit.)*, be for 'fantasy to seize reality.' To do this would of course be much more ordered, systematic and easy to control . . . but it would not be 'real'.

And modern mission is arguably one such 'fantasy'. Mission (and what is expected missiologically of a convert or a newly planted church) may have been systematised and packaged into such a 'whole' or singular form that it does not recognise the value of individual responses to truth. More profoundly, the 'whole' of the church as a body of Christ and family of God may often not have been allowed or encouraged to outwork its divine uniqueness in a variety of different ways through heart-initiated responses to the living God, or just through normal lives lived anew, now, under the headship of Christ.

Lyotard's proposal was simple: to 'wage war on totality.' In our case this would mean to 'wage war' on the 'totalitarian' system of 'missions' that may risk straightjacketing personal responses to Jesus Christ and which may (albeit unknowingly and even not deliberately) prevent an outworking of a genuine life of love for, and faith in God, and a simple trust of where He has put us, and what His purposes may be for us, in the world.

Mission is so organised. It is Evangelism. It is Social Action. It is Church Growth. It is Cross Cultural. It is Practical. It is Funded. It is about Conversion and Salvation and Conferences. It has become a totalitarian entity that exists in and of itself: it has a life of its own; even a theology of its own. And we ask God to bless it, instead of ensuring that 'it' is the dynamic, diverse and often invisible essence of what God may desire 'it' to be!

Another thing suggested by Lyotard was to be 'witnesses to the unpresentable.'

There is a note of familiarity here for Christian people because in many ways our faith is, and certainly Christian faith in modernity/postmodernity has become in a way 'unpresentable': a private 'thing'—a personal value. Indeed the almost 'unpresentable' intangible Kingdom of God over which people may be 'ever seeing but never perceiving, and ever hearing but never understanding' (Mk. 4:12) is not a new thing. And to a certain extent mission(s) today does witness to this unpresentable aspect of the faith.

But what about the 'unpresentable', unspeakable ecclesial 'crime' of not feeling 'called' to mission or evangelism: of being called, or led simply to a God-centred, God-relating Christian life of integrity and honesty in (for example) one's marriage, and family and secular place of work? This is often taboo in the church: but is it not the value of this 'unpresentable' position that should be witnessed to? Is there not sufficient precedent and biblical teaching that honours the place of family, pure hard work with one's hands and the ambition of a quiet life, in subservience to and honour for God?

That is the perceived value, finally, of Lyotard's call for us to 'activate the differences' and by so doing to 'save the honor of the name' (*op. cit.*).

As Christian people the implication for ourselves is simple: we need to be open and honest about our differences and (in evangelism and discipleship) not simply to clone our ecclesial fathers or spiritual parents in whatever traditional or denominational form that may take. We need to work in new ways with the Spirit, in order that the 'name' of the absolute Other—the honour of the name of the One who brought all things and all unique people and circumstances into being—may be saved.

These are sharp and risky challenges to an evangelical and even to an ecumenical mind as we consider the meaning of mission in our age.

Assessment

What appears to have happened during the Enlightenment as well as in post-Enlightenment (where its effects have been felt) is that the very things that gave light to so many, and liberated whole populations of people, have in turn become burdens and controlling forces.

The challenge from postmodernity reinforces the idea that the Enlightenment did not produce the goods it once promised to deliver, and that the danger remaining in its wake is akin to pre-Enlightenment medievalism.

Perhaps people have simply lost their focus along the way, as the once promising light of Enlightenment has become 'harsh [and] chilly' (*op. cit.*). Perhaps contemporary mission has just been another Enlightenment project after all: sucking the marrow of faith out of the church. Perhaps it is only now possible to see the way in which one-dimensional reason has driven modern mission in the place of a richer Spirit-filled wisdom: a prescriptive reason in the place of a progressive, alive outworking of truth in culture. Now, only, it seems, can we start to appreciate the distortive value of prioritising the self (even 'saved' self) and our own models of mission over against God and His 'missiological' purposes in our world. And we are only just becoming aware of the poverty of individualism as an absolute ideal over against the importance of community and the value of self-worth being determined in relation to, and in relationship with God alone.

Because of the inadequacy of the basic principles of Enlightenment, then, and because the tenets of contemporary mission so closely shadow those of the Enlightenment as an age of reaction and change rather than systematisation of truth *per se,* we conclude again, here, that mission has become thoroughly humanistic, and can only become what it was authentically meant to be from a place of total God-centredness and beginning in the full being of God.

Chapter 6

Linguistic and Hermeneutical Considerations

WHILST AN ATTEMPT TO put God back into the absolute centre of our lives and world may sound good and right, it could turn out to be a futile exercise and even a disastrous move. The primary risk involved is the role of individuals along the way, and the subjectivity of the interpretations of Scripture upon which they may end up living their lives and putting 'God' first.

These individuals are all taken from the same 'stock' of fallen humanity: all are inherently sinful; all are at differing stages of a spiritual journey and all are almost certainly closer to the beginning of that journey than the end. The confidence and authority of many is the bible, and yet most are not necessarily equipped to correctly interpret it.

As a result, certain teachings can take root in Christian sub-cultures, churches and in the hearts and minds of even well-meaning and sincere individuals, and can be propagated despite not being necessarily correct. Because these teachings ostensibly arise out of Scripture, they may even tend towards new dominant and 'totalizing' practices in the church: they may be regarded as 'objective' doctrines; they may even be considered to be 'given' and 'bible-based' . . . but they still may not be right!

Stanley Fish discussed this problem of the subjectivity of individual interpretations ('solipsism', quoted below, referring to aloneness or individualism, and the theory that only one's own existence is certain). He wrote (1980: 49—italics added):

> Of course, it would be easy for someone to point out that I have not answered the charge of solipsism but merely presented a rationale for a solipsistic procedure; but such an objection would have force only if a better mode of procedure were available. The

> one usually offered is to regard the work as a thing in itself, as an object [the objective meaning in a text]; but as I have argued above, this is a false and dangerously self-validating objectivity. I suppose that what I am saying is that *I would rather have an acknowledged and controlled subjectivity than an objectivity which is finally an illusion.*

Fish's observation was that when an 'objective' meaning is read out of a biblical text, the objectivity of that meaning may itself be nothing more than an illusion. As it stands, however, that meaning may take over and become a totalitarian regime (if that is not too strong a word to use in this context, though reference has already been made to the same, and the reason has been outlined). This is an astounding warning against forming superficial and wrong interpretations from our readings of Scripture. Fish has added substance to the same fear expressed by postmodernity and discussed briefly already (Lyotard 1984:81–82): that even a 'Christian', 'biblical' interpretation and/or theology can be erroneous and can become a 'totalizing' (*op. cit.*), controlling power over us.

Applied more directly to our own missiological enquiry, Fish's 'illusion' may be the simple, 'objective, biblical' meaning of mission that has been assumed by modern mission advocates. And the totalitarian 'regime' may in our instance be 'modern mission' itself.

This is not an unreasonable supposition. Van Engen (1993:28) observed not long ago that 'a significant global consensus' had emerged with regard to the bible and mission: that not everything we call mission is indeed mission (*ibid.*). This was a penetrating statement, and should encourage us towards a profound re-examination of the foundations upon which contemporary mission is based. In order both to ensure the authenticity of mission and to prevent the church from becoming a 'club of religious folklore' (*ibid.*), the church must unceasingly challenge itself with the 'true *biblical* foundation of mission' (*ibid.*). So, for example, Van Engen called for the preservation of 'the unique authority of Scripture as our only rule of faith and practice' (1993:35).

However, in view of the observations made here, it is questionable how truly biblical 'biblical' is. Certainly many comprehensive 'biblical foundations' of mission (like Senior and Stuhlmuellers' *The Biblical Foundations for Mission* [London: SCM Press, 1983]) have been outlined in support of modern mission. But in order to arrive at an authentic theology of mission, the legitimacy of what has been considered 'biblical' hitherto should be assessed in the light of the diversity of different hermeneutical approaches to the bible that may exist, and in light of the complexities of the operation of language and determination of meaning.

Language and the Determination of Meaning

Underlying any attempt to determine textual meaning are the inherent complexities and imprecisions of language. This is shown by the contribution of various people:

Charles S. Peirce (1839–1914) argued that language is a sign and that it points to either a deeper reality, or to other signs (Thiselton 1992:4). Either way, it is wrong to just seek out superficial interpretations of bible passages. The bible interpreter should (in our missional instance) be careful about what 'signs' certain 'mission' texts are pointing to. It could be that what modern mission 'means' to me is what it meant to my missionary parents, or what the books that I enjoy reading about mission suggest it to mean, or what my pastor says it means. These meanings are derived from secondary signs, rather than primary and/or causal ones (like God Himself, and the authentic meaning of a passage).

Ferdinand de Saussure (1857–1913)—who together with Peirce is reputed to have founded the modern discipline of semiotics (so Thiselton, *ibid.*:47,83)—similarly equated language with 'the arbitrary nature of the sign' (*ibid.*:83). It is arbitrary, for example, that the French use two words (*bon marché*) to describe what the English use only one word for: *cheap* (*ibid.*:84). He argued that meaning is not just about equating language with a linguistic network of possibility (i.e. looking up a word in a dictionary): for 'meaning is generated by relationships of difference' (*ibid.*:83). 'Orange', for example, is given meaning in relation to other colours on the colour spectrum rather than by simply pointing to an orange on a tree (*ibid.*). And we know what 'white' is because of what 'black' is; and we can show what something is, by saying what it is not. Perhaps in mission, then, we may better understand mission by doing exactly what we are doing here: deconstructing past understandings of mission—showing/telling what mission is not, in order to better understand what it is.

Saussure also argued that written language may be regarded as inferior to oral language. The reason for this is that it has been 'robbed of its phonetic component' (Cotterell 1997:135). More: both the speaker and the referents are absent in a piece of writing. Writing, for Saussure, entailed an 'absence of signatory . . . [and] referent. Writing is the name of these two absences' (so Derrida in Thiselton 1992:05). Because of this (he would suggest) we do not need to just read the words, but to understand what is being said—even hear and see what is being said—or what was being said at that time. It is the event that is important, and not just the words. The implications of this for mission are clear: we need not just to read mission texts, but to hear and see what was being 'said' then, and what (in relation to the living God, and His present, ministering Holy Spirit) may now be being 'said' to us, today.

In contrast, the opinion that we are adequately able to determine meaning in writing was represented by Jacques Derrida (in Thiselton *ibid.*:105) who argued (*ibid.*) that 'we think only in signs' anyway—be they phonetic or written. He also argued that 'the self-identity of the signified conceals itself unceasingly and is always on the move' (*ibid.*), thus implying that—whether in writing or the spoken word—we are always seeking meaning in conversation. He argued that a symbol is never a 'mere' or an 'empty' symbol. A bit like Peirce, earlier, he is pointing us to the meaning to which the symbol is pointing. We must, therefore, keep on seeking meaning: it is not an easy task—but a possible and a necessary one. Thus, concerning our reading of the bible, we should always be seeking its potential and fuller meaning, especially allowing former preconceptions to be revisited and corrected, where necessary.

Gerhard Ebeling pointed out the importance of looking not just at particular words—but at the whole. Interpretation is 'not a matter of understanding single words but of understanding the word itself' (1961:16). Thus he insisted that the meaning of the word is determined by its context. Whilst it is possible to understand the individual words, it is still possible to misunderstand the actual message. As has already been suggested, the context of Matthew 28:16–20 suggests that the message of the 'Great Commission' is arguably more about the presence of the risen Christ in the world than about 'going forth to tell'. Without the context, and without a full understanding of the message (despite 'having' the words), one's telling will be largely ineffective.

Similar, but beyond context alone, Ludwig Wittgenstein talked about a 'language-game', suggesting that the influence of a language on thought is not merely a matter of 'vocabulary-stock' or 'surface-grammar' but of how language is used (Thiselton 1980:135). Thus when language is used differently, the concepts change and the meaning of words also change (*ibid.*:138;375). One is forced to consider how words and writings now regarded simplistically as 'mission texts' were meant to have been understood: what meaning was intended by the language of the whole.

Hans-Georg Gadamer pointed behind Enlightenment's preoccupation with methodology and drew attention to the important fact that understanding and conscious judgements are founded on broader realities than mere method. Hermeneutics, thus, is more of an event than simply a methodological discovery. 'The fundamental thing, here, is that something is happening... The actual event is made possible only because the word that has come down to us... and to which we are to listen really ENCOUNTERS US and does so in such a way that it ADDRESSES US and is CONCERNED WITH US' (Gadamer 1975:419). Gadamer is thus advocating and proposing an ontological system of hermeneutics—one that we can identify with even from our brief exegesis of Matthew's final pericope.

James Barr (1961:288) pointed out the 'unsound method of using linguistic evidence in theological thinking.' He argued that mere translation was not enough to determine meaning, and that reliable exegesis is not possible without a profound understanding of the way in which language itself functions to communicate meaning—another challenge to a simplistic 'understanding' of 'mission' texts.

Paul Ricoeur, finally, has drawn attention to a necessary principle of suspicion in the determination of meaning, for by it (through the use of the critical tools available to us) we 'destroy the idols which we project into the sacred word' (Thiselton 1992:13–14). The 'idols' that we may be projecting (without even thinking of them) onto the 'objective' text (so Ricoeur 1981:211) may be the way in which our parents, or generations before us, all did missions. Those 'idols' that we project onto the biblical text may be the interpretations and exhortations of our beloved mentors or pastors, or the charismatic preacher who came to our church, last Sunday, entreating us to get involved in missions. We may have made idols of the way we've always 'done' mission and the way global mission conferences have always assumed what it is (who are we to question them, after all?!). We would do well as faithful exegetes, however, to engage the principle of suspicion to destroy any such idol that we may have projected onto the sacred word.

All these points show that a simplistic perception of mission is not doing justice to a faithful interpretation of Scripture or showing sensitivity to the way in which the language of the Scriptures that we exegete in mission (or others that we tend to ignore) may operate. This is not to say that models of mission represented by modern mission have no place in a theology of mission. Rather, for the purpose of determining a right concept and theology of Christian mission we need to be more cautious about our start point, so that a more complete Christian life and/or understanding of mission may be thoroughly appreciated and encouraged.

The Spectrum of Hermeneutical Approaches to Interpretation

Having considered how the complexities of language may affect our determination of the meaning of mission we need now to consider the complexities of the diverse ways in which Scripture can be read. Differing approaches to the text form a spectrum that can be represented by three distinct hermeneutical positions.

At one end of the spectrum, meaning is said to reside in *the world behind the text*: it is either unreachable (being buried with the author and the meaning intended by him) or, if particular to the context within which it was written, determinable only through textual methods of interpretation such as historical criticism.

At the other end of the spectrum, the existence of textual meaning is denied. Meaning is said to reside *in the world in front of the text*: it is accessible through, or determined by the reader of the text.

Between the two is *the world of the text*, where meaning is derived from the text itself, rather than through a world in relation to it. There may, here, be a sense of the text being allowed to stand 'over against us as resistance, opposition, and tension' (so Wink 1973:32) and to correct us 'from outside' (so Johnson 1990:54–69). But also human individuality may be appreciated through either sensitivity towards the historical context of the author, on the one hand, or the particular needs and contexts of present readers of the biblical text, on the other.

Whilst none is without its own particular problems, each approach, to a greater or lesser extent, represents an approach to interpretation that does exist in our modern day churches.

Meaning Behind the Text: Authorial Intent

Where meaning is said to reside in the world behind the text, various methods of interpretation can be adopted. However, just one representative approach will be looked at here: the hermeneutic of Authorial Intent, which is an attempt to determine meaning behind the text through the meaning that the original author intended in writing that particular text.

E.D. Hirsch contended that the only real meaning in the text was the one which the author intended. The reader should therefore do his or her best to honour this original intention: 'A text cannot be interpreted from a perspective different from the original author's . . . Any other procedure is not interpretation but authorship' (1976:49)! A failure to grasp the one, right meaning would begin a re-authorship process and, thus, a shift away from the objective text and a lapse into relativity. 'When critics deliberately banished the original author,' wrote Hirsch, 'they themselves usurped his place . . . To banish the original author as the determiner of meaning was to reject the only compelling normative principle that could lend validity to an interpretation' (1967:5).

Johnson (1990:54–69) defended Hirsch's model of meaning and intention as the major theoretical model for biblical interpretation, but others like Lentricchia (in Thiselton 1992:13) suggested that Hirsch represents a '"hermeneutics of innocence" which cannot be sustained in the post-Gadamerian era.'

Indeed, Hirsch's point of view does have its problems.

The first of these is that the authors of the biblical texts are now all dead and it is impossible to access their intentions with any degree of certainty. In Barthes' words (in Thiselton 1992:99): 'As an institution the author is dead: his civil status, his biological person has disappeared.' So although texts are an expression of the authors' thoughts, they may be regarded as secondary forms of communication, themselves subject to the linguistical limitations already highlighted. Even if one does discover the originally intended meaning of the author, one will never have any assurance or certainty of that fact. Hirsch himself has admitted: 'Even if by some accident we could [reproduce the author's intended meaning], we still would not be certain that we had done so' (1967:14). (This is despite him arguing that it is 'a logical mistake to confuse the impossibility of certainty in understanding with the impossibility of understanding' [*ibid.*:1]).

A second problem is that of the linguistic competence of the author and concerns whether or not that which was intended was actually written. For example (Cotterell 1997:141), although 1 Corinthians 14:22 reads 'tongues are a sign not for believers but for unbelievers, while prophecy is not for unbelievers but for believers,' the immediate context suggests an opposite meaning: that tongues are for believers (lest the unbeliever should be cynical towards them) and prophecy is for unbelievers (in order that they may understand the words spoken, and for God's truth to convict them). Although knowledge of authorial intention would, in one sense, override linguistic incompetence, the reader is only in a position to make a guess at that intention. This would never provide any certainty sufficient for determining meaning with any level of confidence (Hirsch 1967:14,17).

Thirdly, there is the difficulty of identifying the different levels of authorship inherent within a text: there are at least four such potential 'levels' (so Cotterell and Turner 1989:42). Luke, for example, would have used Mark (or Q) as a source to 'hear' what the likes of John the Baptist 'said', with a fourth level of authorial intention for those who believe in inspiration: the Holy Spirit (*ibid.*). It is impossible to determine whose intention should be sought in a case like this.

Closely related to this is the criticism that the authors may not have understood the full significance of what they were writing.

This need not be seen problematically, however. Hindsight, for example, gives clarity and significance to a text that the author was bound not to have had (like seeing the sacrifice of Isaac as a type of the sacrifice of Christ, or understanding 'the virgin shall conceive' passage in Is. 7:14, or the 'out of Egypt' passage in Ho. 11:1, in terms of Christ). However Plato, for example, observed that even certain poets could not explain various elaborate passages in their writings (Plato, *Apology*, 22b–c, cited in Hirsch *ibid.*:19). In the same way, Kant 'insisted that not even Plato knew what he meant, and that he, Kant, could understand some of Plato's writings better than Plato did himself' (in Hirsch, *ibid.*). Kant observed (1933:310–311) that 'it is by no means unusual, upon comparing the thoughts which an author has experienced in regard to his subject, whether in ordinary conversation or in writing, to find that we understand him better than he has understood himself.'

Thus, despite criticisms that can be made against this method of interpretation, there is also a sense in which faithfulness to a deeper, hidden meaning can produce a hermeneutic of integrity. Although an attempt to restrict meaning to that which was intended by the author may be to discount a 'fuller' meaning of the text (so Lasor 1986:61), there may also be value in this hermeneutic to the extent to which a meaning of integrity and the meaning of the original author, God, is being sought (albeit under the auspices of looking for the author's meaning), and openness to truth itself is being maintained.

Location of Meaning in the Text: Canon within the Canon

Where meaning is said to be located within the biblical text, it appears that biblical meaning is still not clear but is influenced (amongst other things) by the relational stance of the reader or community of readers.

A representative approach to the determination of meaning from within biblical texts is the method of Canonical Criticism. This involves determining a canon from within the canon of Scripture as a whole, that will serve as a hermeneutical key. Luther's *Christum treibet* ('what teaches Christ') is one such example, and another is to take recourse to the oldest proclamation of the New Testament: the kerygma (Maier 1977:16). One missiological attempt to locate a canon within the canon may be Brownson's understanding of 'the "gospel"' (1996:241) as determined through what he would regard to be a '*missional* hermeneutic' (*ibid.*:232).

However, several objections should be made which are representative of criticisms against the method of Canonical Criticism in general, and against claims to the existence of a clear biblical meaning within a text.

In the first place, the determination of a canon within a canon may be none other than a reader response. In this most recent example, it is Brownson's own hermeneutic which determines his canon. This is markedly problematic because his 'missional' hermeneutic is determined from within the above-disputed field of 'mission *enterprise*' (*ibid.*:233). That his canon is none other than a reader response is suggested, further, by his stress on the importance of 'dialogic interpretation' which implies that meaning is determined (or at least controlled) by the reading community, as discussed, rather than existing in and of itself.

A second objection against the process of Canonical Criticism is with regard to the problem involved in adequately defining the selected 'canon'. The chosen sub-canon is usually so precise yet profound a motif that a real understanding of it may be neither immediately accessible nor conveyable within the space of a single word or phrase. This is because what may be self-evident and relevant to one person may be incoherent and irrelevant to the needs and pre-understandings of another. Brownson, for example, struggled to adequately define his own perceived canon within the canon (*ibid.*:250–258), noting that 'the gospel could be articulated in many different ways' (*ibid.*:251).

Gerhard Maier talked about a 'failed and misconceived attempt to find a canon within the canon which could function as a hermeneutical control to guide interpretation' (1977:16ff). In reviewing the allegedly vain attempts of Protestants to arrive at such a canon, he concluded that 'Scripture itself does not offer a canon in the canon, but . . . that the latter is exacted forcibly and against its will' (*ibid.*:49). However, Stuhlmacher's valid response (1977:6) was that an outright rejection of a canon within the canon is too simplistic.

Brevard Childs, one of canonical criticism's leading practitioners, proposed not only that a canon within the canon should be sought, but that it should be determined ontologically rather than literally or textually. He observed that a special dynamic arises out of the New Testament's canonical function: a dynamic which is 'not exhausted by either literary or historical analysis but calls for a theological description of its shape and function' (1984:36). What is needed is 'a new vision of the biblical text which does justice not only to the demands of a thoroughly post-Enlightenment age, but also to the confessional stance of the Christian faith for which the sacred Scripture provides a true and faithful vehicle for understanding the will of God' (*ibid.*:37). Thus 'canonical', in Christian understanding means, for Childs, 'to see that both testaments of the Bible are "witnesses" to a single "reality," that is, "two distinct witnesses to a common subject matter who is Jesus Christ"' (so Brueggemann 1993:279). The doing of theological interpretation, further, is to deal 'not only with texts and with witnesses but finally with "the reality, the substance," that is, with the truth of God' (*ibid.*:280).

James Sanders's work preceded Childs's in defending a similar approach to a canon within the canon. Representing 'a theocentric hermeneutic' he argued for 'Christ as canon' (1987:41–60) and that 'God is the unity of Scripture' (*ibid.*:61). He has (it should be noted) been accused of both an 'existential strain of hermeneutics' (so Dunn 1987:156) through the use of 'strong rhetoric', 'repetition', and 'vague wording' (*ibid.*:156–215), and a handling of biblical evidence which has been 'too speculative and too slight in substance' (*ibid.*:15).

Childs in turn has been accused of advocating a hermeneutic of innocence (Brueggemann 1993:282). However, Stephen Fowl (1984:173, citing Childs) has argued that 'Childs does *not* suggest that scholarship return to a pre-critical stance. Rather, "the issue is not whether to be critical or not, but what kind of critical understanding can best serve the Christian church in her theological task of proclamation to the world in the twentieth century." Dale Brueggemann, similarly, is adamant that Childs is not returning to a pre-critical, fundamentalist position (as suggested by Barr 1980:14), and suggests instead that he is in the third of Ricoeur's three moments of naive understanding, criticism and post-criticism or post-critical naiveté (Brueggemann 1989:312, citing Ricoeur; so too Mudge 1981:1–40).

One of Brueggemann's main criticisms against Childs parallels the criticism made above against Brownson's work: the 'canonical restraints' required by Childs are only viable insofar as he himself has determined what counts as 'canonical' (Brueggemann 1993:281–282). And yet Child's overall insistence must be heard: the goal of interpretation is not the reading individual or even community. It is not 'excitement' (a criterion of the Enlightenment) but (akin to Sanders) theocentricity: not man and his accomplishments, but God (1980:58).

The canon is, then, for Childs, a 'rule-of-faith' (*ibid.*:52), and the genuine theological task 'can be carried on successfully only when it begins within an explicit framework of faith' (Childs 1964:438).

Despite the benefits of his articulation, Childs's reference to 'faith' may be the fundamental weakness of his approach: although he has consistently advocated a canonical reading, he has not clearly defined what this canon of faith actually is. Barr put it this way (1980:13): 'The things Childs does really well, like the history of critical exegesis, are in the end valued rather lightly, while something like canon, which he values very highly, is handled rather poorly and vaguely . . . Canon in this book is vaguely and unanalytically treated.'

However his work has, like Sanders's, been significant in pointing to a reality behind the text, and the canon within the canon as to do with something more than the text: something more of an ontological than locational or schematic reality or motif.

This achievement will be picked up on later in our own investigations.

Meaning in Front of the Text: a Reader Response

Schuyler Brown well represents Reader Response Criticism through his suggestion (1988:232) that 'meaning exists formally only in human beings.' In the case where that human being is specifically a reader, 'meaning is generated by a reader re-reading of a text' (*ibid.*). Meaning does not even exist without a reading of the text: 'apart from a reader and a reading, a text is simply ink on paper' (*ibid.*).

Thus it is the interest of the reader which ultimately guides the reading experience (*ibid.*:232–233). As a result, Brown advocates a literary reading of the text in which an encounter with it should be sought in order to better understand both the reader's own existence and the state of the world. 'The reader is truly a reader and not a critic. He does not stand over the text, presuming to interpret it for others, [but] through openness and attention, the reader may experience a dynamic passivity which can border on the ecstatic or transcendent' (*ibid.*, 234). In this way, 'the interest of the reader may generate new meanings hitherto unknown in the history of interpretation' (*ibid.*:235).

Brown is here suggesting something that a vast spectrum of modern day Christianity ('born-again', Pentecostal, even evangelical Christianity) will be able to identify with, in its own reading of the bible.

Other advocates of a reader response hermeneutic—Wolfgang Iser and Stanley Fish—must also be heard.

Central to Iser's theory is the notion of the reader's activity (1978:9) in 'filling' in 'blanks' or 'gaps'. The reader 'actualises' (1974:184) and 'concretises' or realises (1978:171–176) dimensions of meaning that are 'otherwise only potential' (1974:184). Thus he is proposing '*meaning as an event*' (*ibid.*:28) in which both reader and text are integral to making a written work what it is. The convergence of text and reader brings the literary work into existence, and this convergence can never be precisely pinpointed; it must always remain virtual, as it is not to be identified either with the reality of the text or with the individual disposition of the reader (*ibid.*:274–275).

Fish, cited at the outset of this chapter, puts it this way: the text *per se* does not have a meaning; rather, the meaning of the text is determined by what it does for the reader. 'The reader's response is not to the meaning; it is the meaning, or at least the medium in which what I wanted to call the meaning comes into being' (1980:3). Fish even goes so far as to suggest that a text does not even exist without the reader. He argued that we cannot 'speak meaningfully of a text that is simply there, waiting for a reader who is, at least potentially, wholly free' (in Thiselton 1992:523). Thus 'it is *the reader who objectifies the text* and its characteristics in the first place, and thus controls it (Fowler 1985:14—italics added).' Fowler suggests (*ibid.*) that Fish 'has helpfully highlighted . . . what must be simultaneous foci for reader-oriented criticism . . . [the] *text* and *reader* meeting *in the context of the critical community*.'

'Control' is a clearly important aspect of reader-determined meaning, and for Fish such control exists in this very form of the interpretive community or 'critical community' of which the reader is a part.

Another control may be the stable text. Iser suggests that control over a subjective construction of 'virtual' meaning comes from maintaining a balance between the 'actual texts' (Iser 1974:xi—or what he terms the 'stable text' as per Thiselton 1992:51) and the meaning of those texts that is realised by the readers (Iser 1974:274).

However, the implied need for an 'appropriate reading competence which is aware of textual features such as interconnections and code' (*ibid.*) narrows down an effective readership whilst introducing the possibility of 'infinite polyvalency' (Thiselton 1992:518). Here too, where embodied meaning in the text is denied, 'no claim can be ranked in relation to any other claim' (*ibid.*:550), and with an incompetent reading of the text comes a danger that a whole community, even over an extensive period of time, may have wrongly advocated a particular interpretation (as, for example, in gay, feminist or liberation communities). The result would be that 'if the reader's expectations and assumptions, especially those which have been ingrained by individual or corporate habit, transform the text into a reflection of the reader's own local and domestic concerns, the text's capacity to speak from within a horizon of otherness has evaporated' (*ibid.*:36).

This of course speaks clearly into a missional community concerning the dangers of a missional hermeneutic, despite it having been accepted by all those in favour of it, even over many generations. What was said of Wagner above (*op. cit.*) may be said of all of us: that 'speculations on one page [may] tend to escalate into assumptions on the next.' We may start with a 'biblical' assumption of what mission is, and we may validate this assumption and explore it and defend it 'biblically'. But none of this necessarily authenticates that original assumption. No place should ever be allowed for a detached or merely theoretical or even emotive determination of meaning.

Of value in this Reader Response approach, then, is the way in which it acknowledges both the significance of the reader and his or her unique circumstances in the event of determining textual meaning, and the need for a control beyond the text which an encounter with the Lord of the text can provide.

Conclusion

It is the concept of the 'reality' of God which is common in addressing both the complexities of language in determining meaning, and the diversity of hermeneutical approaches that may exist in relation to the biblical text.

Beyond the problems of syntax and grammar, interpretation and translation, is the undergirding need for a living relationship with God to guide the event, and to provide true meaning.

Spanning hermeneutical extremes is a similar commonality: the need for a relationship with the true and living God. This is as much the case for Reader Response Criticism (reacting against a potentially totalitarian objectivity and at the same time striving for authenticity and ultimate truth), as for Authorial Intent (attempting to access deeper and perhaps unspoken yet intended meanings in the text) and for Canonical Criticism (with its recognition of the need for an ontological approach to a canon of reality).

All hermeneutical perspectives are ingrained by the same, inherent need for a relationship with God.

And, in the same way, meaning can only be determined through an encounter with the living God and an appropriate response to Him.

Mere reference to, and citing of a biblical text does not ensure an adequate determination of the meaning of that text or, in our case, of Christian mission. This is almost certainly one of the major causes of over-pragmatism in modern mission—one of the main reasons for a crisis in mission in our age.

CHAPTER 7

Simplistic Doctrines

ONE LAST CONTRIBUTING FACTOR to the problem in modern mission is worth looking at briefly: the simplistic unpacking of the major doctrines of the Christian faith that appears to be a feature of it.

Soteriology and ecclesiology are just two examples taken from the whole spectrum of Christian doctrine that plays into what mission is and should represent. Similar examples could be drawn from the doctrines of eschatology, pneumatology, anthropology or even the doctrine of God Himself, for all of these are integral to missiology as a 'multi-disciplinary' discipline (Van Engen 1996a:18–19). But from amongst these rich teachings of the Christian faith, the doctrines of salvation and the church have been chosen for our purposes. Both are core goals of modern mission, but neither of them is ever considered in any great theological depth in mission writings. Such an omission can risk emptiness, or even error in the heart of what mission represents.

To show that these doctrines can be simple, without lapsing into bland simplicity or unintentional heresy, a brief outline of their profundity needs to be sketched.

Salvation

A devotion penned by Oswald Chambers (*My Utmost for His Highest*—daily devotions, 5 May) expresses an appreciation of an easy-to-forget aspect of authentic salvation: 'The Christian servant must never forget that salvation is God's idea, not man's; therefore, it has an unfathomable depth. Experience is simply the door through which salvation comes into the conscious level of our life so that we are aware of what has taken place on a much deeper level. Never preach the experience—preach the great thought of God behind the experience.'

This warning was given to combat that natural tendency in our age towards experience. Salvation is often only thought to be valid or significant if accompanied by a tangible experience of that salvation. Too easily salvation's focus is on the self (though now it is a 'saved' self) and too often it overlooks the realities of God and sin. For background to the doctrine of salvation is the full being of God, out of whose presence mankind staggered on expulsion from Eden.

To this end, further core background to the doctrine of salvation is also the weighty reality of sin and what it is. Not just to do with moral failure, sin is about more than just doing wrong, it is about being wrong: being in a wrong place. Sin is about the human condition: the broken relationship that exists between God and Man.

Salvation, then, is all about God and all God has done in revealing Himself to mankind in order to restore that broken relationship. It is a 'Him' thing—not a 'me' or 'how-it-makes-me-feel' thing.

God made the strength of His wrath known through the incident of Noah and the destruction of wickedness through the flood. How Noah failed despite the mercy shown to him, illustrated that salvation of the 'old' man was inadequate: the creation of a brand new man was needed.

And so it was that God showed the overriding reality of His mercy through the calling into being of Israel (made miraculously through barren Sarah, and then also barren Rebekah) as a people who would not have existed outside of His specific intention, design and favour. Through Moses He delivered the nation of Israel from bondage in Egypt. More significantly, He showed Israel His presence on Sinai, and presenced Himself with them, in the tabernacle which He had constructed for that purpose. He gave laws to govern society, and commands so that His people would live at peace with Him and with each other. And, knowing that that this was an impossible ask, He introduced the concept and practice of sacrifice to atone for sin. Through this model of sacrifice, God showed in simple overview His love of good and hatred of evil, and by so doing He created vocabulary by which nations would understand the One Eternal sacrifice for the sin of all, in His Son.

For ultimately, God's mercy was shown through the fulfilment of 'Israel' and its 'Law' in Jesus Christ: in His life, death and resurrection.

His ultimate atonement for all people in all time was through the cross of Christ. In Jesus' blood, the demands of God's purity and justice were sufficiently met. Jesus was the 'lamb without blemish' who would have to be sacrificed for the sin of a wicked world, in rebellion against God.

Integral to these otherwise external and distant-sounding concepts and events, it is important to underline that it is God who initiates salvation in the hearts and minds of individual people. This He has done in history; and this He continues to do in history through the ministry of the Holy Spirit: rekindling 'true life' within mankind, breathing life, again, into lifeless man: speaking His living, creating word into their lives, in regeneration.

And so conversion happens, not as something in the past (or through own efforts that a man can boast about), but rather as an ongoing process as people continue to turn away, and to be turned away from self towards the full being and ever-real presence of God. Growth and belonging in community are integral concepts of conversion, properly understood. Through justification we have been saved; through sanctification we are being saved; through glorification we will be saved.

Integral to the miracle of salvation is true repentance, which is not just being 'sorry' for wrong done, but a Godly grief over past action and past condition and neglect of God. It is an awareness that comes from being confronted by the living God. As spoken by Job (42:5): 'My ears had heard of you but now my eyes have seen you. Therefore I despise myself and repent in dust and ashes.'

And repentance is also a commitment, proactively, to a right way of living and a real relationship with God in the future. In Johannine terminology it involves rebirth, and in Pauline terminology a 'putting off' of the old self, and a 'putting on' of the new self, which has been created for us 'to be like God in true righteousness and holiness' (Ep. 4:24).

The Christian faith, then, is not just a set of doctrines. It is not merely subscribing to certain dogmas. It is about a real 'organic' life with eternal implications. It involves completely entrusting a former way of life to a Person who is trustworthy—having faith to let go of one's own destiny to a Person who is faithful—the living God. Faith is, thus, a heart certainty of how things are, because of Who we are trusting. It is, because of the life of Christ, a revised worldview and a confidence and future hope that will influence our very cultures and the essence of who we are.

Thus it is that we are justified not simply because of a confession that we make, or a lifestyle that we adopt. We are justified because of Christ's work, and God the Father's gracious consideration of us as righteous, and the rebirth He has performed so that we may be His children. God it is and only He who has enabled a relationship to be restored and re-established with Himself. God alone has held out to us this new condition, and He alone has made a living response possible in us, through the miracle of rebirth, and the recreating work of the Holy Spirit in our lives day by day.

So, confession is one thing (and often the primary thing sought by missiologists and missional statisticians), whilst reconciliation between God and ourselves is (if it happens) a far more involved and substantial thing: a miraculous work of God and Life in our otherwise dead, lost existences.

How far authentic, relational salvation is from that gospel-hardened status so often measured in missiometrics!

Church

Where evangelism's aim is for a relationship to be restored, rather than for a club or cult to be created, this should have direct implications not just on our relationship with God but on our relationships with others as well. We have been 'redeemed'—bought by Another—and so our lives are not our own any more. They belong to God; and out of respect for and obedience to God, they also belong to each other.

Thus the 'end product' of authentic soteriology is the group or people that are brought into being because of salvation: the Christian church.

The meaning of *ekklēsia* as a New Testament, Greek word is paralleled by the Old Testament, Hebrew word and concept of *qahal*. Both can be understood as an assembly of God's people: a people called into being by God Himself and gathered around the very person of God (tabernacled with His people, in the Temple, and later in flesh, through Christ's incarnation).

Of course the question we have to ask ourselves is whether the full presence of God is integral to our church gatherings today, and the churches that missiologists strive to plant.

Beyond being characterised by the presence of God, past gatherings of the people of God were distinctive because of the covenant-agreement that existed between God and Israel. Though we are in a dispensation of a new covenant, the basic features of older covenants still apply to us today, and always will.

These are, first, the centrality of God, in and of Himself. God, in whom we have come to faith, is the great 'I AM' of Judeo-Christian history: there is none like Him, as articulated by the covenant 'Preamble' or 'Introduction'. And yet God is often the last concern of people 'doing church', despite theological language often used and spiritual activity engaged in.

Second, a covenant tells of the historical faithfulness of God to His people through the 'Historical Prologue'. Our historical tradition is not our own: it should not be about our own lives of faith, but about God's dealings in the world, and His faithfulness to all people. And church is about a real relationship of God with His people, being told about, thought about, celebrated and remembered. All-too-often He appears to be absent from peoples' lives! In contrast, His faithful presence and outreach to His people over millennia should be central to ecclesial reality.

Third, the Suzerain overlord required certain things from his vassal people and, similarly, God required certain things of Israel in the past (as shown in the Ten, and many other commandments) and requires certain things of us, His church, even today (put as simply as possible: to love Him, and to love each other). Is the church that 'mission' makes, a church of love for the unlovable in obedience to what God requires of His people? Or is it just an internally affirming community which is itself fragmented and ineffective in permeating the rest of society?!

Fourth, the 'Document Clause' required that the vassal nation read out the written treaty to the people. So too, today, we are implored to be devoted to the 'public reading of Scripture' (1Ti. 4:13). Does the mission church prioritise Scripture, and the reading of the Word, or does it, today, pursue a mere 'experience' of God, or confession of faith?

Next (fifth) the dynamic of 'Witness' is introduced: the dynamic of the public nature of the original treaties that were 'cut' which may in our own day equate to the public nature of our Christian lives. We may not call down the mountains, seas and rivers, trees or rocks to witness our covenant with God, but we have entered into a covenant relationship with Him that is public. It is a confession and life of faith conducted before both the community of saints both past, present and future, and the sceptical onlookers of a world in conflict with Christ. Our Christian faith should be a tangible aspect of the breadth of our global and eternal heritage in a real world of sin, not just an isolated affair behind closed doors.

Sixth is the less popular covenant feature of 'Curses'. We are aware of the consequences of error under the Jewish 'law', but we tend not to think of these under (what we like to think of as) our covenant of mercy. However there is still, for all, a day up ahead where all will be raised to judgement (2 Cor. 5:10 'For we must all appear before the judgment seat of Christ, that each one may receive what is due him for the things done while in the body, whether good or bad' and Rev. 20:12-13: 'the dead were judged according to what they had done'). Ultimately, of course, the curse over all mankind in rebellion to God is Hell. All-too-often 'Christian' mankind appears to feel itself to be immune from this sentence, rather than naturally (and outside of Christ continually) deserving of it.

More thought is given (though often still inadequate thought, and often only in a materialistic/this worldly sense) to the seventh element of 'Blessing'. Immediate blessing that we can enjoy is a restored relationship with God, and ultimate blessing that we can concretely anticipate is the hope of a future home with God forever ('in my Father's house are many rooms . . . I am going there to prepare a place for you!' Jn. 14:2).

Is this blessing enough to 'sell' church in our world today, or is a more materialistic, immediate and illusory 'blessing' of prosperity being promised?

Thus we see a clear continuity between the covenant that gave shape to the people of God gathered around the person of God in the past, and the gathering of His people, the church, today. Beyond this is the aspect of church already touched on that is even more significant than the gatherings of the past or the present, and this is the gatherings (or the one gathering) of the future, around the full being of God.

For eschatology is an integral part of ecclesiology. Moltmann wrote that eschatology is 'not one element *of* Christianity, but . . . *the medium of Christian faith . . . the key* within which everything in it is set' (1967:16). Zizioulas similarly wrote that 'ecclesial identity . . . has its roots in the future and its branches in the present' (1985a:59). And McPartlan put it this way: 'The church's centre of gravity lies in the future . . . Her roots and her continuity lie ahead' (1993:187).

And of course New Testament writing is also clear about the future dimension of the church's existence and the importance and cost beyond superficial confessions of commitment to real growth and life in new believers. Jesus was clear about this (Lk. 14:28–33): 'Suppose one of you wants to build a tower. Will he not first sit down and estimate the cost?' The question we need to ask ourselves, then, is whether today's 'converts' really are being shown into this costly and long-term, covenant relationship with God and the community of believers. Often, from the evangelists view point, people are being brought into the 'church' simply to add more numbers. From the 'convert's' view point, it could be that people are converting to 'Christianity' in the hope of getting something more out of the evangelist than the gospel. Both side-step the core dynamic of the convert's new relationship with God, and the work that is involved in nurturing it, though neither would probably want to acknowledge any oversight!

In view of this, we need to carefully consider our goals for and relationships with new mission churches. We need to ensure that converts are really committing themselves to the church past, present and future: to the bride of Jesus Christ who is its cornerstone and essence, and to each other in the church, for eternity. We need to look at the expectations that we place on converts in terms of baptisms that are required, the Lord's Supper that is to be taken, tithing that becomes mandatory and oppressive, not to mention patterns and forms of 'worship'—and expectations that are fuelled in return.

So beyond confession and numbers, the church should be committing itself in the presence of the living God to a life of love for, and relationship with Him and all those who are also gathered around Him as a 'fellowship of love' (Moltmann 1977:65). For more than being just 'an institution' (Zizioulas 1985a:15), church is 'a "mode of existence", a *way of being* . . . a way of relationship' (*ibid.*)—a 'reality imbued with the hidden presence of God' (Pope Paul VI in McBrien 1991: 88).

Conclusion

Volf captured the profundity of what is trying to be conveyed here when he talked about salvation in the church as 'an ontological deindividualization that actualises personhood' (1998:5). There is such a depth and correctness of doctrine that needs to be recognised in, grasped and applied fully throughout missional thinking.

It is essential that the two goals of mission looked at in this brief section (salvation and the church) should be rightly understood and integrated into our expectations of what mission is, and what it should be. But they are just representative of the need to faithfully outwork the fullness of all other Christian doctrines into mission as well.

Without a deep and accurate understanding of the basic doctrines of Christianity our missiology is at best impoverished, or at worst (and most likely to be) distortive and dangerously erroneous.

The profound, albeit simple realities of the essence of our Christian faith need to be better represented and thought through if any missiology is to be deemed authentic.

Chapter 8

Summary and Conclusion to Part I

THE INTENTION OF PART I was to establish what 'current' or 'modern' mission is, in order to identify the cause of the problems and crisis associated with it. By so doing, our hope is to determine the authentic Christian concept of mission that a contemporary expression of it may be seeking to represent.

Definition of the 'old' has always been difficult, as shown in this comment made by a former missiology student of Willem Saayman's (in Hayes 2002:113.):

> As a first year student at the beginning of the 1980s, that chapter was the beginning of my dialogue with Willem Saayman's missiology. And I found it very difficult, because Willem was not talking to me, he was talking to himself. The 'old model of mission,' as it was sometimes later called, was never described, never discussed. We were told that in the 1930s mission had problems and by the 1960s it had itself become a problem. But the poor first-year students were never told what 'it' was. Year after year they would dutifully write assignments and exams about the problems of mission in the 1930s and then note that in the 1960s mission was itself a problem, and would no doubt hope that it might mean something to whoever was marking the papers.

The 'old model of mission' has hopefully been thoroughly exposed in our own work by now. We have been attempting to unravel what Saayman clearly referred to as the problematic mission of the sixties by identifying the 'crisis' in modern mission, and the possible reasons for it.

Symptoms of the problem have been articulated and discussed, the main one being activism. Mission in our age is essentially measurable, numerical, tangible, and all about what one is doing in the world. It has been systematised and modularised and programmed to such an extent that it is often no longer affecting the people on the ground. It has indeed become what it has come to be labelled: an 'enterprise'.

This is reflected in the whole spectrum of contemporary mission from the mission agency itself, through the mission school to all the mission literature that surrounds it. The dominant understanding and model of modern mission seemed to be based on the 'Great Commission mandate' to 'Go!' and the nature of the crisis in mission appeared in turn to be a crisis of identity. Any quest for the identity of mission is more often than not rapidly eclipsed by proposed solutions to missional problems and/or other deviations.

For the purpose of better defining the 'problem' and thus the identity of authentic mission, two foundation stones of modern mission were critiqued: the 'Great Commission' and the programmatic *Enquiry* and resulting model of mission introduced by William Carey. Both of these, together with the shape of mission that has been popularised and appears to be practised all-too-often without question, were found to be inadequate start points. The 'Great Commission mandate' was shown to be part of a much bigger whole, the implications of which are rarely considered beside popular missional interpretations and uses of a selected text. And Carey's *Enquiry* and resulting model of mission was found to be primarily secular rather than theological or biblical.

In addition to the above, and in part to evaluate secularism itself, modern thought was critiqued. It was argued that rationalism, whilst valued and important, should be subject to wisdom that comes from above. Self-motivated projects, similarly, are valid only to the extent to which God Himself has brought them into being. In addition, it was observed that the strength of individual as opposed to community efforts (which hold individuals accountable) often lack integrity. Postmodernity was seen to offer a poignant enough critique of its 'predecessor' suggesting that modernity was not an end in itself.

The ultimate end is the person and purpose of God.

A brief investigation of the complexities of language and the diversity of the hermeneutical spectrum that exists also brought into question the simplicity of the more commonly held concept of mission.

In view of how language operates, further, it is incumbent upon us as readers of the text to be faithful to the way in which language was used in passages that we take to be missional. In the same way, our determination of meaning (hermeneutically) should be subject to the real meaning of the text 'encountering us' (in the words of Gadamer *op. cit.*).

We do this by subjecting ourselves to the real being of God, the living Word.

The same was shown by digging a bit deeper into (again) simplistically portrayed doctrines—in particular the reality of what it means to be 'saved' and the nature of the 'church'. Salvation is not just a vocal utterance of consent: it involves a new life; a restored relationship with God; something that is difficult to determine with the tools that modernity alone gives us. And it involves a restored and new level of relating to each other. The church, then, is not just about numbers and the building up of an institution: it is about a community of God; a people gathered around the very being and full presence of God; a covenant community.

As a result of the above deconstruction of contemporary mission, it is being suggested that functionalism has dominated—even distorted missiology throughout the development of the era of the church. In contrast, the dynamic of ontology, though a largely moribund concept in relation to modern rationalism, should be revived in order to rightly determine and outwork what authentic Christian mission may be.

Mission is in crisis, in other words, because of the domination of these wrong foundations and inadequate pre-understandings of what mission is. What is needed is more than the likes of Köstenberger and O'Brien attempted in their search for a biblical theology of mission between the ambits of 'Eden and the eternal state, Abraham and Armageddon' (2001:19). Although the scope of their biblical awareness was valuable and right, it is even more important, in view of what has been proposed above, to put aside the concept of mission as we know it, in order not to read our perceptions of what it is back into the texts.

Through the ontological as opposed to functional approach to mission that is being proposed here, the missiological implication already seems clear. The extent to which God's life is being outworked in us and to which our lives are being remade, recreated by Him, is the extent to which we are being a true missional dynamic in a world that needs salvation.

Simple though this is, the implication may be that, like the Reformers, we may need to be prepared to openly risk having an undeveloped missiology in order that all theology and the whole of the Christian life may regain missiological relevance.

To flesh out this proposition, the concept of 'ontology' as it is being used in this work needs clarification and definition. This is our purpose for Part II. In exploring 'ontology' our aim is not just to validate it in contrast to the current functional approach to mission, but to determine its nuances and to find out what it will bring to our understanding about how to say 'mission'—or even whether or not to say it at all—and what that may involve.

PART II

RECONSTRUCTION:
Ontology—a Right Foundation for Mission

Chapter 9

Preliminary Thoughts on 'Ontology'

A FRESH FOUNDATION FOR Christian mission needs to be laid in order to determine what mission could and should be (or should *not* be) in our age.

It is not our intention to replace any viable mission of the past; any valid aspects of 'former' mission clearly need to be retained. But this should not stop us critiquing wrong aspects of it, or approaches to it, in looking for a more authentic theology and practice of Christian mission.

When Bosch (1991:4) observed that a paradigm shift was taking place 'not only in mission or theology, but in the experience and thinking of the whole world,' he recognized (*ibid*.:366) that it would involve not just the new but the old as well: 'both continuity and change, both faithfulness to the past and boldness to engage the future, both constancy and contingency, both tradition and transformation.' Indeed, the place of the 'new yet old' (Treier 2008:11) is often affirmed in broader theological trends and expressions. For it appears that continuity between the 'new' and the 'old' highlighted here is valid, to the extent to which we have heard truth in the 'old' correctly, and to which it equates faithfully to what has been revealed through Judeo-Christian revelation (i.e. ultimately in the person and work of Jesus Christ) rather than through any derived ecclesial traditions.

It is important, then, to point out that the reconstruction of 'mission' being embarked on here in Part II is not just about change for the sake of change. Continuity with authentic past is integral to it.

And it is by assessing both past and present that the oft-eclipsed dimension of the ontological has been identified as that which should be core to a right understanding and expression of mission.

Indicators of 'Ontology' So Far

This lost dynamic of 'ontology' has been given meaning by recognising the integral role and full person of God that is essential to, but often lacking in formulations of what mission is: God, made known in Christ, presenced in the world by the Holy Spirit and encountered in and through a living relationship.

An absence of reference to the living God has been sensed in various ways: for example, in as little as the stagnation of the growth of Christianity as a percentage of the world population, despite all the efforts of the modern mission enterprise with all its resources and efforts.

Missional writings themselves appeared, on the whole, to have been based more on tradition and proof texting than theological reflection and biblical exegesis.

Exegetically, the risen, Danielic Son of Man of Matthew 28:16–20, with all His authority over heaven and earth, is more often than not totally eclipsed by the prescriptive mandate of the 'Great Commission'. Historically, the strategies of modern mission have evolved out of secular rationalism and been inspired by the likes of William Carey's humanistic, activistic exhortations towards 'conversion of the heathen' through secular motivations rather than (necessarily) the love of God or (as noted above) an abiding in God.

Through the Enlightenment, and beyond superstition, a real aspect of humankind was identified which dovetailed with the core message of Judeo-Christian identity: the place of worship of the true and living God, and belonging to Him. The Enlightenment had not been a conscious movement against God, but the essence of sin ended up 'enthroned' by the era: the individual self. In contrast, the overriding message of the Enlightenment for Christian believers is not to throw out the baby with the bathwater or, put another way, not to throw out God with religion and/or superstition. This would be to impoverish the once saved heart of man for eternity. God, made known in the nation of Israel, and ultimately in the person of Jesus Christ and witness of the Holy Spirit—and the Christian story to which mankind can belong—must be regained and retained beyond modernity's ventures.

Linguistically, it was observed that determination of meaning is not just about cold translation or methods of interpretation but about an encounter with the Word, and the reality of the person of God as He approaches us in and through the text. Hermeneutically, then, we identified a commonality between all approaches to, and positions that can be occupied in relation to the text, again: the reality of the person of God, made known personally in Christ through Judeo-Christian history, and present with those who confess His name and who have had their hearts and lives remade by the Holy Spirit.

Even the simple concepts of salvation and the church are represented all-too-often in mission thinking and writing in terms of numbers and structures: things that reflect a mere outward appearance of conversion over against the authenticity of a restored life with God, from whom people were formerly cut off, lost in sin.

All these indicate the importance of an ontological priority over against mere functionalism.

But in addition to the above, the place of ontology ingrains at least two other key missiological concepts.

Ontological Essence of 'Being Sent'

First, looking back, and forward, a basic etymological glance at mission would beg that we investigate the meaning of 'sent-ness'. For the word 'mission' derives from the Latin word *missio*, meaning 'sent', and its Greek parallel *apostelō*—also meaning 'sent' or 'to send'. As both of these words suggest that mission is about sent-ness, our questions would have to address (amongst other things) who did the sending; who was sent; where and why they were sent; and whether any of that 'biblical sending' has any relevance in our own lives today.

In responding to these questions we glimpse that underlying importance of the ontological—because 'sending' is about the person who does the sending, and the message that he or she has thought worth communicating through an emissary.

At one level, it was God who did the choosing and the sending, and it was the patriarchs, prophets, priests, judges and kings who were sent, representing God, representing Israel (and thus God) in a Godless world.

At another level it was again God who sent, but this time (also in the line of prophet, priest and king) it was Jesus who was sent, to Israel, 2,000 years ago: again representing God; again representing Israel; but, more than this, representing the 'new' Israel, the new covenant: the 'absolute' in relation to which the old Israel and old covenant were just models.

God was sending His own, to dwell among us.

This is communicated in many places in the bible, but it is especially clear in the Gospel of John (e.g. Jn. 5:36, '... the Father has sent me'; 5:37, '... the Father who sent me'; 5:38, 'you do not believe the one he sent'; 6:29, 'believe in the one he has sent'; 6:38, 'the will of him who sent me'; 6:44, 'the Father who sent me'; 6:57, 'as the living Father sent me'; and so on).

The purpose of Jesus' life here on earth was to bring eternal life, which (expressed in Jn. 17:3) is 'that they may know you, the only true God, and Jesus Christ, whom you have sent.'

Integral to His sent-ness, further, was the concept of return: return to a home in heaven which had room enough for everybody (Jn. 14:2), but more importantly a return to the One who has done the sending (Jn. 16:5, 'yet none of you ask me, "Where are you going?"') and to eternal dwelling and belonging with the Father.

To miss the reality of God the Father and God the Son in Jesus Christ, and their ongoing eternal relationship, is to miss the whole point of any dynamic of sent-ness in the Christian faith (whether Christ's, the early apostles or our own and others in our age).

So God the Father sent God the Son. And the Son then returned to the Father.

But God the Father 'sent' again, a second time: sent Himself, again (presenced Himself in the world, again)—though, this time, not in the Son but rather, through the Son, in the Holy Spirit—to all who would receive Him ('when the Counsellor comes, whom I will send to you from the Father, the Spirit of truth who goes out from the Father...' [Jn. 15:26]; 'I am going to send you what my Father has promised, but wait in the city until you have been clothed with power from on high' [Lk. 24:49]; 'the Holy Spirit whom the Father will send in my name...' [Jn. 14:26]).

'Sent-ness', biblically, is inherently about the presence of God, and the ministry of God: first in Abraham and the nation of Israel; next in Christ Himself; and then in the Holy Spirit.

Yes, another level of 'sending' is that God the Son, Jesus of Nazareth—Jesus the Christ—sent His disciples (Jn. 4:38, 'I sent you to reap what you have not worked for'; Jn. 17:18, 'As you sent me into the world, I have sent them into the world'; Jn. 20:21, 'As the Father sent me so am I sending you').

Preliminary Thoughts on 'Ontology' 133

However an obvious concern is the difference in 'sending' that is reflected on these occasions (not to mention the obvious difference between these sendings and the Divine sending of the Divine just outlined): first (Jn. 4:38) presumably as an evangelistic outreach; second and similarly (Jn. 17:18), presumably, as witnesses of Christ's life and ministry; but then, thirdly, in a new post-resurrection era and on the Johannine 'Pentecost' occasion of Christ's giving of the Spirit (Jn. 20:21) being sent out just as the Father had sent the Son, empowered and indwelt by His presence in the Holy Spirit.

Clearly, if we might be bold enough to appropriate any of these 'sendings' to ourselves, two millennia later, it should be an appropriation of the last of these.

Looked at slightly differently, it may be important to determine the actual extent to which we are also Jesus' 'disciples'. Is it right to associate ourselves with Jesus' disciples as prayed for in John 17:6–19 who, it seems, had already been 'sent into the world' (pre-Christ's crucifixion, resurrection and Pentecost)? Or are we, rather, just some of those 'future believers' of John 17:20–26 ('those who will believe in me through their message' [Jn. 17:20])? And does it matter? Is there much of a difference between the two?

Unlike those occasions of evangelistic outreach during Jesus' days on earth, we are not 'eyewitnesses' to His life and ministry; and we are not living with Him physically side-by-side: discipled by Him day by day. Yet even here this may not be important as (arguably) we have indeed 'met with Jesus': we have indeed been 'discipled by him' and we are indeed eyewitnesses of His life and ministry in (perhaps) more profound ways (doing 'greater things than these . . .' [Jn. 14:12]), to the extent to which we have met with Him through the ministry of the Holy Spirit, and to which Jesus is now with the Father ('. . . I am going to the Father' [Jn. 14:12]) in a place of indisputable authority.

Either way, interestingly, Jesus' prayer for these future believers was not that they would in turn pick up the mantle of sent-ness or apostleship but, rather, that the world may know 'that *you sent me* and have loved them even as you have loved me' (17:23—italics added). It is the sending of the Son by the Father that is the one, key thing of missional importance in history.

And the communicating of this to the world by others was to be not through aggressive evangelism, but through both the disciples' abiding in the Father and the Son, by the Spirit—and also their abiding in peace and wellbeing with each other. For Jesus prayed 'that all of them may be one' (Jn. 17:21), and that they may be 'brought to complete unity to let the world know [again] *that you sent me* and have loved them even as you have loved me' (Jn. 17:23—italics added again).

Jesus' prayer was not for workers; He did not have a 'passion for mission' (a common catchphrase of modern mission). Instead, His prayer was that people would know that He, Jesus, had been sent from the Father. And it was for believers to '*be in us so that* the world may believe *that you have sent me*' (17:21—italics added).

Salvation would not come through mission or missionaries in the future. It has already come in Jesus Christ Himself.

A priority of Jesus in the Gospels never seemed to be the sending of believers. Such would be to distract from His own sent-ness. Far more of a priority for Him was their relationship and state of dwelling with the Father: Jesus prayed that believers might dwell in fellowship with the Father, Himself (the Son) and the Holy Spirit. For this is how others would know He had come from God.

Abiding in the triune God; the fullness of God abiding in all believers through the Holy Spirit; believers abiding with each other, in love!

If anything, this is the essence of sent-ness or mission in Christianity: not the secular machinations of 'mission enterprise' and sending of mission personnel in the global modern church—but the love and presence of God in this fallen world.

What has clearly come out of even just the brief outline we have sketched here, is that 'sent-ness' in the Christian life is inherently a Divine thing, not a human thing. It is about God the Father sending God the Son to make His Father known; it is about God the Son returning to the Father, to dwell with Him; and it is about God the Father and Son sending God the Holy Spirit to indwell all who turn back to Him, through faith in Christ.

Unbelieving people will come to know this by God's people simply abiding in Him.

Ontological Essence of Missio Dei

To a certain extent this has been reflected upon in contemporary missiology through consideration of a second missiological concept: *missio Dei*—the sending of God.

Traditionally the term has referred to the dynamic of sending in the relationships within the Trinity already mentioned: the Father sending the Son, and the Father and Son both sending out the Holy Spirit. However in Protestant missiology since the mid-twentieth century in particular, *missio Dei* has taken on a more particular meaning. The once purely Trinitarian term has been broadened to include a sending of the church by God. *Missio Dei* has, in other words, been 'expanded to include yet another "movement": Father, Son and Holy Spirit sending the church into the world' (Bosch 1991:390).

There is a certain amount of validity about this development. There is value, for example, in this observation made at Willingen (1952): 'Our mission has no life of its own: only in the hands of the sending God can it truly be called mission' (*ibid.*). This involves a right recognition that anything we do must be sourced in God, which is a good thing to recognise. It is as though 'mission' had tumbled off a bicycle, but picked itself up, looked around (to see who was watching), dusted itself off and, recalling which direction it was going in before the tumble, started off in the 'right' direction again.

That would be all very well, but one has to ask whether modern mission was a valid entity before the 'tumble'. Although 'mission' identified its source correctly, in God, had God actually determined or shaped 'what' was recognising Him? Does 'mission' itself not need to be critiqued? Wright, as already considered, would insist: Yes it does need to be, in order to escape an 'extraordinary shallowness' (*op. cit.*). We have stated already that this should involve a critique in terms of identity and even existence (i.e. assessing the validity of what mission is: the 'rightness' of it even existing, in the first place). But tied in with the question of identity is determining whether God does indeed 'send the church' and whether it is legitimate to incorporate another 'movement' into a Trinitarian dynamic, or not.

What appears to have happened is that the predetermined entity of modern mission (or 'our mission'—our programmes; our initiatives) has been imposed on God, even to the extent of describing God's attributes in terms of what it (mission) is, by saying that 'God is a missionary God' (for example Aagaard in Bosch 1991:390). This should not be! By so doing, contemporary mission has been projecting its own image onto God, rather than allowing God to determine it (as He determined and made humanity) in *His own* image (if indeed He has even determined 'mission' at all; for it may just be a human construct).

So, the positive aspect of *missio Dei* (as used missiologically from the twentieth century onwards), in other words, is that it has recognised the need for mission to be sourced in God.

However, the negative is threefold. First, most seriously, it has (albeit almost unconsciously) distorted orthodox doctrine by imposing modern Protestant forms of mission onto the being of God. Second, the concept of modern mission is being retained as a given, and as a start point, instead of being laid aside in order to 'hear' what is being 'said', missiologically, in the bible and Christian Story. Thus, thirdly: even from the restored vantage point of its source in God, mission has still not been determined for what 'it' is or should be (if different from what it currently is), or even whether it should 'be' at all. If it should have an existence, its own identity and culture has not been adequately scrutinized, critiqued or defined. God as source has not significantly informed mission identity or praxis; it has remained in the mould of modern mission.

Consideration should be given, for example, to whether the dynamic of sending or sent-ness in the Godhead has any implications for the Christian life and church or, indeed, whether these implications (if there are any) should even be regarded as separate to the Christian life (i.e. as 'mission'). These and similar considerations should be made independently of any 'mission' traditions that exist in modernity or even church history (hence the need to include a Theology of Mission strand under Christian Thought rather than Practical Theology in the seminary). They should be made in relation to the very being of God, made known in Jesus Christ, present with His people by the Holy Spirit, as revealed in Judeo-Christianity.

So the principle being highlighted here is basic to this Part II 'Reconstruction': that prior to any human activity should be a full recognition of, and relationship with the one true God, and that a correct and relevant Christian praxis can only derive from God and from His purposes.

This pre-empts the priority that German theologian and philosopher Friedrich Schleiermacher gives to Being over against Doing or even Knowing, as discussed below.

The Meaning and Place of 'Ontology'

What remains, then, is to amplify and add meaning to the way in which the term 'ontology' is being used and, thus, what the proposed 'ontological' foundation as alternative to praxis may involve. This will be done by reviewing how 'post-modern' trends or core aspects of theology have picked up on that lost dimension of ontology, and by considering how exactly we can 'know' what we know about mission, and what it is.

Finally, by way of summary and conclusion, Part III will attempt to sketch the effect that an ontological foundation may have on the practice and meaning of authentic Christian mission.

CHAPTER 10

Schleiermacher: The Priority of Being

SCHLEIERMACHER'S WORK IS IMPORTANT for our investigation because it is an early theological response to modernity, some of the shortcomings of which we have already considered. His critique of the Enlightenment from the early part of the nineteenth century was keen, and his developed thinking is classical in its articulation of what has been labelled 'ontological' in this work.

The importance of this has been noted already: it was a breath of fresh air against the background of cold rationalism and self-centredness that had come about in the Enlightenment. What ontology may mean for mission breathes hope into often lifeless mission enterprises and presuppositions which have come about despite the warnings of many. Bosch, for example, pointed out that 'even the attempt to list some dimensions of mission is fraught with danger because it . . . suggests that we can define what is infinite' (Bosch 1991:512). And yet, definitions of mission and what it involves have all continued to develop out of preconceptions of it as a functional arm of the church.

This common perception of mission is being referred to here as *contemporary mission* or *modern mission*. A similar term used is *pragmatic* or *functional mission*—'functional' in the sense of extreme pragmatism, strategisation and technique. The term 'functional' may also helpfully be associated with the term 'praxis' in the sense given it by a Hegelian/Marxist philosopher from Poland towards the end of the nineteenth century. August von Cieszkowski proposed a philosophy of action, suggesting that the future of philosophy was 'to become a practical philosophy . . . a philosophy of practical activity, of praxis, exercising a direct influence on social life and developing the future in the realm of concrete activity' (in Braaten, 1985:97).

This praxeological philosophy and thinking appears to have worked itself into the church in terms of mission itself being largely understood only 'in the realm of concrete activity' (*ibid.*).

Schleiermacher's contribution is to have articulated something that is beyond mere praxis: the prior and broader dimension of ontology that had been lost in the Enlightenment.

Moltmann (1981:2) pointed to Schleiermacher as the one 'who first understood the way in which [the] modern concept of experience and truth was related to actual existence.' The son of a Prussian army chaplain, Schleiermacher was never content to simply accept doctrines just for the sake of accepting them; Christian teaching had to mean something: it had to resolve and satisfy spiritual angst and questioning. His reputation, then, was as one who 'consistently remoulded "dogmatic theology" into "the doctrine of faith"' (*ibid.*). Even Reformation doctrine, it appears, could get dry and meaningless, but Schleiermacher could not accept that. He was essentially an existential theologian and would argue, for example, that 'the experience of the self in faith points towards God' (*ibid.*).

As such, his contribution was a refreshing response to the one-sidedness of the Enlightenment. His thought serves to articulate and undergird the priority here given to ontology, and is evidenced particularly through his discussion on the essence and action of the church.

What is Church?

Schleiermacher's perception of what church is, or should be, was insightful.

He saw it as more than just the buildings or the institution. It was more, even, than the people themselves (gathered in fellowship). Church was about the faith of its people. Indeed, his systematic theology *Glaubenslehre*, or *Der Christliche Glaube* (*The Christian Faith*) is based on an attempt to determine what makes the Christian church different from any other society of faith or life (Schleiermacher 1989:3).

Certain concepts are integral to his ecclesiology.

A 'Feeling' of Piety

Scientific empiricism—or numbers—were not important for Schleiermacher. What mattered more was the *feeling* (*gefühl*) of the believer, and *'piety'* in particular. 'Piety' was not the sort of proud religiosity that it may sometimes be taken to mean. For Schleiermacher, it referred to that which makes a fundamental difference to the church: a religious 'feeling' or 'consciousness' of communion (i.e. feeling about, or consciousness of the relationships which are brought into being and that exist in the church between God and others [*ibid*:5–6]). He quotes Steffen's account of *feeling* as being closely akin to his own in that it concerns 'the immediate presence of whole undivided Being' (*ibid*.:7).

The real and 'immediate presence' of God—the 'whole undivided Being' of God—is what makes 'church' *church* for us, and what makes our Christian community what it should be!

In other words, the essence of church is a person's living relationship with God and his or her sense of community. Through ongoing relationships with God and with each other, the church shows God's consistent representation of Himself through Judeo-Christian history, to the world. As mentioned, this is not a new teaching; Schleiermacher's work was simply to communicate the Christian faith (so Madges [1996:51] and Gerrish [1987:122,130]) rather than to defend it at all costs (Clendenin 1990:290).

In the same way, our own appreciation of the ontological is not something new: it is simply an attempt to regain what was and always should be core to the Christian faith. If a person's living relationship with God and others is basic to ecclesial identity, it follows that Christian mission should develop from out of such relationships and should be concerned with the same. It should not be merely about human wants and needs, and (equally) it should not let human wants or needs determine what it is.

Absolute Dependence on an Other

This is not the place to critique Schleiermacher's thinking. The purpose of referring to him and other theologians below is to simply celebrate a post-Enlightenment recognition of the ontological dynamic of the Christian life, lost during that era, and to find vocabulary that will help restate basic biblical truths.

So another contribution made by Schleiermacher, then, was his recognition of mankind's absolute dependence on an Other. He saw in humanity the capacity for 'consciousness of being absolutely dependent on or, which is the same thing, of being in relation with God' (1989:12). He also identified 'the dependence of everything finite upon one Supreme and Infinite Being' (*ibid*.:34).

Integral to the life of faith and to the church is God: God, who is really real and who exists in His own right; God as Other; God as Supreme and Infinite Being. And our absolute dependence on Him!

A sense of this reality of God as Other comes in the first place through our own self-consciousness. Our awareness of 'who we are'—or at least how we perceive ourselves—can change, from time to time. Indeed, 'every consciousness of self is at the same time the consciousness of a variable state of being' (*ibid*.:12), and this comes not from ourselves. It comes from a 'non-self-caused' element (*ibid*. 13)—a 'having-by-some-means-come-to-be' element (*ibid*.)—which in turn points to the existence of an Other, the 'whence of our ... existence' (*ibid*.:16) beyond ourselves.

Thus, Schleiermacher's feelings of piety, noted above, are not 'feelings of joy or sadness, but ... an awareness of one's existence and one's receptivity to an Other as one changes and faces change' (*ibid*.:17). This, argues Schleiermacher, is how 'God is given to us ... in an original way' (*ibid*.). We are, because of Him (a far cry from Descartes' 'I think, therefore I am')!

Core to basic humanity and human existence is this 'Other'; so, core to any missiological identity, too, must be the pulsating reality of this very same 'Other'.

Revelation, Redemption, Inspiration

How does fallen mankind become conscious of an Other, and of his or her absolute dependence on that Other, but through revelation. For Schleiermacher, revelation signified an 'illumination of what was obscure, confused, unobserved' (*ibid*.:49). It is 'the disclosing and unveiling of what was hitherto concealed and kept secret' (*ibid*.).

And it is a public unveiling from without, not just some sort of private, Gnostic enlightenment; revelation 'presupposes a divine communication and declaration' (*ibid*.:50).

This is significant because it discounts the possibility of any one faith or religion's idea of an ultimate Being from being established as a universal truth by mere assertion of that fact by that particular community. Even within Christianity, it is not right for believers to 'read into Jesus whatever they are able to conceive as ideal in this sphere' (*ibid.*:378). Truth concerns fact, communicated from beyond, and should always concern fact, revealed from beyond. For Schleiermacher, 'complete truth would mean that God made Himself known as He is in and for Himself' (*ibid.*:52). God is the source of truth, and so God should be core to our understanding of who He is!

(A direct implication of this for our specific area of interest, here, is that God, and only God, should be the beginning and end of any understanding of Christian mission.)

Integral to our absolute dependence on an Other, too, is the fact that all mankind is in need of being redeemed by God. Right consciousness before God thus involves an act of redemption by which all people are enabled to relate directly with God for the first time since the schism back in Eden.

Redemption is the 'passage from an evil condition . . . into a better condition' (*ibid.*:54). Evil itself was regarded by Schleiermacher (*ibid.*) as 'an obstruction or arrest of the vitality of the higher self-consciousness' (self-consciousness being, as noted, not consciousness of self but of one self's absolute dependence on an Other).

Therefore redemption is a way out of a state of '*God-lessness* or, better, *God-forgetfulness*' (*ibid.*:55). And faith, in turn, constitutes a 'certainty that the influence of Christ puts an end to' this state of being separate from God (*ibid.*:68). Indeed, the term '"faith in Christ" relates the state of redemption, as effect, to Christ as cause' (*ibid.*).

Schleiermacher so rightly notes that 'if we conceive of religious moments in which all reference to redemption is absent, and the image of the Redeemer is not introduced at all, these moments must be judged to belong no more intimately to Christianity than to any other monotheistic faith' (*ibid.*:56). Thus it is only through Christ's redemption that relationships can be rightly restored. 'It is indisputable that all Christians trace back to Christ the communion to which they belong . . . [and, further] that the term *Redemption* is one to which they all confess' (*ibid.*:54). Schleiermacher writes: 'We have fellowship with God only in a living fellowship with the Redeemer' (*ibid.*:371).

Integral to the Christian life and message is this divinely vitalised new life with the living God.

Inspired life! 'Inspiration' for Schleiermacher is to do with the communication of the whole being of Christ through Scripture: 'an impulse towards the awakening of a fuller self-consciousness and towards the winning of a total impression of Christ' (*ibid.*:76). An inward thing! But a vibrant, living thing!

Yes, it is about an outward fact—a 'purely factual certainty' (*ibid.*:68)—but the church's faith is 'certainty of a fact which is entirely inward' (*ibid.*). For Schleiermacher, 'to be a religious man and to pray are really one and the same thing' (cited in Clements 1987:185). Despite tangible communication of Himself in history, on one level, the Christian life involves knowing and relating to God and other people on a personal level (Schleiermacher 1966:15).

And church growth is about what God Himself works in people's hearts and lives: for 'when we trace to the divine causality our consciousness of fellowship with God, restored through the efficacy of redemption, we posit the planting and extension of the Christian Church as the object of the divine government of the world' (Schleiermacher 1989:723).

It is beyond the scope of our work to engage in any real depth with Schleiermacher's propositions. But we can appreciate the deeply relational, ontological thrust that this 'father of modern theology' (Gunton 1980:94) has given to us. A right self-consciousness and right 'feelings' of piety are determined only in relation to who He is. Only inspired by an impulse towards the awakening of a total impression of Christ, and through the divine revelatory communication of God with mankind can people find a way back into a direct relationship with Him: redeemed out a state of God-forgetfulness, to God-centeredness.

The Priority of Being Over Doing

Beyond the ontological unpacking of standard theological terms (such as revelation, redemption, faith and inspiration), Schleiermacher helpfully discussed the ontological priority over praxis or functionality: the priority of Being over Doing, or 'Feeling' over 'Knowing' or 'Doing'.

In his assessment of these three different states of self-consciousness, he proposed (*ibid.*:8) that Knowing and Feeling constitute an 'abiding-in-self (*Insichbleiben*)' whilst Doing—clearly an Activity—is a 'passing-beyond-self (*Aussichheraustreten*)'. Although Knowing corresponds with Activity (through the act of Knowing [*ibid.*]), Feeling, only, involves Receptivity. Because of our absolute dependence on an Other for faith and salvation, we require Receptivity, first. Doing, on the other hand, as a passing beyond the self, outworks a prior possession of knowledge.

Thus, of primary importance is Feeling (as defined already as consciousness in relation to God and as associated with the essence of piety, or absolute dependence) through which Knowledge is gained and one is able to pass beyond self by outworking this practically in some sort of Action or Doing. It follows, then, that Receptivity is prior to Activity (*ibid.*).

Looked at another way, Schleiermacher argues against either a Knowing or a Doing as basic to an authentic Christian life (*ibid.*:9).

The reason for this, as regards the first of these, is that if authentic Christianity was about Knowledge (like an entire knowledge of Christian Dogmatics), then 'the most perfect master of Christian Dogmatics would always be likewise the most pious Christian. And no one will admit this to be the case' (*ibid.*)! Thus true Christianity is not just about knowing all there is to know about it.

Neither is 'some previous knowledge about God' (*ibid.*:17) a valid 'first principle' of the Christian life, because it risks being contaminated by prior and erroneous forms of knowing. In other words, we cannot claim to be true Christians because of some former knowledge about God because what we 'knew' about Him (or about that which we may in the past have referred to as 'God') may not be correct. In fact, it will almost certainly be a 'corruption' (*ibid.*:18). God, instead, needs to reveal Himself to us as He is.

Applying this to our own area of interest, it follows that although our former missiological 'knowledge' or presupposition about what 'mission' is may appear to be right, it may not be: this 'knowledge' about mission may not necessarily be of God.

We would also do well to take Schleiermacher's observation as a warning not to simply move off into mission on a mere assumption of who we think God may be, and where He may be leading us. We need to know God's own purposes with absolute certainty. Indeed, we need God, in and of Himself, to encounter us from beyond ourselves and to give us a right knowledge both of Himself and of what He desires of us.

But for Schleiermacher, not only is Knowing an inadequate first principle of the Christian life—neither is Doing.

This is because 'not only the most admirable but also the most abominable, not only the most useful but also the most inane and meaningless things, are done as pious and out of piety' (*ibid.*:10). Just because we are doing something—involved in something(s)—does not make those actions necessarily right; nor does it mean that we are necessarily Christian people.

Anyone, for example (whether born of God, or totally opposed to Him), can do charitable works, or be involved in social welfare. Just because things are being done does not make them things of God, and doing them does not make us people of God.

Applying this again to our own field of mission one may, for example, have conscientiously developed a mission praxis in accordance with one's own understandings of God. However, that perception of need and praxis may be no different from a secular perception of need and, thus, whilst 'good' to do, doing these things may not necessarily be in line with what God is requiring of us in a particular instance, at a particular time. And doing these things does not ensure that we are living as the people of God, or conveying what really matters in the gospel (a restored relationship with God) to other people. More, if 'in these instances an Other is determined by us' (*ibid.*:14), then our formulations will just be self-made projects anyway.

Despite any level of conscientiousness, a missional praxis may actually be wrong because it has derived from a wrong (or even merely theoretical) perception of who God is and (thus) what 'He' desires.

We may have done many 'things' for God, but these may not necessarily have been 'things' that He had desired or asked of us.

Thus it does appear that the essence of the Christian faith 'in its diverse expressions remains essentially a state of Feeling' (*ibid.*:11). It is only through the clarification and honing of this Feeling that a correct Knowing can give rise to a wholly relevant Doing. And so it falls 'to piety to stimulate Knowing and Doing' (*ibid.*:9).

Schleiermacher puts it this way: unless Receptivity is prior to Activity, the Doing that will result will be little more than a spontaneous movement outwards from the self: little more than 'an urge outwards, an indefinite "agility" without form or colour' (1989:13).

One has, therefore, first to receive in order for one's action to have any level of significance.

It follows that authentic Christian mission can only flow from a correct receptivity to God Himself. It cannot derive from prescriptive mandates concerning what we should be doing as people of God. Schleiermacher offered a poignant warning, with regard to the advance of the church (1966:102): 'Certain indications should be drawn up for recognizing whether [this Activity] is properly motivated. For it is possible to err in both directions here: in hasty self-confidence and in anxious hesitation.'

Christian mission would do well to avoid both these extremes, and take time to consider the purposes of God.

Diversity of Action

The distinction between Being and Doing just highlighted has a logical application in Schleiermacher's thought: that the 'activities' which emerge from different people in response to, and as a result of their distinctive 'receptivity' to God, may be authentically multifarious. For: 'a different Doing may proceed from the same Knowing in different people according as a different determination of self-consciousness enters in' (1989:9).

Applying this to our own field, it follows that the extent of this diversity will match both the diversity of Christian people and the cultural contexts of the world. Further, to limit mission to being the responsibility of just a prominent few in the church is to stunt it, and to stunt the church. Finally, if mission can be rightly understood it will be an integral aspect of the life of all believers.

Dealing with Critique

The importance of these perspectives is largely overlooked because of various strong criticisms and discomfort that people have with Schleiermacher's work.

People struggle, for example, with one of his core concepts (noted already): that of 'Feeling' or 'piety' or, as he describes it, self-consciousness. For some this indicates self-centredness or the very egocentricity that is being contended in this work. Indeed Schleiermacher's theology has been accused of being 'less concerned with God than with man's consciousness of God' (so Mackintosh 1964:94). It may also—as such—be perceived as the projection of ourselves outwards, as was Feuerbach's argument: that 'the knowledge of God is nothing else than a knowledge of man' (1957:121,207) or the 'identity of the self in eternity' (so Massey 1976:371) or the 'projection of an image of the human ego onto the cosmos' (so Newbigin 1986:45).

Whilst there may be certain substance in these criticisms, this crucial concept of 'Feeling' has clearly been misunderstood as indicative of feelings of pleasure and anger (for example) rather than as '"the immediate presence of the whole, undivided personal existence"' (Roy 1997:218).

Another criticism has been that such 'feeling' may be a highly subjective thing. Barth considered Schleiermacher's innovative systemisation of theology to have pulled it into an inevitable realm of subjectivism and anthropocentricity (so Sykes 1984:101; see also Almond 1978:437,438). But Schleiermacher's work would dispute this criticism by his argument that the personal existence to which he is referring is always 'intimately bound up with... the awareness of God' (Roy 1997:218). 'Feeling' is, for Schleiermacher (1989:140), far more than mere anthropocentricity: it is to do with a 'state of our heart and soul (*Gemüthszustand*)'—in other words *theocentricity*. Roy (*ibid.*) suggests that whilst self-consciousness may appear to be too subjective a phenomenon on which to base theology, 'the inner life of the human self, this stable feeling is by no means merely subjective, since it has to do as much with the general (*allgemeine*) as with the individual self-consciousness.' 'General', in the context in which he uses it means, for Schleiermacher, that 'the experience (*Erfahrung*) is "expected of everyone"' (*ibid.*). Moltmann (1990:59) observes that by 'Feeling', Schleiermacher means: 'the fundamental tenor of human existence, not sentimental emotions.' Thus: 'far from being subjectivistic, this sense of personal existence is always intimately bound up with the awareness of the world and the awareness of God' (Roy 1997:218).

Still another criticism may be that Schleiermacher is proposing thought-lessness (in view of the fact that he is referring to a mere state of consciousness).

This is, however, to miss Schleiermacher's proposition of 'Feeling' as pertaining to a '*prereflective* consciousness... a *Zustand*, a "mental state," that consists in "self-consciousness"' (*ibid.*:217,218, citing Schleiermacher 1989:6). It is not an unconscious, or unthinking state of mind, but something that is common to all people (religion being 'rooted in human experience and, consequently . . . accessible to every person—from the least educated to the most sophisticated' (so Madges 1996:48).

Despite Barth's criticism of Schleiermacher—his 'love/hate and . . . even older hate/love' relationship with Schleiermacher (so Clendenin 1990:281)—they both held that 'one must be *determined* in order to be free . . . [that] *unless it is God who determines*, we are under the power of a demon, not the truth' (Gunton 1986:321—italics added). Thus perhaps giving clarity to Schleiermacher's similar thought (in this regard), we note that for Barth 'it is the transcendence of God, rather than God's identification with the human condition, which guarantees human freedom' (Campbell 1986:331).

The theological integrity of this 'father of modern theology' (*op. cit.*) is thus difficult to refute. For Schleiermacher did not stop at establishing the anthropological 'norm' of absolute dependence; he went on to explain what this meant theologically: focus on the Other who is ultimately knowable.

The focus of his theology, the essence of being truly human (which follows, as man has been made in the image of God), and core to the Christian life and church, therefore, is the living person of God.

Assessment and Summary

Schleiermacher's work has given us valuable concepts and vocabulary.

First, it validates the concept of ontology as crucial and foundational to a right theological awareness.

Further, it clarifies the meaning that 'ontology' is being given, here: relationship with God—not mere personal being, or self-centred selfhood, but Being in relation to who God is, in and of Himself.

Schleiermacher's concept of the church as that which has been brought into being and which exists in relation to Christ as cause, and which is distinctive because of its faith in and relationship with God, is equally useful in stressing the centrality of an ongoing encounter with the founder and focus of the church.

His recognition of 'an Other'—in other words the way in which he equates Christ with the 'Other' who is common to all mankind—suggests two things. First, Christ is more than just our own formulations of who He is, and more than just our own perceptions and understandings of God (in some sort of Deistic manner). Second (in terms of evangelism), we should not be seeking to reach others and convert others to our way of thinking but to God (a concept of which perhaps they already hold, which will need explaining in relation to [and in most cases usurping by] the Christ event and salvation history): God, the one and only personal creator and saviour.

And then, of course, we are indebted to Schleiermacher for his incredible articulation of, and argument for the priority of Being over Doing. The implication of this is that any praxis a Christian person engages in missiologically needs to have been derived from a deep and real relationship with God: from sitting at His feet, from knowing Him and being known by Him. Thus, any right missiology and missional action must derive authentically from God, and not ourselves (or even our own pious understandings of who He is) as individuals.

We are also grateful to Schleiermacher for pointing out that because a right Action derives from within the person of God Himself, that Action will (as a result) be creatively diverse, and that it will involve all Christian people, not just a select few.

The implications and warnings of these (and almost certainly other aspects) of Schleiermacher's work for contemporary mission are profound: unless mission is determined within a relationship with God and the people of God, independent praxes will result which may be at best a waste of time or, at worst, counterproductive in their distortion of *missio Dei* rather than their furtherance of it!

CHAPTER 11

Postliberals: Pointing Us Back to Basics

KNOWN NOT ONLY AS the father of *modern* theology, Schleiermacher was also known as the father of modern *liberal* theology. It is therefore appropriate that the 'next' response to modernity for us to listen to is that of postliberalism.

Lesslie Newbigin (1991:3) noted that for too long the church has been 'trying to counter scepticism by calling in the help of philosophy to prove the existence of God, rather than by inviting people to believe in God's own revelation of himself in Jesus Christ.' And postliberalism appears to have been arguing the same: that the Christian faith and church should not be defended philosophically so much as with 'God's own revelation of himself in Jesus Christ' (*ibid.*).

Outline in Brief

The postliberal programme evolved, essentially, from the Yale Divinity School (so Phillips and Okholm 1996:11). It represented (*ibid.*): 'a new theological coalition which confesses Jesus Christ and the core biblical framework of salvation history as the norm for the Christian's life. Instead of conforming the confession of Christ to American culture or to Enlightenment epistemology, this coalition insists that Jesus Christ is not subject to some higher authority. Compromise on this point—even for mission strategy—would ensure the dilution, even the distortion, of Christianity.'

Hans Frei pioneered postliberalism as a response to the perception that 'all across the theological spectrum great reversal [has] taken place; interpretation [is now] a matter of fitting the biblical story into another world with another story rather than incorporating that world into the biblical story' (Frei 1974:130).

By way of an alternative, instead of trying to fit the bible story into our alien world, Frei proposed the importance, rather, of fitting a rebellious world back into the biblical story. His younger contemporary, George Lindbeck, talked about this as 'the ancient practice of absorbing the universe into the biblical world' (Lindbeck 1984:135).

It is the biblical story, or the *biblical world* which is normative, not our own world today: not 'American culture' or even 'Enlightenment epistemology' (*op.cit.*), nor even African culture or any other epistemology. The issue concerns absolute authority, and the postliberal, as noted, would vest it solely in the person of 'Jesus Christ and the core biblical framework of salvation history as the norm for the Christian's life' (*op. cit.*).

This is a right and a necessary corrective in our age. A mere concept of an 'Other', accessible universally, could tend erroneously towards a general sort of Deism.

And so the norms of the Christian faith have had to be articulated. The control of Scripture has been highlighted as being of key importance, Frei prioritising it over against any concept of a universally accessible reality, and contending against an experiential form of reality usurping Scripture's foundational role (Phillips and Okholm 1996:11). It is Scripture that should be foundational to a right understanding of the grand, universal narrative (*ibid.*), not subjective experience.

Lindbeck also stressed the form of the text over against any existential interpretation of it, for without the text there is no common framework from within which to compare and assess religions, truth claims and/or experience (1984:49).

It followed too, for Lindbeck, that postliberalism's stress should be on 'ancient catechesis more than modern translation' (*ibid.*:132) in biblical interpretation. It was 'the Gnostics, not the Catholics, who were most inclined to redescribe the biblical materials in a new interpretive framework' (*ibid.*). 'Catechetical instruction', in contrast, involves practising new modes of behaviour and learning the stories of Israel and their fulfilment in Christ (*ibid*). The Christian story is old and tried by time.

Important, then, is to regain the world of the biblical narrative as the specific framework of the Christian faith in favour of a mere personalised (and thus almost syncretistic) translation of the text or existential spirituality in relation to our 'modern' or 'postmodern' contexts.

The relevance of all this for mission is that postliberalism is clearly pointing to a source of truth beyond our selves that is rooted not just in Scripture but in the person of Christ, and salvation history. It is addressing the key issue of authority or (even more than this) epistemology, and locating these in God who has reached out into human history, rather than in humanity's imaginative thoughts or own clever works. As noted already (*op. cit.*): 'Compromise on this point—even for mission strategy—would ensure the dilution, even the distortion, of Christianity.'

The issue being addressed, then, is clearly of critical, foundational importance for the future of the Christian faith, and an outworking of it. Postliberalism is pointing us back to absolute basics.

Criticisms Against Postliberalism

Certain criticisms have been made against postliberalism and although they are potentially confusing and irrelevant, a deeper understanding of our own ontological proposition can be gleaned by considering them.

Antirealism

Because of its stress on the bible, postliberalism has firstly been criticised for having fallen short of the 'reality' that exists behind the narrative of the text.

Lindbeck, for example, has been accused of being 'inherently antirealist' (Hensley 1996:71) and of conceiving theology as '"primarily descriptive rather than ontologically normative"' (Bloesch in Hensley, *ibid.*). McGrath (1996:16) has echoed this criticism by asking whether postliberalism does 'make ontological claims when confessing the Christian faith' or whether it is 'a form of antirealism?'

In some ways the criticism is understandable: Lindbeck underlines the age-old teachings of the church; Frei advocates the sole adequacy of the bible through comments like 'Belief in the divine authority of Scripture is for me simply that we do not need more' (1987:22), and: 'The text is sufficient for our reference . . . It is enough to have the reference to Christ crucified and risen' (*ibid.*). These may both be understood as 'antireal' statements.

However, such criticism appears to be focused only on Frei's methodological use of 'Scripture' and text as 'reference', and to be missing his reference to Christ: his recognition of 'authority' in 'Jesus Christ' Himself, 'crucified and risen'—the actual 'reality' behind and beyond the text which makes it what it is.

Indeed Frei stressed just this point when he wrote of the 'truth' to which Scripture points: 'The truth to which we refer, we cannot state apart from the biblical language which we employ to do so' (*ibid.*). His reference to 'the truth' as existing beyond the text is an acknowledgement of the reality of this truth.

Yes, the postliberals' 'Christ' may appear to be packaged within the text, but He is certainly not confined to the text. For example Frei states: 'I can talk about "Jesus" [as a "fact" like other historical facts] . . . but can I talk about the eternal Word made flesh in him in that way? I don't think so . . .' (*ibid.*:24). Christ is, for Frei, too big, too *real* a reality to talk of in that way. His recognition of who Christ is may start in the text, but because of the text and because of who Christ is, it has to move beyond it, and would never remain 'in' it.

In articulating the sufficiency of Scripture he is implying that we do and should look beyond Scripture to the reality to which it faithfully attests.

Another defence against antirealism is postliberalism's aim to prevent Christianity from being moulded into the shape of the secular world (so Ochs 1997:609). Basic to postliberalism's *raison d'être* is its recognition of the substance of the biblical world in contrast to the inadequacy of the secular worlds. In order for religion to survive in recent times, it has tended to appeal to 'some form of inwardness as the source and center of authentic religiousness' (Lindbeck 1984:24)—a form of existentialism. And yes, postliberalism has spoken against this worldly inwardness, appealing for the bible and revelation of Jesus Christ to be true Christianity's defence. But it has also pointed to a deeper, more real reality than experience: the person of God Himself, who is prior not only to the writing of the bible, but to an interpretation of it, and who is also prior to and independent of our 'experiences' of Him.

This, then, is a highly valuable contribution because as has rightly been noted by many scholars it is impossible to return to a 'pre-critical, fundamentalist position of naive understanding' (Barr 1980:14; so, too, Brueggemann 1989:312, citing Ricoeur's 'Preface to Bultmann' in Mudge

1981:58, and of course Mudge himself in that work). It is impossible, in other words, once having believed, and critiqued the Christian faith, to then return to the position of naiveté occupied before that spiritual journey was embarked on. Although postliberalism may appear guilty of attempting such a return, it is seeking not so much a pre-critical mode of thought as a post-critical perspective on an external reality: a Christian teleology based not on critically derived existentialism so much as post-critical acceptance of a reality that exists in and of itself.

Christianity is more than just a human response to a 'core experience of the transcendent' (so McGrath 1996:26): it is about the transcendent One Himself. And in order to articulate this 'One', the explanatory and revelatory significance of Christian theology becomes apparent. It has to involve much more than mere 'experience' (*ibid.*), and so postliberalism is far from being 'antireal' in that it points to much more than just the framework of the bible and Christian history: it points to the actual person of Christ and, indeed, the being of God Himself as authentic 'Other'.

Socialisation

A second criticism made against postliberalism is that it is simply an endeavour to preserve the religion of Christianity: a mere attempt to give continuity to the Christian religion by socialising people into it.

There is of course certain grounding for this criticism. For example Lindbeck had perceived a 'growing dissatisfaction' with Christianity and 'the doctrines or dogmas of churches' (1984:7), and suggested that 'in order to survive, mainstream Christianity will become more concerned about developing distinctive and encompassing forms of minority communal life than it has been since Constantine' (*ibid.*:164). Ochs held that postliberalism had indeed aimed to create a mode of survival for the Christian religion, rather than simply to express or interpret it (1997:609). Phillips and Okholm (1996:16) pondered whether a stress on 'biblical narrative and the significance of Jesus Christ' was based on 'anything more than the community process of socialization.' And Hans Frei clearly underlined this survival incentive with these words: '[T]he most fateful issue for Christian self-description is that of regaining its autonomous vocation as a religion, after its defeat in its secondary vocation of providing ideological coherence, foundation, and stability to Western culture' (1986:74).

However postliberalism's purpose was never about the survival of Christianity at any cost. Its arguments have not been unreasonable or in any way distorted to achieve this aim. For example, despite its observation that 'reasonableness... has something of [an] aesthetic character... [and is something of an] unformalizable skill' (*ibid.*), postliberalism has recognised 'reason' as a necessary norm with which to adhere. Indeed its propositions have focused upon the very norms of reasonableness which for them 'are like the rules of depth grammar, which linguists search for and may at times approximate but never grasp' (*ibid.*).

Further, its appreciation of religion has been for its positive effects on society primarily through the way in which religion operates. Lindbeck associated religion with the culture and language of belief (*ibid.*:18) and doctrines, in turn, with the linguistic rules (*ibid.*:84) of those cultures. The whole task of a doctrine, then, was to serve as a rule (*ibid.*:19); in other words, a doctrine does not make first-order truth claims, but rather regulates them (excluding some and permitting others). And because doctrines operate regulatively, not propositionally (*ibid.*), religion itself exercises 'immense influence on the way people experience themselves and their world even when it is no longer explicitly adhered to ... [It] can be viewed as a kind of cultural and/or linguistic framework or medium that shapes the entirety of life and thought' (*ibid.*:33).

So, postliberalism's goal is not just the survival of religion at any cost. Based on reasonableness, and regulated by doctrine, it is about the real and beneficial impact that it can have on society.

More than this, Christianity's association with the norms of reasonableness, and its appeal to the biblical narrative and revelation of the true and living God in Jesus Christ does not constitute a socialisation programme. Instead, it is an appeal to an external standard of truth located in the 'only real world' of the bible (so Erich Auerbach who greatly influenced Frei, as noted by Phillips and Okholm 1996:12).

A social totalitarianism is not being posited but a relational one and (more) one that exists in relation to an objective Being. Affirming dogma and church doctrine, rationality, textuality, and revelation, points beyond mere formalisation to the essence and reality of God who exists in and of Himself!

Against Classical Foundationalism

A third criticism against postliberalism is its apparent rejection of classical foundationalism as necessary for the survival of Christianity.

Foundationalism's quest for a reliable epistemology represents a mindset and way of thinking that ingrains modern thinking and, importantly, the way in which we have come to 'know' what mission is, in modernity. It insists that for something to be rationally acceptable, (1) there should be evidence for it (so Plantinga 1983:47), (2) that evidence should be 'properly basic', i.e. 'indubitable' (absolutely certain or unquestionable) through being 'self-evident or incorrigible [habitual; consistent; regular] or evident to the senses' (*ibid.*:59), or (3) that such evidence should be traceable to something which *is* 'properly basic' (*ibid.*:55).

Although this summary is very brief, it helps to better understand foundationalism's remarkable far-reaching relevance. It 'remains the dominant way of thinking about these topics [viz. faith, knowledge, justified belief, rationality, and allied topics] . . . The vast majority of those in the western world who have thought about our topic have accepted some form of classical foundationalism' (*ibid.*:48).

It is no wonder, then, that postliberalism's apparent rejection of it has attracted criticism.

And yet despite the stronghold that classical foundationalism has in the modern mind, Nicholas Wolterstorff (1976:29) observed that towards the end of the twentieth century it had 'suffered a series of deadly blows . . . [and that] it now looks all but dead.' Alvin Plantinga, further, exposed foundationalism's failure to fulfil the criteria which it had itself once set for other epistemological foundations. He observed that there is actually 'no satisfactory criterion for properly basic belief in classical foundationalism which is itself properly basic or based on evidence traceable to properly basic beliefs' (so Zeis 1990:174). Although something may be self-evident, incorrigible and evident to the senses, some people may still not necessarily regard it as truth. Further, although something may be accepted as basic by nearly everyone, that 'something' may not necessarily be true, or properly basic. Plantinga (1983:62) writes: '*Not* nearly everyone takes [this basic formula of foundationalism] as basic; I do not, for example. Nor is it self-evident, incorrigible, or evident to the senses.'

His conclusion was radical: that classical foundationalism is 'both false and self-referentially incoherent' (*ibid.*:17), is 'bankrupt . . . [and] poorly rooted' (*ibid.*:62) and 'should therefore be summarily rejected' (*ibid.*:17).

In view of this, postliberalism's rejection of foundationalism could be seen not as a criticism but as a commendation: that it is not blinkered by it, and that it is looking for something even more reliable than proper basicality.

For postliberalism is not rejecting foundationalism *per se* but, rather, is seeking something even more authentic—more 'basic'—than classical foundationalism in something more akin to Plantinga's theological foundationalism. Theological foundationalism, Plantinga suggested, like its classical namesake, seeks a control beyond itself and its own perception of proper basicality and reliability, and religious beliefs can under certain conditions be regarded as epistemologically basic (Zeis 1990:174,177).

To this end, postliberalism's perceived rejection of foundationalism is not a rejection of realism either, as already discussed. Indeed, Lindbeck has been described as 'an anti-foundationalist thinker who is in principle open to metaphysical realism' (Hensley 1996:80). In other words Lindbeck is open to 'believe that reality exists "out there," independent of [a person's] mental and linguistic representations of [that] world in the form of beliefs, experiences and theories' (*ibid.*:70). By arguing for the priority of Scripture and the world of the text, Lindbeck is in no way rejecting the objective external reality of God (Lindbeck 1984:40). In fact it is this very aspect of reality that postliberalism claims to be the responsibility of the church to bring to life, through embodiment of the biblical narrative.

Ronald Thiemann's response to classical foundationalism was similar to Plantinga's in its favouring of the Christian epistemological doctrine of revelation. He proposed a descriptive theology which 'makes normative proposals but does not seek to justify those proposals by developing a foundational explanatory theory' (1985:72). Those normative proposals, he suggested, are located within the Christian narrative.

Thiemann's thesis has itself attracted certain criticism, for example as involving too much of an 'interpretive activity' (*ibid.*:72) and, thus, as being an essentially subjective, individualistic exercise (for interpretation 'is never without an individually and culturally relative context' [so

Topping 1991:45–46]). However, if it is a context of 'previously justified beliefs' (*ibid.*:45) which 'determines the validity of the arguments offered' in any situation (*ibid.*), and if the context of that belief is true (as God's existence and revelation of Himself is true), then the 'norms' which one determines are justified.

A related criticism could be that Thiemann, in searching to 'illuminate the structures' (1985:72) of Christianity, is merely searching for a foundationalist-like proper basicality (*ibid.*:75). This should not be necessary if theology is open to being informed from outside of itself (even though that theology should, desirably, be 'appropriate to Jesus Christ as humans experience him . . . and credible to human existence as any woman or man experiences him' [Ogden 1996:7]). For that is what Christianity is—determined from beyond—and to deny a 'reality beyond the realm of human language is incompatible with Christian belief in divine prevenience' (so Placher 1987:49).

But Thiemann does appear to have been mindful of this by determining Christian 'norms' from within the Christian narrative, rather than simply searching for properly basic structures of faith.

The common thread running through all the above is that truth can only be known when truth's own story is heard and when truth itself, as 'Other', is encountered, and in turn encounters.

To this end, postliberalism's operation outside of the now questionable bounds of classical foundationalism is authenticated by the locus of its investigations in the revealed truths of God. This in turn validates our own location of absolute truth and epistemological integrity in the person of God.

Summary and Assessment of the Postliberal Contribution

All this enquiry is relevant because of poignant questions such as the following, offered by Brownson (1996:230): 'What does it mean to be called to speak of the gospel as *truth* in a world that declares that religious speech can never be true, but only "true-for-you"?'

Postliberalism's start point and thus its benefit for us in our search for ontological definition and clarity, is the world of the bible and the person of Jesus Christ, and the norms of the Christian narrative. It points unashamedly to the objective 'Other' of which the bible talks, as the place where truth resides. By so doing, it has succeeded in articulating the truth of the reality of the Being of God, and the authentic reality of who He is.

In its appeal to an external reality, postliberalism has created the space within which particular denominational claims to truth can be circumvented, if not reconciled. Thus, although it clearly does attempt to formulate a mode for the survival of Christianity, postliberalism's ultimate reference is not to the Christian religion or even the Christian community *per se*, but to the being of God who gives that religion and community its identity. Therein alone—in the person of God (attested to by the faithful witness of Scripture and prompting by the Holy Spirit, rather than 'proper basicality')—does true knowledge and understanding reside: and therein alone can it be adequately grasped.

Thus, postliberalism serves us in our own thinking, to point beyond methodology (even the critical reflection of 'theology') to *Theos* Himself: God, made known in Jesus Christ, and present by His Holy Spirit in our lives, even today. Moltmann (1974:19) puts it this way: 'Ultimately, one's belief is not in one's own faith . . . [O]ne believes in someone else who is more than one's own faith. Christian identity can be understood only as an act of identification with the crucified Christ.'

All this adds clarity to what is meant by 'ontology' in our proposition of the eclipsed, ontological foundation of Christian mission, namely the reality of, and not just reference to the true and living God.

Chapter 12

Engaging with the Other

IT IS ONE THING to recognise and talk of God as 'Other', but it is important to address just how one engages with that 'Other': how a conscientious enquirer could ever begin to know Him and any purposes (like the specifically 'missiological' or related purposes that we are interested in) that He may or may not have for His people.

This question can be approached in a number of ways.

Wright's Concept of Critical Realism

N.T. Wright's voice is helpful to hear for what it adds to our understanding of a relational or ontological approach to knowing God, in particular through his concept of critical realism. 'Critical realism,' he posits (1992b:35), is:

> a way of describing the process of 'knowing' that acknowledges the *reality of the thing known, as something other than the knower* (hence 'realism'), whilst also fully acknowledging that the only access we have to this reality lies along the spiralling path of *appropriate dialogue or conversation between the knower and the thing known* (hence 'critical'). This path leads to critical reflection on the products of our enquiry into 'reality', so that our assertions about 'reality' acknowledge their own provisionality. Knowledge, in other words, although in principle concerning realities independent of the knower, is never itself independent of the knower.

Wright's first achievement (for our own purposes) is his articulation of the reality of God (the 'thing known') who exists independently of our selves. Just as Schleiermacher acknowledged the real and independent existence of the 'Other', and just as postliberalism acknowledges the need to look beyond philosophy to God's own revelation of Himself in Jesus Christ, Wright acknowledges, and in his own way successfully articulates the same: the real existence of a real God ('the *reality of the thing known*') who is knowable—or certainly get-to-knowable!

We ourselves (us believers) are the 'knowers': the ones who seek to know the 'thing known', who is God, and who seek to engage with Him.

This 'knowing' (Wright clarifies) involves a process: a 'dialogue'—and not just one dialogue or a one-off dialogue (if indeed that is possible) but a 'spiralling path' of dialogue between these two 'parties': between the knowers (ourselves) and the thing known (who is God). In the context of a living and growing relationship with God, we could call this dialogue 'prayer'.

So 'realism' refers to the reality of God (He is not just a figment of our imaginations), and 'criticism' refers to that spiralling dialogue involved in getting to know God.

'Critical realism', then, is about the real person of God and 'critical reflection' upon Him, in order to known Him better. This does not involve criticising God. It involves critiquing and reflecting upon our own perceptions and formulations of who God is: God, who opens Himself up to our critical enquiry. Our formulations about who God is, are 'the products of our enquiry into "reality"', or our 'assertions about "reality"' (*op. cit.*).

In this way, Wright's concept of critical realism fleshes out our understanding of the ontological priority, here: our focus on the being of God as core to any of our knowing. For integral to the very process of knowing, Wright has recognised the reality of the 'thing known' (the reality of the 'Other' outside of ourselves); the need for focusing on God in and of Himself; and the need for conversation between ourselves and that 'Other' in order to correctly 'know' (Him!).

If asked how we are to develop an authentic theology of Christian mission, the response is simple: through knowing God. Yes, our knowledge—or formulations—may be provisional as the 'reality' in focus is independent of us, as knowers. As Wright says: 'Our assertions about "reality" acknowledge their own provisionality' (*ibid.*). And yet Wright also notes that knowledge 'is never independent of the knower' (*ibid.*). The 'reality' in focus is independent of us, but our knowledge of that reality always engages us. God works with us—works in us—to reveal His purposes and truth as we wait for Him.

The gaining of knowledge is, therefore, a real and personal quest for truth that happens within a living relationship with God.

Subjectivity?

An obvious observation, here, may be that Wright's process of gaining knowledge will always be a highly subjective exercise because it involves ourselves, and our own perceptions of God's truth. And what is true for me may not necessarily be true for you or, worse still, may not even be true at all.

And yet Wright recognised that certain controls are in place, all of them to do with publicness.

One is the tradition of Christianity itself: a faith which is committed to its own 'irreducible publicness' (*ibid.*:135). Another control is God Himself who has revealed Himself publically. Yet another 'control' is the fact that any relationship between the 'knower' and the 'thing known' is (ultimately) a public relationship because the whole nature of the Christian narrative and the restored fellowship with God that results has always been and always will be a public thing.

The importance of this publicness is that it is an inherent aspect of the Christian faith, as evidenced in a whole variety of ways.

The historical Jesus Himself, for one, is best understood in relation to the broader and public narrative within which His story has taken place (so Wright 1986:189–210). Closely related to this, the Christian faith is itself represented by a number of symbols which are all committed to publicness (1992b:232): for example, the Temple, Land, the Torah and Racial Identity in Jewish history (*ibid.*:224). These symbols in turn articulate the essence of the grand narrative and act like the 'constraints' of the story (1986:200). Symbols provide 'fixed points' (1992b:232) which function as 'signals' (*ibid.*) to oneself and to one's neighbour that one has heard the story and is living by it (*ibid.*). 'Symbols ... bring worldview into visible and tangible reality' (*ibid.*:224). Thus 'symbol and story are mutually reinforcing' (*ibid.*:232).

Clearly core to the public Christian faith, then, is its story, the focus of which is not just a private God of individuals' imaginations, but the public *creator* God who has made Himself known publically through Judeo-Christian history. Christianity is the story about 'the creator and his world' (*ibid.*:135). It is committed (*ibid.*) to speaking about 'the creator and redeemer god as God, the one God: not a Deist god, an absentee landlord, nor one of the many gods that litter the world of paganism, nor yet the god who, in pantheism, is identified with the world; but the God who made and sustains all that is, who is active within the world but not contained within it.'

This central importance of the Christian Story and the One of whom it tells, stands in direct contradiction to postmodernity's 'incredulity [or scepticism] toward metanarratives' (so Lyotard 1984:xxiv). Lyotard suggests that the concept of 'the grand narrative has lost its credibility, regardless of what mode of unification it uses, regardless of whether it is a speculative narrative or a narrative of emancipation' (*ibid.*:37). Wright, in contrast, is arguing for the validity of the one, Christian narrative. Postmodernity's mere rejection of the category of narrative does not necessarily invalidate that category; it does not mean that one grand narrative does not exist for all humanity and truth.

And so it is publicness that guards against a subjective interaction with the reality to whom Wright draws attention: the publicness of the Christian faith; the publicness of the creator God Himself; the public relationship that Christian people have with God through their public confession and outworking of faith; and all this illustrated, as it were, by the publicness of Jesus Christ's own life in Ancient Israel; the publicness of symbol; and the publicness of the Christian Story.

Whilst critical realism may be 'subjective', it is not without a comprehensively firm control.

Foundationalism?

There are apparent similarities between Wright's 'narrative' and Thiemann's 'tradition' (1985:72) assessed earlier as an alternative to foundationalism. The fundamental difference, though, is Wright's aspect of relationship between 'knower and the thing known' (1992b:35) that is involved in the process of knowing.

It is important to touch on 'foundationalism' again, albeit briefly, because of what may be basic or foundational in any process of 'knowing' truth. And it is important to hear Wright's relational contribution because of our own interest in the significance of the ontological, and our supposition that 'knowing' does not necessarily depend on mere tradition, but what that tradition points to.

Thiemann's stress on the importance of 'tradition' is almost absolute. However where he simply stops short of denying that an external reality is contrary to the Christian faith (so Placher 1987:49), Wright makes it specifically clear that a relationship with this reality is the subject of his investigations.

And although Thiemann attempts to describe the structures of the Christian religion (1985:72), Wright—in view of the perceived subjectivity involved in such a process—points to the objectifying influence of reality on the process of knowing, as focused in a real knowledge of Jesus of Nazareth. This knowledge of Jesus should be authentic, not just mythical. Indeed: 'It is not only possible,' he writes, 'but highly likely, that the church has distorted the real Jesus' (1992c:18). And so it is that 'without the real human Jesus of Nazareth,' he writes, 'we are at the mercy of anybody who tells us that Christ is this, or that' (*ibid.*:93).

Further, where Thiemann's descriptive theology presumes a certain practice of faith which seeks to understand itself more fully through critical reflection upon itself (1985:75), Wright's approach is to critique (and by so doing advocate) reality itself and, thus, the process of knowing, not merely a system of faith. His *Who is Jesus?*, for example, gives a useful survey of the 'old', the 'new' and the 'third quest' for the historical Jesus, and insists upon faithfulness to the Jewish context and the gospel records of who Jesus was and is (1992c:94–97).

Admittedly 'we seldom, if ever, "know" enough, in terms of positive indubitable proof, to give the kind of account we want to give of any period, incident or character from the past' (Wright 1996:8), and so Wright acknowledges that 'there is always a leap to be made between the actual evidence and the fully-blown reconstruction' (*ibid.*). He suggests this to be the leap of faith. Real faith, is 'the constant exploration of, and trust in, a god whom Christians believe to be, among other things, intimately and passionately involved in the historical process' (*ibid.*:8–9).

It is ultimately, then (and this again is the value of his contribution), a relationship of faith with reality that Wright is suggesting to be the essence and focus of such a system of faith. The system or story of faith itself is just the way in which this reality is presented in a trustworthy way in the public sphere. It is through '*telling the story of Jesus*' (1992b:139)— not just the story of the Christian tradition—that the Christian religion is fairly presented on a public scale.

As such, it is the story of the real being of God, made known to humanity, which provides a critical standard for, or foundation to any or all of our knowing.

Praxis?

In all that has been considered thus far, it is right to ask where all this contemplation on reality, dialogue, conversation in knowing, and the motifs of story and symbol leave one practically.

Not surprisingly 'praxis' is, for Wright, an important but inherently relational concept. Arising from within the 'normally . . . unexamined and indeed unnoticed' elements of a Christian worldview (1992a:185), praxis involves a 'particular mode of being-in-the-world' (1992b:133) or 'being-*for*-the-world' (*ibid*.). This is because 'humans in general are part of the creator's designed means of looking after his world, and Christians in particular are part of his means of bringing healing to the world' (*ibid*.:133–134).

In a way this echoes the activist presupposition of mission questioned above: that God needs Christians to further His kingdom, as shown (for example) by Van Engen's concept of God's need for people to spread the gospel (1996b:227). But here, the paradigm of story-symbol-praxis is given as rationale for Wright's statement and, accordingly, a more ontologically (and thus more accurate) than functionally derived praxis is in mind.

Wright's praxis has been drawn from within the structure of the Christian narrative: from God's own being, and dealings with humanity. It stems from the ontological core of the Judeo-Christian faith. Referring to the '*covenant faithfulness of Israel's god*' (1992a:203) and to God's '*fulfilment of his covenant purposes*' (*ibid*.) in Israel for all peoples of the world, Wright notes in reference to Pauline theology that '*the gentile mission grows precisely out of this strange covenant purpose*' (*ibid*.:205). Responsibility '*for*' (1992b:133) the world exists only—and primarily—in relation to the hub of the Christian story: the person of God, the creator/saviour. For it is in Christ (and thus in the redefinition of God and Israel 'by means of christology and pneumatology' [1991:1]) that the 'covenant faithfulness of God' (*ibid*.:236) has been made known on a public scale—not through human efforts in this regard. 'The events of Israel's rejection of the gospel of Jesus Christ are the paradoxical outworking of God's covenant faithfulness' (*ibid.*), and the climax of this covenant is none less than 'the loving justice of the one creator God, now revealed in the gospel' (*ibid.*:256).

And so it is through God that the truth of the gospel is communicated to the world—and through praxis in terms of one's relationship with God. It is in relation to God and His covenant with Israel that Wright stresses a *being*-in-the-world rather than a *doing*-in-the-world (*op. cit.*).

Symbol and praxis together, then, 'point beyond themselves to a controlling story or set of controlling stories which invest them with wider significance' (1992b:124). Like Judaism, Christianity is 'not a "faith", but a way of life . . .' (*ibid.*:233) and 'if one is to keep the symbols alive one must quite simply live by them' (*ibid.*). This way of life, further, is specifically 'Christ-shaped' (1991:256), and dependent upon His work and being in us, not just our own cold, empty efforts and deeds for Him.

Thus Wright lucidly articulates the ontological stress of the present work. Praxis derives from a right state of being, namely being in a relationship with God.

Summary and Assessment of Wright's Contribution

Through both the '*reality of the thing known*' (1992b:35) and through his understanding of criticism as dialogue '*between the knower and the thing known*' (*ibid.*), Wright represents one of several valuable, contemporary approaches to theology that recognises an ontological dimension based on a relationship with God as integral to a Christian epistemology.

Because of the ingrained relationship involved in gaining knowledge, the issue of subjectivity arises. However, controls over this 'subjectivity' do exist, which are the publicness of the text and the Christian faith, symbols and story (outplayed in human history), and the publicness of the God of Judeo-Christianity Himself.

Through a brief consideration of the value of foundationalism, we appreciate Wright's response to the seduction of empirical norm's by pointing instead to the person of God and to a living relationship with Him as foundational to all knowing.

It is no wonder, then, that 'praxis', for Wright, is not just an activity or methodology: it is a response to God and an outworking of our love for Him and others in our world.

In all this, Wright has articulated valuable aspects of an ontological approach to knowing.

Polanyi On How Best to Know What We Know

This is exactly what we are investigating here in this chapter: the issue of how we know; of how 'knowing' involves an inherently ontological paradigm; of how we can better know what mission is, in particular from this start point of ontology over against praxis; of how we can know with certainty that such an ontological approach to mission is valid; and of how to know the significance of that approach for the meaning and practical outworking of what 'mission' may be.

The name given to this field of the study of 'knowing' is epistemology, and an appropriate thinker in this field, particularly for our own purposes, is Michael Polanyi. This is largely because of his recognition that knowing is an inherently 'ontological' exercise, and that it involves relating to an external reality. His propositions are quite striking against the background of the epistemological climate of the past few centuries.

In brief, two great paradigms of knowledge have been separately pursued in modernity and especially in its aftermath. The first of these is Science, which has on the whole been considered to be a 'seemingly clear and distinct kind of knowledge' (Apcyzynski 1977:3). The second, a more opaque type of knowledge, is that of the human, or Humanities, which has also been respected as a 'distinct sphere of knowledge [albeit that it is exists] *apart* from the objectivity of scientific knowledge' [*ibid.* —italics added—and Gill 1972:247]).

Of late, however, these two paradigms of knowledge appear to have been converging. In contrast to what was once regarded as the 'ideal' of total objectivity (i.e. fact), the equal validity of the existential—of morals and personal values—has been increasingly recognised, despite the 'risk' of subjectivity. Fact and Value, in other words, have come to be seen as competing and equally valid paradigms of knowledge.

The emergence of this existential paradigm as a reaction to the rationalism of the Enlightenment has already been touched on. Through that era, the validity and complete objectivity of 'fact' came increasingly into question (so Apcyzynski 1977:9 and Lyotard 1984:29) and the place of personal experience and value in all forms of knowing started to be recognised.

Polanyi is a beacon representative of this convergence between Fact and Value because of his experience and contributions in both, for his station as a philosopher of knowledge developed almost as an 'afterthought' (Polanyi 1983:3) to his career as a scientist.

Ernest Nagel, in his 1961 *The Structure of Science*, admitted that we do not know 'whether or not the current premises of science are true, and furthermore that if we tried to justify them we would find most of the premises doubtful' (cited in Apcyzynski 1977:9). Nagel's rather fatalistic response was (in Polanyi's words, also cited by Apcyzynski, *ibid.*) 'that we must save our belief in the truth of scientific explanations by refraining from asking what they are based upon.'

Polanyi, in contrast, refused to simply overlook or ignore the problem expressed by Nagel. Instead, he made the problem into a feature: he proposed the tangible existence of a subjective realm to all forms of knowing (similar, in a way, to the priority given by Schleiermacher to Feeling over Knowing). This proposition is focused in Polanyi's dictum (1983:4): 'We can know more than we can tell.' Through this, he was suggesting that knowledge—or, as he describes it, 'tacit knowledge'—constitutes a realm of pre-understanding with regard to truth (*ibid.*:7).

His epistemology stands out as a credible and influential response to the 'crisis of credibility' of the Christian faith: a predicament which involves Christians not knowing whether their faith is credible or not any more. Puddefoot (1980:28) described it like this: 'Christians have been told so often and for so long by so many people . . . that what they believe is irrational, impossible or simply absurd, that now they almost believe it themselves'!

By making a feature of the tacit dimension, however, Polanyi created space wherein a personal, living faith could be accepted as viable and legitimate. His place in the convergence of science and the human is reflected by Gunton's analysis (1988:68) of the two positions:

> The former [science] . . . has among its distinguishing features that it is an epistemology of spatial distance . . . [Here] the essence of knowledge is the proposition, in which the distant object is described in words which attempt to mirror what is there . . . In the Polanyian approach, the reverse is the case. The central

metaphor here is that of 'indwelling'. The knower knows the world by indwelling body, tools, concepts and the like, which, by being known tacitly, become the bridge by which other parts of the world can be known . . .

This leads us into a slightly more technical look at Polanyi's propositions.

Tacit Knowing

As noted already, Polanyi's concept of 'tacit knowing' describes mankind's capacity to 'know more than we can tell' (*op. cit.*), and there are four aspects of it that need to be clarified.

First, describing its 'functional structure', he suggests that knowing involves a movement—a movement from certain features of an object to the face of that object—and he employs two terms in relation to this tacit knowing: the proximal and the distal.

The 'proximal' relates to those particulars which are more accessible to us and from which one can comprehend or make (better) sense of a more distant, 'distal' object. Thus, the functional structure represents the movement from a nearer (proximal) feature to a further, more separate or detached (distal) one (Polanyi 1983:10). Gill labels this aspect of tacit knowing 'mediation', noting that some of the things which we 'experience and know about . . . engage us *by means of* or *in and through* others' (1978:143).

For example: we 'encounter the aesthetic meaning of a painting or piece of music through the particulars which comprise them, such as light, colour, shape and line, tone, pitch, rhythm, and harmonization' (*ibid.*).

Polanyi (1983:10) describes this function of 'mediation' as the attendance '*from* something . . . *to* something else; namely, *from* the first term *to* the second term of the tacit relation.'

The second aspect of 'tacit knowing' is what Polanyi calls the 'phenomenal structure' (as opposed to the functional structure). This involves the process of the two functional features of tacit knowing appearing and then coming together. It is about the '*appearance* of . . . that *from* which we are attending *to* another' (*ibid.*:11). Often only in and through the appearance of distal terms (the object) does one become aware of the proximal terms of knowing (those which make up that object). (So Apcyzynski 1977:104.) And it is through the coming together of these two terms of knowing (the distal and the proximal) that the meaning of the 'comprehensive entity' (Polanyi 1983:13) is determined.

Apcyzynski (1977:106) expounds this point as follows: 'We tacitly know the interiorized particulars through the meaning they attain when this meaning refers to a coherent entity . . . All our knowledge possesses this directedness or intentionality. This is due to its being grounded in our bodily indwelling . . . Human thought is dependent on the particulars it embodies. Through the integration of these particulars, the reality which they comprise is endowed with meaning.'

As the two terms are held together in relation to a comprehensive entity, a certain meaning is determined in the knower.

So the phenomenon of the two terms coming together, and meaning being determined, is what the second aspect of tacit knowledge is about.

The third, '*ontological* aspect' (Polanyi 1983:13), is about the involvement of the knower in that process. Knowledge is not just about meaning being determined, but about the indwelling of that meaning within the knower.

Meaning occurs when distal facts or objects and tacit, proximal features appear and start to take on particular significance.

Polanyi understands indwelling not in terms of formal reasoning, but in terms of 'skilled imaginative integration . . . a sort of power built into each of us . . . [an] intuition . . . [a] leap of imagination' (Scott 1985:52).

A fourth aspect of tacit knowledge, and basic to this ontological whole, is the way in which these functional, phenomenal and ontological aspects of knowing all progress in a cyclical way. Through interiorisation, or indwelling, that which was once a distal term in turn becomes a proximal one (Polanyi 1983:17). As we learn, that which was once distal, becomes a new proximal of yet another distal term or object. Through learning about things, we internalise and respond to yet more objects. As regards certain moral teachings, for example, interiorisation 'is to identify ourselves with the teachings in question, by making them function as the proximal term of a tacit moral knowledge, as applied to practice' (*ibid.*). Interiorised teachings in turn become the terms from which we attend to some other thing: they, themselves, now, forming 'the tacit framework for our moral acts and judgments' (*ibid.*) in an ongoing, dynamic and cyclical progression.

In summary, these four aspects of tacit knowledge have been identified: the functional structure of tacit knowledge (the proximal and distal elements, and movement between them); the phenomenal structure of that knowing (how the appearance of a distal object makes one aware of certain proximal terms within us); the ontological aspect of knowing (meaning is not something that is external, but internal: something that involves the knower and comes from indwelling the knower); and the cyclical dynamic of knowing (how what was once distal becomes the new proximal in determining new meanings, and in the extension of knowledge).

Application For a Missiological Epistemology

These observations have direct relevance for the determination of the meaning of mission and whether or not we have understood 'it' correctly.

First, as regards the functional structure of tacit knowing (i.e. that through the proximal features one relates to the distal ones) we should acknowledge the pre-existing 'features' of understandings about 'mission' that we have.

We need on the one hand to check out the proximal features through which we may be relating to the whole in our particular field of interest. It may be that we are reading certain parts of the bible only: perhaps just those emotive, romanticised texts that fuel a passion for 'mission', for example. Or it may be that we are just motivated by any or all of those powerful missionary quotes, like C.T. Studd's: 'If Jesus Christ be God and died for me, then no sacrifice can be too great for me to make for him,' or Jim Elliott's: 'He is no fool who gives up what he cannot keep to gain what he cannot lose.' It could be, and almost often is, that our presuppositions concerning the identity of mission are determined from past missiological traditions and 'churchmanship', or from the seduction of our own self-importance and self-worth or desires to be useful, rather than the specific purposes of God in individual situations. It may be that we are comfortable and accredited in—that we are actually masters in—a sophisticated missional hermeneutic through which we read Scripture, and approach the world, and which very probably we may be teaching to others as well.

On the other hand, we need also to check out what distal objects portray 'mission' to us. More often than not, missional distal objects would include any or all of the following: big voluntary, humanitarian or church-based projects or enterprises; cross-cultural 'work' in foreign lands; partnering with cultures more responsive to, or ignorant of the gospel than our own; funding foreign initiatives; 'other' cultures and faiths turning to Christ; 'Christianisation'; social welfare and development programmes; exotic lifestyles and experiences; outreach and visions often more about my own 'call' or wants and purpose in life than about the spiritual need of others, or about God's way forward; new disaster zones, or the latest appeals for help or openings for ministry opportunity; and so on.

So that is the first thing we have to do, missiologically: be aware of the features from which we attend to other features, and what those other features are which we commonly refer to as missional. And we should ask ourselves whether or not there may be any other functional structures of mission—anything else that God may be wanting of His people—that we do not regard as missional or (therefore) important and (thus) which we do not attend to adequately.

Second, then, as regards the phenomenal structure of tacit knowing, we must ask about the sense that we make of these (and other, omitted) functional structures. We have to ask just what the 'whole' of our understanding of mission is, and whether it is adequate, or a distraction to a fuller knowledge about the purposes of God in the world. How valid is the 'mission' that comes to mind when any of the above, standard proximal or distal features of so-called 'mission' arise? Is this really an authentic meaning of mission, or is it just something determined through the lenses of our own pre-understandings, traditions and churchmanships?

What represents the distal object which, when it appears, makes us aware of its more proximal features? It could be the emergence of need or tragedy. How do we determine which needs are within our capacity to respond to—part of God's purposes for us, at a particular time—and which others to overlook? So, for example: how did Jesus, on one occasion, turn down the ministry of healing, in preference for the ministry of preaching?

And, as we consider distal situations or events, what makes us view them 'missiologically'—what constitutes 'missiological' in our thinking?

What proximal features are we drawing from; presumably those listed under 'functional structure' above—but what makes these particularly 'missiological' features, and are we confident that these are the only ones that should be informing our understanding about Christian mission or, more importantly (because this phrase could become restrictive), about God's purposes in the world? It could be that other unmentioned, unknown features not traditionally associated with mission are eclipsed behind those more commonly accepted as 'missional'.

If other less familiar proximal features could become part of our presupposition pool, then a much broader distal 'mission' would come into focus. If it drew on the ontological realities that this work has been attempting to highlight, for example, then 'mission' might be something much larger, more divine and beyond our human comprehension in terms of it being about God's own involvement in, and love for our fallen world of sin (perhaps a priority of, or focus on eternal salvation over against immanent humanitarian need), and about the Christian life of love lived in response to His salvific working in our lives.

For it is in the appearance of these distal objects of 'mission' that we become aware of the proximal features from which we attend to them. If the distal object of 'mission' is a narrow, more traditional approach to mission already noted, then we will be drawing on the usual 'mission' texts and traditions to enable understandings of and responses to distal situations. If, however, a broader understanding of mission is allowed, real but more commonly overshadowed features of the gospel and Christian life will be being drawn upon and incorporated, rather than overlooked; for example: the critical importance of loving not just in words and tongue but with true deeds that are of God; the requirement to lay down one's life; the advice to be content in any and every situation; the quiet and real working of the Holy Spirit; the fact that the Lord looks not at outward appearances, but at the heart; the way that God chooses the weak things of the world, to shame the wise; the instruction to turn the other cheek, and love our enemies; and so on.

This, then, is where Polanyi's third, ontological aspect of knowing would come into play. Here, a person's whole life is shown to be involved in the reality of Christian mission. On the one hand, it could be that an almost secular, humanistic activity is internalised and comes to be lived by; on the other hand, the full being of God may be encountered, and His love, truths and purposes for the world may indwell the knower and the community of knowers, drawing them into what He is doing in the world. God's purposes would indwell the community of believers, or even just the faithful individual who is open to the leading of the Spirit.

Of course it is the latter which we should be aiming for. The whole of us should be involved, through relationship with God, as we grow in the Christian faith—in contrast to a derived, almost sectarian church movement based on praxis.

Polanyi warned that to concentrate on either proximal or distal features of the functional or phenomenal structures of knowing would cause the whole to lose meaning and to become hollow (*ibid*.:18). Although a recovery of meaning would be possible through subsequent refocusing on the whole, the original meaning would never be brought back (*ibid*.:19). A '*deeper* understanding' (*ibid*.) may be attained in the process, but it is only primarily in relation to the whole—through a relationship between the whole and the knower—that something is truly known. To narrow an understanding of mission to a derived, mandatory understanding of what it is, is to minimise it: to risk distorting the whole; to endanger a recovery of the whole of what God is doing in the world, in and of Himself (despite mankind!).

Here again the importance of a living relationship with God is being featured as (in this instance) an epistemological norm that Christian people should be striving to realise. Only to the extent to which God and His missional/sending salvific purposes in the world are exposed for what they are, and only to the extent that Christian people engage in a living relationship with Him, will true mission ever be known for what it truly is and should be.

Of course the fourth, spiralling element of continued and relational growth and knowledge means that we become more and more convinced of the way that we do things: we will become confirmed in whichever approach we have taken to understanding mission, as our presupposition pools concerning those 'norm's of mission become more and more what we understand it to be.

What was once a distal feature (such as the mandate of the 'Great Commission') in relation to less tangible, proximal elements (such as consciousness of God, love of neighbour, or a desire to share good with others) may itself, through indwelling, become a proximal element in relation to the appearance of new distal elements (such as a newly observed need, a fresh challenge to serve on the 'mission field', exposure to a new mission society, or fresh news of an unreached people group).

The danger of this is that if an erroneous or narrow term is indwelt and in turn becomes a proximal term, affecting the way in which we respond to new distal terms, it follows that we will be engaged in an overall false, distorted system of 'truth' and practice of mission. Because of this, we should be warned then (for example) that the 'Great Commission' concept or basis for mission should never be taken as a primary, proximal term in an epistemology of mission, because it is a secondary (derived/interpreted [and questionably so, as discussed earlier]) 'term' itself.

Thus it is of crucial importance to ensure the authenticity of the proximal terms that are being 'activated' or stimulated in the process of missiological knowing and meaning.

Polanyi (*ibid.*:10) cautions that one is 'usually unable to specify these elementary acts' of knowledge. However, through something even as simple as a 'problem' (*ibid.*:21)—or in our instance a 'crisis' in mission—we should admit to being made aware of something deeper that is going on. Even just 'to *know* that a statement is true [or not!] is *to know more than we can tell*' (*ibid.*:23). Thus, in our missiological instance, even simply to have perceived a crisis in mission, or to have been made aware of mission casualties on the field, is to be aware of something 'more than we can tell'.

It is our duty, then, to be honest about what we hear (in terms of dissatisfaction with regard to modern mission), and to scrutinise our missiological presuppositions, and to ensure that we are engaged in a living relationship with God as we seek to determine what authentic mission is.

Reality As Tacit Dimension of All Human Knowing

Polanyi describes the subsidiary dimension of tacit knowing in terms of a hidden reality, writing (*ibid.*:24): 'All the time we are guided by sensing the presence of a hidden reality toward which our clues are pointing.'

In this way, he goes beyond an Enlightenment paradigm of objective knowledge not simply by stressing the integral place of the knower in the process of knowing, but by proposing an almost relational, external reality in that process. 'An empirical statement is true,' for example, only 'to the extent to which it reveals an aspect of reality, a reality largely hidden to us, and *existing therefore independently of our knowing it*' (Polanyi 1958:311).

It may be objected that Polanyi's thought is too centred in the self, or in the individual. For example, it has been noted (Apcyzynski 1977:3) that the tacit dimension 'resides in a person, indeed could be *called* the person insofar as he has assimilated his culture's tools—be they skills, word, logics, or theoretical disciplines—and by dwelling in them is enabled to relate *to* reality.'

And yet his own defence in this regard is that his proposed 'reality' is not determined in relation to self, but to external, distal elements which have been indwelt. Polanyi (1983:25) writes: 'It is personal, in the sense of involving the personality of him who holds it, and also in the sense of being, as a rule, solitary; but there is no trace in it of self-indulgence.' Torrance (cited by Gunton in Torrance 1980:97) has similarly argued that Polanyi's 'personal knowledge . . . has nothing to do with the inclusion of a personal, far less a subjective, factor in the content of knowledge, for the personal participation on the part of the scientist relates to the bearing of all his thought and statement upon objective reality, insofar as it is accessible to human understanding and description.'

That Polanyi's 'reality' may be equated with the being of God is suggested by the fact that he 'is always willing to point out theological or religious implications of his thought' (Weightman 1994:125). An example of this would be his statement 'that his interpretation of society "would seem to call for an extension in the direction towards God," and his comment . . . that this conception of knowing opens the way to the possibility of knowing God' (*ibid.*). It has also been pointed out (*ibid.*:17) that these words were influential in weaning Polanyi off scientism—words written by Dostoevsky (1976:292) in his novel *The Brothers Karamazov*: 'Look at the worldly and all who set themselves up above the people of God, has not God's image and His truth been distorted in them? They have science: but in science there is nothing but what is the object of sense. The spiritual world, the higher part of man's being is rejected altogether, dismissed with a sort of triumph, even with hatred. The world has proclaimed the reign of freedom, especially of late but what do we see in this freedom of theirs? Nothing but slavery and self-destruction!'

The void represented by the 'hatred . . . slavery and self-destruction' of this world points back to the antithetical position of all that has been lost in the process of reaching this state of 'freedom' from religion: the spiritual though external and relational reality of God.

So Polanyi is clearly committed to belief in this external reality beyond the more obvious, incorrigible fact: a reality that is, often, inaccessible by merely factual and/or empirical observation, as shown here (1960:133): 'We can account for this capacity of ours to know more than we can tell if we believe in the presence of an external reality with which we can make contact. This I do. I declare myself committed to the belief in an external reality gradually accessible to knowing, and I regard all true understanding as an intimation of such a reality.'

Integral to true knowledge, then, are the personalities not just of the knower but also of the full Being of God. Knowledge for Polanyi involves the indwelling of meaning (which is otherwise outside of a person) within the knower (1983:13). Torrance (1971:181) puts it this way: 'Theological knowledge must take the road from God to man before it takes the road from man to God.'

Being (of God and of ourselves in relation to God) is the underlying reality of human knowledge.

The value of all this for our own investigations is Polanyi's clear articulation and scientific, philosophical defence of the integral place of that external reality (whom we would call God) in knowing, and that through an internal, tacit and genuinely personal happening (which we would call prayer and/or a personal relationship with God) we can engage with that external reality, in order to 'know' more fully.

Implications of a Relationally Based Epistemology

One of the outcomes of Polanyi's ontological epistemology is that the reality on which he focuses, 'being real, may yet reveal itself to future eyes in an indefinite range of unexpected manifestations' (Polanyi 1983:24). Elsewhere (1960:133) he writes the same: that the reality in which he declares belief, 'being real, may yet reveal itself to our deepened understanding in an indefinite range of unexpected manifestations.'

So, a relationship with God may work itself out in an 'indefinite range' of ways, and (missiologically) may require an indefinite range and number of things from different people.

This implies both that previously held understandings of mission should be continually reassessed and, where necessary discarded, and that new patterns of mission should always be explored and 'allowed' as the Spirit leads. A living determination of what God may be requiring of us, rather than a rigid formulation of what mission means should be basic to a right missiological outworking of a Christian life.

Polanyi (1983:20) warns against ignoring this personal, external reality in human knowledge. He writes: 'The declared aim of modern science is to establish a strictly detached, objective knowledge. Any falling short of this ideal is accepted only as a temporary imperfection, which we must aim at eliminating. But suppose that tacit thought forms an indispensable part of all knowledge, then the ideal of eliminating all personal elements of knowledge would, in effect, aim at the destruction of all knowledge. The ideal of exact science would turn out to be fundamentally misleading and possibly a source of devastating fallacies.'

An 'exact science' (*ibid.*) of contemporary mission is represented by, for example, any school of world mission or enterprise. Although these schools and enterprises may have formed an indispensable part of twentieth century mission practice, such practices may have been developed on dispensable aspects of knowledge (wrong or time-particular presuppositions). To contemplate an exact 'science' (*ibid.*) of missiology based on modern (or any era-bound) practices of mission, then, and (further) to consider it indispensable, may constitute a 'devastating fallacy' (*ibid.*) with regard to an authentic understanding of Christian mission. Certainly with the benefit of Polanyi's insights we should be reticent to talk even of a 'science' of mission—or 'missiometrics' as Barrett has called it (*op. cit.*)—for if we may not even have an 'explicit knowledge of . . . scientific truth' (Polanyi 1983:23), then to label a derived aspect of theology a 'science' is confusing, if not incongruous.

This is not to deny that there may have been certain cognitive, objective and 'right' manifestations of mission in the past and/or in the present. But to make just the cognitive and/or objective foundational to any other living understandings of what mission is and may be in the Christian life may result (or may have already resulted!) in a devastating fallacy.

The essence of authentic mission appears to have been sacrificed on the altar of 'science' and cognitivity—perhaps in an attempt to attract funding and mission personnel. In Polanyi's thought, by way of contrast, we have seen a logical defence of the validity not only of fact and objectivity, but value and the subjective. Gill (1972:274–275), on Polanyi, puts it this way: '[If a] knowledge of God is related to the factual realm too exclusively, it is impossible for it to meet the requirements of cognitivity; if it is related to the valuational realm too exclusively it loses its cognitive significance . . . [T]he contemporary dichotomy between fact and value [may be] replaced with a view of language and knowledge based upon dimensional and contextual significance. In this way knowledge [may be] seen to be a continuum between the tacit and explicit poles, which in turn are the function of the interaction between awareness and response.'

This 'continuum' is related to Polanyi's tacit knowing through both the functional and phenomenal structures and the ontological structure of meaning as a whole. All aspects of any relevant knowing, and in our case knowledge about 'mission' are important: its 'cognitivity'; its 'cognitive significance'; how one perceives mission or becomes aware of it; how one internalises that perceived meaning and how one responds to it practically; how awareness and response affects future perceptions about what mission is; and so on.

The temptation in mission in particular (where people passionately want to get involved and to 'do' something because of their faith), is to narrow down what God may require to something tangible, definable and do-able as an easy 'prescription'. But there is obvious danger in this. Lyotard (1984:65) suggested that whereas in the pragmatics of science it is possible to determine those denotative utterances upon which institutions of learning are built, social pragmatics, in contrast, 'is a monster formed by the interweaving of various networks of heteromorphous classes of utterances (denotative, prescriptive, performative, technical, evaluative, etc.).' Because different people in society all 'think' that they are doing mission right, and want to see results in almost secularist terms, the social pragmatics of mission has become something of 'a monster'.

However, in contrast to 'an ideology of the "system," with its pretensions to totality' (*ibid.*:65), if the One Grand Narrative of God and His dealings with the world is recognised, and if an ontological 'system'—a pragmatics deriving from a living relationship with God—becomes the norm of the Christian life, then 'the monster' will be chained and bound, and people will be freed to be who they are, and to live and to outwork a liberated life in service to Him Who loves all, and has died for all.

Such a dynamic of totality has been suggested by Schleiermacher, the postliberals and Wright, and now, here, by Polanyi through the inherent relationality of his thought. Gunton's comment (1988:65) is astute: '[I]n place of an ontology of spatial distance, we find [in Polanyi] one of acquaintance. Knowledge is a relation of knower and known before it is propositional.' Where the 'known' is fundamentally to do with the heart of God—in relation to His reaching down to the lost—it follows that a relationship with God is prior, and fundamental to any mission praxis, and foundational to a missional epistemology.

As both the prime feature from which praxis is derived, and the integrated 'whole' of Christian mission involves the real being of God, the development of a missional epistemology would involve more than just 'openness' to God (so Apcyzynski 1977:105): it would involve an actual 'encounter' and living relationship with Him. Apart from a relationship with God, faith is cerebral and love, itself, is mechanical; the praxis of mission itself would be little more than a lone, bleak human act: a mere activity, in no way connected to its subsidial parts or the whole by which those parts are meant to be understood.

Polanyi's work thus gives credible support to the present work which points to a prior and relational dimension as foundational to a missional epistemology. Not only does it address the distinction between the objective and subjective realms of fact and value (as shown by Gill 1972:248–249), affirming the latter, but it supports a worldview that is fundamentally defined in relation to the ultimate reality and person of God.

Summary of Polanyi's Contribution to Missiological Thought

In order to give a few pointers to take away from what may have been a difficult read, a brief summary of certain things that can be deduced from Polanyi's thinking may be helpful.

First, we will 'know' what authentic mission is not by being presented with a proof text, or church tradition, but through a living relationship with God.

Second, mission is not just about the tangible, objective, factual or obvious, but may be about the internal, relational, subjective, 'value' and intangible.

Third, we need to scrutinize our presupposition pool as regards what we understand mission to be. Yes, certain aspects of that knowledge base may be 'right' or valid, but a lot may not be. We need to be prepared to 'unlearn' pre-understandings about mission—even what that label itself represents—that may have been incorrect.

Fourth, equally, we need to critique the more 'distal' objects of mission that we engage with, being careful about what aspects of them we seek to preserve or propagate, and which (other) aspects may be superfluous to the love of God and His purposes and, thus, may be disposable (e.g. mission buildings and programmes, over against the gospel and a growing relationship with God).

Fifth, to know what mission is, involves an ontological exercise: it is essential to seek understanding from within a living relationship with God, so enabling one not to be bound by (for example) false or distortive prior perceptions of what mission is.

Sixth, even if we have 'learnt' various lessons, missiologically, in our relationships with God in the past, it is important as one grows in God to rethink things: to re-assess formerly held 'truths' and subject them to further scrutiny.

Seventh, we should be aware that God may be asking different things of different people: that in our own lives He may be requiring a response that is contra what others may see as the 'norm', and we should have the courage to respond to the living God and not to the pressure of people, even (and especially) within the church.

Eighth, finally: to insist on a particular missiology—or 'science' of mission—may be to propagate a 'devastating fallacy' (*op. cit.*) in the Christian church. Whether it is such a fallacy or not will depend on what God's purposes in particular situations may be. But a blanket 'science' of missiometrics will almost certainly result in the eclipse of the purposes of God behind our own.

Knowing the Word

In order to engage with the 'Other'—the real being of God, made known in Jesus Christ—and in order to gain knowledge and wisdom from Him, one has to first receive what God has revealed to us of Himself: what He has made known of Himself to us, and what He has shown us of how to relate to Him. The most comprehensive record we have concerning this is the Scriptures, the written 'word' of God. More, though, we need to enter into a living relationship with Jesus Christ, the living 'word' of God, and this through the enabling of the Holy Spirit (an outpoured gift of God with us, and to us).

Wright and Polanyi are really just examples amongst many of those who have validated such a relational investigation for the twentieth/twenty-first century rational mind.

That investigation itself still remains to be done: it is required of all people, individually and collectively, and involves a lifetime and more of discipleship.

The framework of Christian understanding is that mankind was dead in its sin, darkened in its understanding, and that God has had both to reveal Himself to humanity and also teach humanity what it was meant to be.

A first move was required by God: having created, having been confronted by disobedience, having grieved over the wicked state of man, and having shown that simply to spare a single 'seed' of wicked man (Noah) was insufficient to purge sin. A word from outside of our selves was required this time, not simply to create but to recreate.

So, then, a word of call and promise to Abraham; two humanly impossible births: Isaac, and then the twins Jacob and Esau; an illustration of how God chooses between two 'heirs': not through birthright but undeserved merit . . . and response to Him, desire for recognition by Him, grasping after blessing and favour in God's sight; then Joseph—endowed with access to the things of God: explanations of dreams; knowledge of the future; wisdom; discernment; and the birth of the nation of Israel in obscurity (humanly—in Egypt) but core to the purposes, plans and promises of God.

Moses: trying to do it alone, perceiving himself as deliverer; brought to nothing by God; rejected; restless herdsman; absolute loss of confidence; and then eventually—as a nobody—being used by God, in the purposes of God, so that God alone would be seen as the saviour of Israel.

A theophany at Sinai: a voice heard only as thunder by the ignorant, but giving life to the nation through law and guidance—more: a presencing of God with His people in the tabernacle.

Now the 'Other' was present—though still invisible; untouchable; to be awed. Accessible yet inaccessible; knowable (at least in outline) yet still unknowable!

A nation fumbling still in ignorance: a host of judges, prophets, even kings, though few with a heart for God or submission to Him.

Then David: a man after God's own heart; a sinful nature, but in a living relationship with God; alive to Him; listening to Him; learning of Him; adoring Him; human failure in many ways, but God-aware; enough to precede One who was not just God-aware, but God Himself...

For at last: a living word, audible to all (except those in rebellion to Him, blinded by wealth, position, power and religion) and knowable! God with us!

But not just One who would speak: One who would also act; not just a living word but a living sacrifice; fulfilment of the Law's demand for perfection to honour the perfect One; appeasement for failure: eternal life for an infinite number of people lost in guilt and sin.

And not just leaving us alone, but dwelling with us; God with Man—poured out, filling-in empty hearts; empty lives.

Lives lived not to the sinful nature, but in the Spirit.

Divine Spirit of that 'Other' in you and me! And us, with Him in us, in this dark God-less world!

Then! And now! And in the years (maybe even centuries) to come!

Yes, we 'know'. But do we *really* know?!

That requires the miracle of rebirth!

Chapter 13

The Age-Old Essence of Orthodoxy

As we highlight and attempt to articulate these ontological aspects of our Christian faith things may, for some of us, be starting to feel familiar. We are at home with the concept of 'ontology' that has been fleshed out in all that has been said thus far. This is because all that we have been suggesting is really little more than a duplication of 'the old'—the 'age old': that which has already been articulated for us by those far more able and lucid through the years of the church's history in traditional, orthodox thinking.

For this reason it should be useful to explore a bit of contemporary orthodox thought as an example of the breadth of ontological awareness still out there, waiting to be (re-)discovered. Just two thinkers will be looked at, and even these cannot be looked at comprehensively. We will just touch on aspects of their thought that help to unravel our own: one from an Anglo- and the other from a Greek-orthodox position.

Walker: Anglo-Orthodoxy

Andrew Walker gives a refreshing representation of orthodox thinking. It has direct relevance for our own because from a living Spirit-filled, Pentecostal beginning, Walker has developed into a place where he expounds and appreciates the narrative hermeneutic we have seen as common to the postliberals (Frei and Lindbeck), Thiemann (in his theological foundationalism) and also Wright (through his concentration on story and symbol). Other writers in other contexts have drawn on the same narrative approach, like Braaten from a liberationist context who writes: 'We... have a story to tell the people' (1985:171). A similarly clear and simple summary of both Walker and the orthodoxy he represents is captured in these words of his: 'There is a story, once widely known, that tells who we are, where we came from and where we are going . . . This story is told by Christians and it is called the gospel' (1996:2).

Expounding this story gives further insights, expressions and confirmation of our ontological stress.

Public Story—Not a Private One

The importance of 'story' or 'narrative' is that it simply expresses one truth for all.

The Christian story in particular is a public one—a story for all people. The publicness of the Christian story derives from the fact that the person of God has revealed and made Himself known in history in and through the historic person, Jesus Christ. As such, although it is a rightly personal and relational faith for some, it is also clearly a public faith for all.

Understandably, then, Walker strongly opposes the way in which the Christian faith has been 'driven from public life into a privatized world of personal choice and leisure pursuits . . . a domain [in which] private opinion rather than public truth rules' (*ibid.*:3). He suggests (as already noted in our own thinking) that this privatisation has come about because of Enlightenment's stress on self, on the autonomy of the individual, and its effective banishment of God to the realm of private, personal value. The Enlightenment is, for him, 'the backdrop against which modernism comes into full focus' (1988:xi). He emphasises that 'without an understanding of the dualistic modes of thought [the private and public] that dominate modernity it is difficult to make sense—let alone plot the course—of modern theologies' (*ibid.*).

This Enlightenment dualism has directly impacted certain aspects of the church, of which mission is just one example. Because the public forum has come to be the place of 'functional rationality' (1992:49, 53), in contrast to private outworkings of faith, mission as an upfront 'public' thing has almost had to become secularised. It has become a secular enterprise rather than necessarily an expression of a person's relationship with God.

Two things are therefore needed: first, to bring Christ Himself out of the realm of private value and back into the arena of public fact and, second, to de-secularise Christian mission.

Story About a Person

It is impossible to overlook Walker's stress on the person around whom the Christian story—the gospel—is centred. Even within the biblical text, the gospel 'is focused . . . in Jesus of Nazareth: the person identified by St John as "the Word": the telling-forth, or self-revealing of God' (1996:16).

Put another way, he points out that the Christian narrative is 'more than a tale about the life of the God-man. It is to discover that its central focus, Jesus himself, is also knowable—unlike the characters in a work of fiction or a history book' (*ibid.*:17). More: Jesus, as God's Word, is also 'the author of the story' (*ibid.*) and, as such, He 'transcends history as the Christ of faith' (*ibid.*).

Thus, following Christ in faith is 'to be drawn into God's story, which then becomes our own' (*ibid.*). This knowable Being is (as noted in different respects, above) the very essence of a 'grand narrative' (*ibid.*:5,6,12,51 and so on). For ourselves, this helpfully stresses that the story is not just about facts—or doctrine—but that Christian facts and doctrine are about a person: the person who authored the Christian story. Further, it stresses that all who follow this author and historic character can be drawn into—and become a part of—His story.

The Sectarian Nature of the Church

An important aspect of Walker's thinking is his positive expression of the sectarian nature of the Christian faith: the fact that it is a distinctive entity and requires distinctive living from its people.

Not portraying sectarianism as a divisive and reactionary concept, he sees the sectarian nature of Christianity as a unified and a Godly entity. It parallels, in a way, the nation of Israel which was called out to be separate from other nations (like Wright's symbol of 'Racial Identity'). Walker was recognising a New Testament parallel in Jesus' words, such as that He had come to bring 'not peace, but a sword, and to turn father against son, daughter against mother', and so on (Mt. 10:37–39).

What is required of the church in the world, then, is to be set apart and seen to be unique.

Within the church, however, an opposite stress is needed. Internal unity should be worked at. Walker argued that 'Christianity [should] harness her impatient but powerful sectarian spirit for the good of the whole Church' (1992:61). Without this harnessing and control, he warns, 'the unbridled sectarian spirit will do what unbridled sectarianism always does: break away ... to be broken in by the forces of apostasy and establishment' (*ibid.*).

So then: sectarianism in the world (the church being seen to be distinct from and different to the world), but unity in the church! The Christian faith should find expression and belonging in the established whole. For as the maturing of sects leads ultimately to 'establishment' (*ibid.*), so the growth of young expressions of the Christian faith and experience should conform to certain orthodox practices.

Liturgy and Mission

One such orthodox practice to be respected in the church is liturgy.

The value and purpose of liturgy is to guard against a 'charismatic sense of excitement, [with] its preference for experience over doctrine, [and] the tendency to value novelty against tradition' (*ibid.*:60). Instead of the 'restless liturgy' of more charismatic expressions of faith, an established, traditional liturgy should be respected.

Walker views liturgy in much the same way that Wright regarded symbol, and so it sounds familiar to hear liturgy talked of as the oral culture which 'socializes us into the mysteries of God' (Walker 1996:194). Liturgy's focus is not on a denomination, but on the universality of the kingdom of God. The New Testament is about 'a Christianity that precedes denominationalism in order to go beyond denominationalism' (1988:126). Drawn from the word 'usage', liturgy is about 'well-worn use, [and, thus, about] the practice of being in the presence of God' (1996:196).

Yes, liturgy is heavily symbolic, but as has been seen with Wright, behind any symbol is the reality that it seeks to represent. Thus, liturgy points beyond itself to the living God.

Walker's stress on the use and purpose of liturgy is paralleled by the likes of Pannenberg, who on the eucharist in particular suggests that 'the rediscovery of the Eucharist may prove to be the most important event in Christian spirituality of our time' (1983:31). It 'manifests the mystery of the church, the communion of believers united by the communion of each with Christ, and symbolizes the eschatological unity of all humanity' (*ibid*.:47). And on symbol, Pannenberg's warning (*ibid*.:49) is important for us, here: 'The symbol is understood as symbol only if it is not mistaken for the thing itself . . . Only if liturgical legalism is avoided can the symbolism of the Eucharist be fully effective.'

In ecclesial contexts where liturgy is more often than not performed legalistically, it helps to remember its evangelistic purpose in re-enacting the heart of the gospel story (Walker 1996:196). 'Holy liturgy . . . is the way to the heart of our story,' writes Walker (*ibid*.). Like the motif of 'symbol' it reinforces the story; it is 'the regular, unceasing dramaturgical re-enactment of the story' (*ibid*.).

Pannenberg (1983:41) also talks of re-enactment in reference to the Lord's Supper: 'There is no other place or event in the worship of the church where the very foundation of its life can be comparably commemorated and symbolized, as well as re-enacted, than in the event of celebration and communion . . . Every celebration of the Eucharist re-enacts the reality that constitutes the foundation of the church.'

Involving a depth and dimension beyond our physical norm of reality, Walker suggests that the symbols of liturgy (of which the eucharist would be just one) 'reach beyond themselves to their source and Creator' (1996:195). Because of this, then—in view of its power to communicate the central character of the grand-narrative—Walker suggests that liturgy is a critical aspect of mission. He even goes so far as to suggest that 'liturgy in postmodern culture *is* mission' (*ibid*.:198), and he expands: 'In this world where icons proliferate but are profane; where texts swarm everywhere but have lost their sting; where images dominate our senses but mirror each other, liturgy is a beacon to show the way out. Instead of abandoning imagery and drama to postmodern popular culture, we must reclaim it for ourselves . . . Liturgy is both mystagogy and mission. It nurtures soul and body and draws us "further up and further in" towards the story.'

Beyond the eucharistic service, the essence of the church's liturgy is in its being 'acted' out in the self-sacrifice of the Christian, eucharistic community. Liturgy for Walker, for example, is not about gathering regularly for worship in a church building, but about a continually gathered community living out what is central to its identity. For liturgy is about living a life out there, not just about performing a ritual in a ghetto community.

Certainly there is a deep need for the Christian community: 'Communities themselves are icons,' writes Walker (*ibid.*:199); 'Icons of paint and wood image God and the saints, but so too do holy communities' (*ibid.*). And (*ibid.*:200): 'local congregations . . . will remain the most visible, viable and typical expressions of Christian community in the future.' Indeed (*ibid.*): 'The church in communion is the icon of the Holy Trinity. It is the picture of God we hold up to the world. Of course icons are only images of their prototypes: God alone is holy. But pictures are telling. If we are indwelling the story, sharing in God's life, we will mediate God's love through his presence in us to the world . . . In postmodernity, most people will not live in community, but we Christians must if we are to show the way home.'

Through the symbolism and imagery of orthodox practices such as liturgy (and the liturgy of a faithful Christian life in particular) then, the heart of the Christian gospel—that which is foundational to mission praxis, and the guarantee against falsehood within its story—is fully expressed: the being of the person of God, made known in Christ, the '*someone*—for whom we should be prepared to die' (*ibid.*:202).

It is this full Being: this 'free' Spirit of God (1993a:106)—symbolised as the 'Dove'—who has the relevance and 'power to radically destroy societal or denominational structures . . . [and] has enough explosive force to shatter sociological shibboleths.'

Summary and Assessment of Walker's 'Story' and 'Liturgy'

Despite this far too brief glimpse of orthodoxy expressed by Andrew Walker, we have caught sight of the same ontological bedrock which has been consistently highlighted up to this point.

Walker outlined that Christianity is both private (i.e. inherently to do with the Christian life, in relation to that which is symbolised and thus beyond or behind, within or internal) and public (in that the Christian story itself is a story which is set in the common history of the world). Beyond this, Walker has helpfully argued that Christianity is about a Person: the very being of God—and that to have missed this point is to have missed the essence of just who we are as Christian people and, hence, what we should do and/or how we should live as Christian people.

Important for Walker, then, is the unified and established church—set apart from the rest of the world, yes, but not divided within itself: united, whole and (as such) an internally consistent entity, incorporating both old tradition and contemporary experience of who God is.

An example of an expression of this unity and melding of both old and new, he suggests, is liturgy which (because of what it is an expression of) is a public testimony: a public re-enactment of the Christian story and faith. This is done (for example) as one remembers and affirms God's faithfulness and giving of the law to Israel (through reminding ourselves of the Ten Commandments); as one remembers and confesses one's own sin and worthiness of death (through the Confession); as one hears God's Word, read out to the community of believers and affirmed in their responses; and as the great sacrifice of His atonement and substitution in taking our sin is re-enacted (though the Lord's Supper). These are just examples of the public witness and outworking of both old tradition and contemporary experience in the public gathering as a Christian body.

An equally important public witness, however, is the living out of one's Christian faith in a public forum, whether individually or (more) in community or as congregations. Both the Christian life (despite being otherworldly—even sectarian) and God Himself (although He is 'Other') are integral parts of our own world (as shown for example through Walker's appreciation [1990:67] of C.S. Lewis's 'big magic' and 'other country' of *The Chronicles of Narnia*).

God as 'Other' yet knowable, who dwells in us and impacts our day-to-day relationship with Him, then, being core to orthodoxy should surely be basic to all Christian understanding (and understanding of Christian 'mission' in our particular instance).

Zizioulas: Greek Orthodoxy

Walker and Anglo-orthodoxy represent the relatively recent Reformation or post-Reformation era. Zizioulas, in contrast, speaks for one of the oldest Christian traditions and more classical heritage of Greek orthodoxy.

Whereas Walker articulates the comprehensive and simple, age-old story of 'what I received [and] what I passed on to you' (1Co. 15:3), Zizioulas explores the depth of the patristic unpacking of that story. As with Walker, this is not the place to examine Zizioulas's systematic work, but his exploration of certain ontological aspects of the Christian faith fleshes out an understanding of the depth of ontology lost over the last two millennia.

Of particular interest to us is how he highlights the ontological content of personhood, in particular through discussion on the non-essential being of God. This in turn suggests certain things about what it means to be truly human and thus has significant implications for the identity and meaning of mission.

Background to an Ontological Concept of 'Person'

The concept of 'person' which we apply to God and to ourselves as human beings has gone through a profound change of meaning.

Ancient Greek thought was 'essentially "non-personal"' (Zizioulas 1985a:27–28). Aristotelian philosophy emphasised the 'concrete and the individual' (*ibid.*:28). It was unable to offer 'continuity and "eternal life," for the total psychosomatic entity of man renders impossible the union of the person with the "substance" (*ousia*) of man, that is, with a true ontology' (*ibid.*). In Platonic thought, the concept of a 'person' was an ontological impossibility because 'the soul, which ensures man's continuity, is not united permanently with the concrete "individual" man' (*ibid.*); it was separated by death: that great tragedy of the ancient Greek world as portrayed in the Greek theatre of the day.

The concept of 'person' got its definition from the ordered whole, the cosmos, of which a 'person' was just a part, and of which even 'God' was merely a part. 'Being' was about 'relationship and "kinship" with the "one" being' (*ibid.*:29), and a 'person' was always just a derivative of the whole. 'Personhood' was about being bound to the whole, and would always end (from an individual point of view) in the tragedy of death.

Over time, however, the word 'person' did come to take on an ontological meaning. One of the reasons for this was because of what the word referred to: the word 'person' (*prosōpon*) in ancient Greek was not just an anatomical reference (to some part of the head [*ibid.*:31]), but almost synonymous (*ibid.*) with the word for a 'face' or for a 'mask' (a *prosōpeion*) which an actor would make use of on the stage (*ibid.*).

One way of understanding a mask is as an empty (old-Greek-type) non-ontological shell. Another way, though, is to understand it for what it enabled: it was something through which free, unbounded being could be explored through a limitless range of different characters. By using masks, both the actors and the audiences were able to experience 'life' beyond that which was defined and bound by the ordered cosmos of the ancient Greek world, and to find out what it meant to be truly free (*ibid*.:32–33). Through a mask, someone could in the first place choose to 'be' (for once, as an unnecessary being, one would not have been forced into existence against own free will). In the second place someone could, behind a mask, 'avoid' or miss out on certain death.

So, although *prosōpon* was still a non-ontological term—limited by its own superficiality (the 'front' or 'face' of a mask)—it also, ironically, signified exploration into the world behind it: into the meaning of true, unbounded (unrestricted) being. Clearly it did refer to the role of an individual rather than to his or her essence (*hypostasis* or being, nature or substance), but the latter was explored through the former.

Slowly, and to the extent to which *hypostasis* came to be signified by the term *prosōpon* (*ibid*.:36), this term started to be used in place of the first, largely through the Latinization of the creed by the Western world. Basil's (Greek) wording of the Nicene Trinitarian formulae had been *mia ousia, treis hypostaseis*, but over time and under Tertullian's influence, the Western (Latin) confession of the Trinity as '*una substantia, tres personae*' was accepted (Mantello and Rigg 1996:275).

This caused understandable concern in the East, where the reference to three *personae* rather than three *hypostases* was perceived as a mere reference to the three roles of God (three functions or modes), which would be to imply the early heresy of Sabellianism (Zizioulas 1985a:37). In order to avoid this, Augustine further amended '*una substantia, tres personae*' to '*una essentia, tres substantiae*'—'*substantia*' being seen as more about the essence beneath the lifeless mask of the *persona* (Mantello and Rigg 1996:276).

All of this shows the efforts made to express the deep ontological reality of the person of God and, by so doing, the concept of 'personhood'. Through that long and involved development, the formerly non-ontological concept of 'person' had taken on an inherently and unavoidably ontological meaning. The term 'person' went beyond the boundary of the 'mask' to become wholly associated with the full essence and being of what was explored through it.

And because of the theological context within which the meaning of 'personhood' developed, it can only fully be understood by first understanding the nature of God. This explains Zizioulas's attempt to show 'how deep and indestructible is the bond that unites the concept of the person with patristic theology and ecclesiology' (1985a:27). In fact, 'The person both as a concept and as a living reality is purely the product of patristic thought. Without this, the deepest meaning of personhood can neither be grasped nor justified' (*ibid.*).

The depth of this patristic thought is due to its subject, the living person of God as ultimate Being: God, Who has lovingly revealed Himself to mankind.

This acutely ontological concept of 'person' outlined here, then, has at least two points of significance for the church and Christian mission: the first concerns how we think of the personhood and true being of God; the second concerns how this in turn affects how we think of ourselves, and true humanity.

The Personhood of God

In line with the way credal statements have developed, as shown briefly above, the personhood of God would imply that He must be an unnecessary being, and that He is not bound by death. We accept these observations on the grounds of Scriptural evidence, which does not in any way suggest that God is bound by Himself or by His own existence; and certainly this is what patristic thought defends.

In other words: there was never a time where God was without the choice to 'be' or not. He was not 'caused' by Himself. This would have made Him a 'necessary' being, and 'necessity' would imply a concept of God akin more to the order of the cosmos of ancient Greek thought (wherein even 'God' is trapped by his own place and role in the world) than to biblical revelation. Neither will there ever be a time when God does not exist.

For God is not a mere derivative of the whole: either of the world which we know, nor even of the thought of another; neither is He bound in existence by His own substance or reality (as may be expected of some simple deism), or the substance or reality of another.

These bounds are not aspects of true personhood. For example, an actor has a choice about whether to put on a mask (*persona*) or not: whether to 'bring to life' a certain character in a theatre production, or not, or, wearing that mask (as that elected person), whether or not to go through death. That is part of the freedom of authentic personhood.

Mankind has no choice about existence, and is bound by the knowledge of its own inevitable death. But God is a truly free, ontologically complete person: not 'necessary'—tied in or determined by His own existence—but one who has chosen in and of Himself to exist; neither is God bound by mortality or inevitable death.

And that is what Zizioulas successfully managed to articulate. He suggested that God has been willed into being by the free will and choice of the Father to exist—that 'God exists on account of a person, the Father, and not on account of the substance' (*ibid*.:42). The personal freedom of God flows from the person of the Father. With the Greek Fathers, Zizioulas argued that 'the unity of God, the one God, and the ontological "principle" or "cause" of the being and life of God does not consist in the one substance of God but in the *hypostasis*, that is, *the person of the Father*' (*ibid*.:40). 'God, as Father and not as substance,' he has suggested (*ibid*.:41), 'perpetually confirms through "being" His *free* will to exist . . . the Father out of love—that is, freely—begets the Son and brings forth the Spirit. If God exists, He exists because the Father exists, that is, He who out of love freely begets the Son and brings forth the Spirit.'

The point for us is this: 'God as person—as the hypostasis of the Father—makes the one divine substance to be that which it is: the one God' (*ibid*.). And Zizioulas adds a word of encouragement to those of us who may be tempted to overlook the importance of this thinking and its implications for us: 'This point is absolutely crucial' (*ibid*.).

This is indeed crucial in order to avoid having an unthinkingly narrow concept of God as a necessary being (having no choice over whether to exist or not), or subject to death (even just in the mind of those for whom He may once have existed like Nietzsche who claimed: 'God is Dead!']). It is crucial, too, in order to prevent us from 'making' God in our own images (instead of accepting things the other way around: that we are made in His). It forces us to consider what we may otherwise not think about: that God is not just an accident—not bound to His own existence, or even our own formulations of who He is and (thus) a 'basic human right' of ours—but that He has freely chosen to *be*, in and of Himself (*ibid*.:44). More (suggests Zizioulas [*ibid*.:44,46]): His choice to exist has stemmed from the very essence of the person of the Father which, in line with biblical thinking, is love.

And this love and life has no end.

This is very different from a vague deism, and has direct implications for what our own relationships and responses to Him should be, as discussed below.

Zizioulas's proposition is, of course, not without its critics. Torrance argued that he 'fails to take proper cognisance of the ontological significance of the union integral to the divine communion and involves projecting a causal ordering into the Godhead' (1996:289). He suggested that if the Father is the cause of divine substance, the implication is that 'the Son (and also the Spirit) is that "than which something greater can be conceived," and that the personhood of the Son is profoundly different from that of the Father' (*ibid.*).

In defence of Zizioulas, however, it can be argued that it is the nature of the Father *as love* which is being raised up as 'cause' and, further, that there is also a biblical recognition of a hierarchy within the Godhead. Paul, for example, writes that 'the Son himself will be made subject to him who put everything under him, so that God may be all in all' (1Co. 15:28).

But more important for us than this technical conversation is that despite his criticism, Torrance has admitted that Zizioulas's 'revision of trinitarian expression by way of the category of "person" stands to breathe new life into the Western debates . . . In short . . . profoundly liberating ways forward are offered by his central theses' (1996:290).

It is these liberating concepts of the personhood of God that we are attempting to pick up on, here, and to explore—in particular Zizioulas's proposition that it is the Father's will to exist that ensures His ontological freedom (as opposed to His necessity). Despite what our criticisms of Zizioulas may be, his work has greatly assisted us by pointing to the personhood of God as ontologically free and independent of who we (His creatures) are.

This of course has direct implications on what it means to have been created in His image: what it means to be truly human.

The Personhood of Man

Modernity's 'quest' for humanity has involved a quest for individual freedom. And yet it ignores the fact that as it apes Greco-Roman thought, death still locks humanity into the cosmos.

Death has unconditionally sentenced humankind to mortality.

Further, despite our achievements (as explored in the Enlightenment survey, earlier), humanity remains 'bound' (Zizioulas 1985a:42) by its createdness and physicality, and lack of choice in the matter. Whereas Zizioulas (*ibid.*:43) observes that 'the authentic person, as absolute ontological freedom, must be "uncreated," that is, unbounded by any "necessity," including its own existence,' mankind is continually confronted by its own necessity: its lack of choice over whether to exist or not.

Zizioulas notes: 'The ultimate challenge to the freedom of the person is the "necessity" of existence' (*ibid.*:42). Humanity acknowledges (from a point of weakness) that it does not possess the absolute expression of freedom through its choice to 'be'—certainly not in a positive sense, in which a person can will to live, as God has, but only in a negative sense, whereby an individual can at most choose to terminate existence, through suicide. The choice of whether to exist was never given to us—and this is part of our humanness. At best, our parents chose that we should 'be' (thus making us to be the consequence of another's purpose, design or passion); at worst we were not 'wanted', or were never intended to 'be' (thus making us a human 'accident').

And yet these human perspectives are not absolute or final.

The Christian story, in contrast, offers to humanity both reality beyond death, and a choice over whether to live or not, in the here and now.

For two things follow from God's unnecessary being, and are communicated to us clearly through the Christian body of truth.

The first is that true personhood involves immortality—ongoing being!

Secular man would argue that as death terminates the body-soul relationship, 'true' non-temporal personhood can never be attained.

But a Christian perspective is contrary and simple: it points beyond the physicality of the Fallen world to the reality of the resurrection modelled in real terms in the person of the historic Christ. Yes, physical death is a boundary that confronts all human beings, but the resurrection is a hope that is equally real. It takes man beyond the (naturally perceived) boundary of death. And it is available to all. This is not just a hope, but a certainty, because Jesus of Nazareth, the Christ, as the 'first-born' of all creation (Ro. 8:29; Co. 1:18), has been raised to a life-beyond-death within our own era of history. This has been witnessed by a vast number of people and groups on independent occasions (over five hundred people at one time [1Co. 15:6]), in other words in totally validating circumstances.

Thus 'createdness' in Christianity does not equate with the ancient Greek concept of mortality: it is a concept embraced by, and allowed in eternity. This is why Zizioulas can insist that death is not an ontological reality (Zizioulas 1985a:48), with these words: 'Theology, unlike philosophy, teaches an ontology which transcends the tragic aspect of death without in the least accepting death as an ontological reality.'

Because of Christ, forgiven Man is now able to reach out, to pluck and eat of the fruit of the Tree of Life, and live forever.

Christianity thus deals with this first problematic issue of human personhood: 'createdness' is no longer a finite thing. Just as Christ the created man sits even now at the right hand of the Father, so created humankind has the promise of being destined for ongoing life.

But a second thing follows from God's unnecessary being: true personhood involves an unforced/voluntary beginning—a choice to exist. Zizoulas observed (*op. cit.*) that 'the authentic person, as absolute ontological freedom, must be "uncreated," that is, unbounded by any "necessity," including its own existence.'

From a physical, purely humanistic point of view, the only aspect of true personhood that can be expressed is the negative aspect: the will or choice *not* to 'be', or to live—in other words the choice to terminate one's physical existence and to take one's life (whether through suicide or euthanasia or whatever one chooses to call it), or not.

But from a spiritual point of view we do see a profound and wholly voluntary beginning to life being offered to all humanity.

This voluntary beginning involves people being able to 'choose life' (De. 30:19). It involves the freedom given to all people to 'believe and to receive ... [and so to] become children of God' (Jn. 1:12) and to be 'born again': 'born from above' (Jn. 3:3–7). Without being forced to!

Thus, Christianity—in at least these two simple respects (its response to the 'problems' of mortality and lack of choice to exist)—offers true humanity, true personhood to all who would hear its message.

But a third thing about the personhood of God impacts human personhood, and that is love: the ability 'to love without exclusiveness ... not out of conformity with a moral commandment ... but out of this "hypostatic constitution"' (Zizioulas 1985a:57–58). Just as the existence of God is owed to the free will to exist of the Father (who is love), so the essence of humanity has its roots in love.

What this means on a practical level is that 'communion is a product of freedom ... not because the divine nature is ecstatic but because the Father as a person freely wills this communion' (*ibid.*). We love, freely, because God desires it of us, and (more) because He enables it in us. We love and affirm each other not because we want to, nor because we have to, but because our own existence is owed to the love and affirmation of the Trinity. Without God's love for us, we would not be; we owe that love in turn to other people.

Volf writes, in commentary on Zizioulas: 'that *God's essence as person* means nothing other than that God *is* love' (1998:78) and, therefore, that 'human beings can become persons only by participating in God's personhood' (*ibid.*): they can only become truly human by participating in the love that is God.

It is because of the love of God and the life that He has given us, in other words, that we in turn are able to love. 'We love because he first loved us' (1Jn. 4:19). Because of God's communion of love with the Son and the Spirit, a similar communion should flow in the life of the church. Pannenberg argues that 'the essence of the church is communion of the faithful on the basis of the communion with Jesus Christ that each individual member shares' (1983:41). This would involve a life that—through being lived—affirms who the church is and who, in turn, Christians are, in relation to the Father who is love and who has freely chosen to exist. Of course this is humanly impossible: a human impulse to love would involve mere moralism. Divine love in us is only possible as a result of that miraculous rebirth and recreation by the Father.

And so this love, without exclusiveness—incorporating love—must be realised as being integral to Christian life and, thus, full human existence.

Thus it is that humanity finds identity in the personhood of God. Volf (1998:83) put it like this: 'Human beings can become persons only in communion with the personal God, who alone merits being called a person in the original sense.'

Implications for Mission

All that has been discussed above should dynamically impact the life of the church and should inform our twenty-first century missiological awareness and outworking of it in the world, in various ways.

The Message of Humanity

First, where modern (or postmodern) humanity may feel hindered by its createdness, the historical event of the resurrection of Christ points people beyond the physicality of this world to the reality (even physicality) of createdness enduring beyond the grave, as Jesus has experienced it.

A characteristic of a Christian, or an ecclesial person, is the future dimension of existence. He exists 'not as that which is but as that which he will be; . . . [for] ecclesial identity is linked with eschatology, that is, with the final outcome of this existence' (Zizioulas 1985a:59).

In other words, 'the Church exists not because Christ died on the cross but because he has risen from the dead, which means, because the kingdom has come.' (1988a:296). Put another way, and as cited already, Zizioulas (1985a:59) has suggested that the roots of 'ecclesial identity' are 'in the future . . . [with only] its branches . . . in the present,' and McPartlan (1993:187) that the 'centre of gravity' of the church 'lies in the future . . . [that] her roots and her continuity lie ahead.'

Thus Christian mission should be characterised by its message about a sure and certain future; it should reflect a sincere hope of life beyond the Greek (human) 'tragedy' of death, and the future salvation of all mankind (in place of an almost sadistic exclusivism).

Second, at the point where modern man may feel frustrated by his or her lack of choice to exist in the first place, the gospel presents an opportunity for each and every person to be born from above: to enter into a new existence, reality and world—but on the basis of their own freewill and choice to 'be'.

It would be tragic to miss the point of what has been proposed here as this is exactly what humankind today is searching for. Zizioulas (1985a:49–50) expresses the crucial significance of these observations in this way: 'The eternal survival of the person as a unique, unrepeatable and free "hypostasis", as loving and being loved, constitutes the quintessence of salvation, the bringing of the Gospel to man . . . The goal of salvation is that the personal life which is realised in God should also be realized on the level of human existence. Consequently salvation is identified with the realization of personhood in man.'

Both permanence of createdness (everlasting life) and a personal choice and ability to 'be' have been core to the quest of human identity throughout time. The Christian gospel offers humanity what it cannot buy or earn or gain elsewhere. These realities should, then, be integral to our understanding of the salvation we hold out to others in Christian mission, and should be understood as basic to ecclesial personhood.

But a third element of ecclesial personhood has been outlined: love. Love should be an integral aspect of humanity—not just as a moral obligation or act, but as an expression of the new creation God has caused in us. God is love, and exists because of love, and has brought us into being in love. This is what He requires of us, and enables in us: to love Him, and to love each other. Love should, as noted, organically ingrain the constitution of the church. Divine love should be basic to any understanding and outworking of Christian mission.

Eucharist as Mission

Integral to the characteristics of true human personhood highlighted above (divine belonging in terms of the choice to exist, and continued physicality and the essential place of love) is the sustaining of the relationships which are so much a part of ecclesial identity.

These, Zizioulas suggests, are brought into focus in the eucharist which, when understood in 'the correct and primitive sense... is first of all an assembly (*synaxis*), a community, a network of relations, in which man "subsists" in a manner different from the biological as a member of a body which transcends every exclusiveness of a biological or social kind' (*ibid.*:60). In the eucharist is 'the historical realization of the philosophical principle *which governs the concept of the person*, the principle that the hypostasis expresses the whole of its nature and not just a part' (*ibid.*).

The eucharist offers 'positively what baptism meant negatively: the death of the old, biological identity was replaced by the birth of the new identity, which was given in the eucharistic community' (1985b:29). Here 'Christ is "parted but not divided"' (1985a:60–61). In contrast to the old life which is based on natural necessity and leads to death, the new life is 'based on free and undying relationships, above all on the eternal filial relationship between the Father and the Son . . . [and] gives eternal life.' (1985b:29).

Volf puts it this way: 'The truth of Christ, indeed, the truth of every person, surpasses the *nous* (mind) and is accessible to human beings only as an *event* of communion' (1998:93).

Thus, Zizioulas would argue, the eucharist may be regarded as a tangible movement: 'a progress towards this realization [of personhood]' (1985a:61). Assembly and movement, together, in his view, make the eucharist *liturgy*—and here the two ontological features of eschatology and the eucharist exist together (*ibid.*:61–62): 'This liturgical, progressive movement of the eucharist, [with] its eschatological orientation, proves that in its eucharistic expression the ecclesial hypostasis is not of this world—it belongs to the eschatological transcendence of history and not simply to history . . . *The truth and the ontology of the person belong to the future, are images of the future.*'

This, then, is an important derivation of Zizioulas's recognition of ontological personhood: the 'functional', or 'pragmatic' outworking of an essentially ontological existence should be the presentation of the church as the '*eikon* of the Kingdom' (1988a:300)—not in the Platonic sense of 'image or shadow, empty of reality' (*ibid.*:301), but, through her existence in Christ, as 'an image of something else that transcends her . . . so *transparent* as to allow the eschatological realities to be reflected in [her institutions and structure] all the time' (*ibid.*).

And the primary means by which this is achieved (in Zizioulas's view) is through the eucharist; for in it, Paul talks of the church receiving 'above all a *Person*—and not ideas' (1985b:190—italics added). This is of utmost importance for him, but also for ourselves, for as noted by McPartlan (1993:133) in commentary on Zizioulas: 'what is primary in Christianity is not a message but a Person . . . a living Presence, to be found in the eucharist; verbal formulations and propositions are *derivative*, from this source.' It is through the eucharist, therefore, that 'the basic structure of the Church herself is organically connected with her essence' (Zizioulas, cited in McPartlan 1993:194).

Through this whole discussion, it is important to note that reference to the eucharist is not a pagan or magical kind of spirituality, or legalism (1985b:31); its fundamental feature is the gathering together of Christian believers (*ibid.*:32) through their participation in the relationships of the eschatological community (*ibid.*) which exist in relationship to God, through Christ and in the Spirit. Although Reformed tendency was to centralise the preaching of the Word over the sacrament, Luther, in his 'Sermon on the Sacrament of the Holy and True Body of Christ', did point out 'that the meaning of this sacrament is a twofold communion: first the communion of the believer with Christ, and secondly the communion among all those who enjoy such unity with Christ and thus form the one body of Christ' (so Pannenberg 1983:39).

So an important effect of the eucharist is its stress on community, rather than individuality. Volf notes that Zizioulas's ontology of person is 'conceived in contrast to any individualism destructive to the community (and thus to life itself)' (1998:75–76). Individualism is a consequence of the Fall: a perversion of human personhood (*ibid.*:81), and so Volf articulately warns against 'naked ecclesial individualism' (*ibid.*:160).

But the key purpose and role of the eucharist is, as mentioned, the focus it brings on the real presence of Christ. Zizioulas (1985b:32) commented that: 'Those who despise the eucharistic community and its head, the bishop, are arrogant and cut themselves off automatically from communion with God and from eternal life.' Although this has, in the past, led to the legalistic axiom '"No salvation outside the church" (*extra ecclesiam nulla salus*)' (*ibid.*), its effective meaning is that, as the Fourth Gospel puts it, 'unless we eat the flesh and drink the blood of the Son of Man we cannot have life' (*ibid.*:34). To this end, Volf also notes poignantly: 'The Logos is not the spoken or even written word, but rather *exclusively* a person' (1998:94).

For Pannenberg, the Reformer's placing of the gospel in the centre of the church's life accorded a 'dangerously authoritarian character to the function of the preacher' (1983:39). More correct, in his view, is that '*The Eucharist, not the sermon, is in the center of the church's life* ... [and that] the sermon should serve, not dominate, in the church. It should serve the presence of Christ which we celebrate in the Eucharist' (*ibid.*:40).

Echoing Wright's recognition of the symbolic, and Walker's recognition even of liturgy, Zizioulas's stress through eucharistic liturgy is on a God-centredness which transcends the natural state of self and which should be the focus of our being and identity as Christian people.

However one understands the dynamics and/or actuality of the symbolic (e.g. when or how 'the moment of the eucharist' [1988a:298] occurs, or when and how the Word is faithfully upheld in a gathering of believers) this ultimate stress on the full being of God and the community that comes into being because of who He is, is wholly appropriate and helpful in articulating our lost ontological dimension. It should in turn be core to the expression and outworking of an active Christian presence in, and mission into the world. Through the eucharist, or through whatever other means of realising and communicating it, it is through the real being of Jesus Christ, the full being of God in our lives and in our fellowship, by His Spirit, that people are brought into communion and community with the full being of the triune God and His people.

To this end, it is surely anathema that mission be 'loaded with ideas of aggressiveness' (1985c:189). Instead, it should be intimately concerned about unity in the Kingdom of God through realisation of true humanity and personhood.

Similarly, just as the identity of the church is determined by an eschatological perspective of humanity as a whole in Christ (1988b:347), the identity of Christian mission is only determinable and effective in relation to the person of God and the reality of the eschaton. With this focus, the church will (attractively) be seen to be '*offering herself to the world for reception* instead of *imposing* herself on it' (ibid.). Thus the church 'becomes the community which *relates the world to God*—and this is essentially what mission should mean. Mission is not a method . . . but an *attribute* related to the nature of the Church' (Zizioulas, cited in McPartlan 1993:289).

Put another way, Zizioulas argues that 'the nature of mission is not to be found in the Church's *addressing* the world but in its being fully in *com-passion* with it' (1985a:224). Thus mission does not simply involve preaching (or evangelism) as a ministry of the Word, for 'the Word of God is not to be separated from his *incarnation* . . . the Word of God is no longer simply a prophetic utterance, as it was in the Old Testament, but "flesh" (John 1:14)' (*ibid.*—footnote 42).

Again, how this is outworked in practical terms may remain debatable. However, stress on the essential life and real person and presence of Christ the Word has been important to try to articulate, and essential to attempt to grasp hold of. As Zizioulas (1988a:303) writes: 'I believe that while we remain unaccustomed to a kind of ontology which I would call "relational", and which is bound up with pneumatology and Trinitarian theology, we shall never be capable of understanding the Mystery of the Church.'

Summary and Assessment

Williams commends Zizioulas for his 'sobering warning to the managerial pragmatism that can so easily dominate ecclesiology these days' (1989:105)—the precise characteristic which is being refuted in this writing.

For in Zizioulas' work we have seen a significant emphasis of the priority of ontology over praxis.

Through consideration of God's unnecessary being and more, we have seen these things that are core to the Christian faith: that human personhood is about life beyond physical death (and that physical death is only temporal); that it involves and offers to all the choice to exist (to be born again, from above, into the family of God—made known to us in the person of Jesus Christ); that human personhood is about inclusive love (not excluding those from other classes or cultures, but belonging together, because of one's belonging in Christ); that human personhood is about future and eternal identity and belonging; and, finally, that core to any ecclesial identity is the relationships that come into being with God and with each other because of who Christ is and because of His very real presence in the centre of our ecclesial communities.

As core to the Christian faith, these should all, in turn, be basic to Christian mission. This is because they constitute what can and should be communicated to unbelievers about what it means to have been made in the image of God.

Thus we see, in McPartlan's words (1993:137), that Christian mission should offer 'not an *improved* life or a *better* life or a *higher* life, but *life* itself.'

CHAPTER 14

Ontology in Other Core Aspects of Christian Thought

AN ONTOLOGICAL DIMENSION UNDERGIRDS all aspects of life, and is being increasingly recognised not just as an essential but (more) as a primary dimension of life. In Christian Ethics, for example, Hauerwas (1984:116) put it like this: 'The question "What ought I to be?" precedes the question "What ought I to do?"'

The same is seen in any area of theology, but to serve as examples, and also to further clarify our understanding of 'ontology' as a lost dynamic that is prior to any correct understanding of Christian mission, it is worth looking at just three aspects of theology and Christian thought here.

What we see should highlight just how functional an approach to mission has been followed by the church in modernity.

Relational Nature of Authority

The first of these, which is a key aspect of the modern determination of what mission is, is the concept of 'authority'—especially with regard to the authority of the biblical text. Despite Dodd's perception of a 'great though largely silent crisis . . . [the] questioning of authority if not a revolt against it' (1944:v), the very act of an approach to the bible suggests that a certain concept of authority is being adhered to in mission thinking. For this is what we have seen, above. Mission has already been shown to have been influenced by the authority of tradition (for example through William Carey's model of mission). But tradition in turn appears to have been motivated by, or has at least appealed to the higher authority of the bible (so, for example, Schneider [1967:1–10], amongst others, claiming that authority for evangelism is 'grounded most deeply and finally in the risen Lord's Great Commission').

The problem with 'biblical' authority being an end in itself (again exemplified in even Carey's modern mission) is that it is often an interpreted authority. 'Biblical' authority can be different things to different people: texts can be read literally and/or prescriptively, and without faithfulness to the linguistic and hermeneutical realities that may surround them. A specifically derived, textual authority was discussed in Part I: an authority that had grown out of a simple exegesis of Matthew 28:19–20a and a literal, prescriptive rendering of that verse (or part of a verse) in contrast to the authority suggested by the broader pericope of Matthew 28:16–20. Here we saw evidenced an authority not of mandate or text but of the supreme Person to whom such mandate has to be attributed.

Admittedly, there may be an element of recognition of this personal authority (as in the case of Schneider, cited above) similar to Max Warren's personification of the 'Great Commission' in his *I Believe in the Great Commission* (London: Hodder & Stoughton, 1976). But these, and other such appeals, are ultimately to a text interpreted in their own ways, and not to the person of God in history: the risen Lord.

For this is where any biblical authority does derive from: the very Being of God of whom it writes.

Authority Derived from the Being of God

Why should we be sceptical about the programmes and methods that our church has come up with—the tried and tested methods of modern mission? Why should we presumptuously assume that it is for us to come to God and attempt to determine His will and purposes, any more than other people have done before us—and to discard their missiological systems and conclusions in the process?

Well, the simple reason is because God is God. Our authority is not Israel or the Law and the Prophets, not the synagogues, rulers and chief priests, not the Archbishop of Canterbury or the Pope (though all of these have authority and position that we do need to respect, in their place). But ultimately it is God who is our authority. Just like the apostles before the Sanhedrin in Acts, when they were told to stop preaching in the temple courts: what was their response (Ac. 5:29)? 'We must obey God, rather than men!' And what was Gamaliel's counsel (Ac. 5:38-39)? 'If their purpose or activity is of human origin, it will fail. But if it is from God, you will not be able to stop these men; you will only find yourselves fighting against God!'

That is our authority: the true and living God—creator of heaven and earth, who has no beginning or end, and who has adopted us, and enabled us to be His children.

It is God who should be determining our footsteps, and who we should be seeking to know and understand in a fresh and daily way in order to determine what His 'sending' may involve in our day and age, our broader context and in our own lives.

This point has been argued in different ways by various people. René Paché (1969:30-31), for example, argued the authority of God from a number of biblical passages such as: 'My word . . . that goeth forth out of my mouth . . . shall not return unto me void' (Is. 55:11), and 'Lord, to whom shall we go? Thou hast the words of eternal life' (Jn. 6:68). But he also traced the authority of the bible to the fact that it stems from God's being through testimonies from the early church, the Reformers and various Protestant Confessions (*ibid.*:233-247). In short: authority derives from the fact that 'God speaks to us directly through [the Scriptures]' (*ibid.*:88).

The centrality of God's Being has been a particular feature of the Christian religion in relation to the 'evolution' of the canon of Scripture. It is the view of the early church that 'Scripture as a fact was also a gift . . . It was a gift from God made primarily to the people of God . . . [And] If it confronted the early church as a fact, it did so ultimately because it had its origin, not just in the prophets and apostles, but in God' (so Bromiley 1983:204). Scripture was authoritative for the Church Fathers because it derived from God, and enshrined the truth of God, and had the authority of God Himself (*ibid.*:207). God was 'the ultimate authority from whom every other authority derives its authorization' (*ibid.*:219).

Michael Ramsey (1962:1) said it well: that Christianity has never been 'a "religion of the Book";' that the central fact of Christianity was never 'a Book but a *Person*—Jesus Christ, himself described as the Word of God' (*ibid.*:1-2). It is 'the relation of the books to the person' (*ibid*:2) that has made the canonical books different. Whereas the Old Testament books were accepted as canon because Jesus Himself appealed to them (*ibid.*:7–8), the New Testament canon arose in relation to the conviction that Jesus Himself was that Word of God (*ibid.*:11, cf. Jn. 1:14, 1Jn. 1:1, Rev. 19:13).

For although there are different approaches to arguing the grounds of the authority of Scripture (e.g. through consideration of inerrancy, inspiration, revelation and so on) authority has always ultimately depended upon whether or not the writings were of God (so Godfrey 1983:199–220).

Authority Derived from that which was 'Handed Over'

Looked at another way, Scripture's authority comes from having been passed down from one Christian generation to another. As suggested by Ramsey (1962:13), authority resides in that which was '"handed over" from Christ to the apostles, and from the apostles to the Church. Here in embryo is the conception of "tradition" . . . the Greek verb "to hand over" (*paradidonai*).'

And yet it was not just a set of teaching that was 'handed over': it was God Himself—it was none less than the presence and being of God 'handed over' to the created world by the Father in the form of Jesus Christ and by Jesus in the form of the Holy Spirit.

Both Roman Catholic and Anglican communions agree on this point (as reflected in the Venice Statement): that within the Christian community 'the peculiar authority of a collection of books, the Bible' derives from God, through Christ (Yarnold and Chadwick 1977:9). Recognition of this authority is shown when, for example, at times where exegesis alone cannot decide between two interpretive positions, 'the Church lends its full authority to one interpretation of Scripture rather than another because that best accords with its living experience of Christ through the Holy Spirit' (*ibid.*:12).

In other words, 'The apostles derive their authority . . . from the Lord of the Church' (*ibid.*:14). The authority of Scripture lies not just in the fact that God inspired it, but that He 'became intelligible to us in the incarnation, the person of Christ' (Rogers and McKim 1979:457–458), and that He persuades the reader, still, through His own Holy Spirit. Indeed, the Gospel of John ends off (20:31) by spelling out the function of Scripture (broadly understood): that by knowing Christ the reader may have life in His name (*ibid.*:461).

Wright (1992b:143) observed the same authority: 'I am proposing a notion of "authority" which is not simply vested in the New Testament, or in "New Testament theology", nor simply in "early Christian history" and the like, conceived positivistically, but in the creator god himself, and this god's story with the world, seen as focused on the story of Israel and hence on the story of Jesus, and told and retold in the Old and New Testaments, and as still requiring completion. This is a far more complex notion of authority than those usually tossed around in theological discourse.'

Authority for Wright, in other words, is 'dynamic' rather than 'static' (*ibid.*:471). New Testament writings have a form of 'intrinsic authority' (*ibid.*:472) and are written in such a way as to 'articulate *and invite their hearers to share* a new worldview which carries at its heart a new view of "god", and even a proposal for a way of saying "God"' (*ibid.*).

In short, our observation is this: authority is not a textual thing, but a relational one. We have proposed that authority—even of a biblical text—comes not from its textuality but from the One who has (ultimately) authored that text: the One who gives it meaning. This relational view of authority is key to what is being highlighted here: that a living relationship with God should ingrain what it means to be a Christian person in today's world.

Relational Nature of Sin

A second core aspect of the Christian life and, thus, mission, is the issue of sin.

Looked at already in relation to soteriology, it has been argued that sin is not just about moral failure, but about being wrong with God: being found outside of a relationship with Him. It has already been suggested that moral failure is really just a symptom of sin: of being apart from God, and not honouring Him as Cosmic Lord. Sin is often misunderstood merely in terms of moral or cultural norms, but a brief investigation shows how deeply ontological sin is and (therefore) how salvation and mission are themselves equally ontological realities.

It helps to think about where sin originated from. Not (as once argued) from those fallen, lustful angels of Genesis 6 mixing with the human race. No! Sin was there before that. Clearly sin became a condition of man soon after the creation, through the first man and woman who had been created, as recorded in the account of the Fall in Genesis 2–3.

Not everyone has viewed these chapters negatively. Indeed, in Genesis 3 Kant saw not a fall, but a rise, 'praising' Adam 'for his willingness to make his own moral judgment rather than blindly following the dictates of another, even if that Other is God' (in Hamilton 1990:211).

But the opening narrative of the bible was for both Augustine and Paul 'the ultimate source and foundation of [their] views with regard to the origin and universality of human sinfulness' (Tennant 1903:1)

And certainly Genesis 2–3 itself heavily underlines the concept of Fall and the negativity of that event (as opposed to a positive maturing of mankind): firstly by its negative portrayal of the individual self and then, on the basis of that, its account of sin.

The Fall's Negative Portrayal of Mankind

This is by no means a comprehensive list, but several features identify fallen humanity.

First, it is insignificant beside the sovereignty and omnipotence of its Creator. God is the Alpha and the Omega, for it was God 'who said of himself: I am the first and the last' (Westermann 1987:ix)—a view depicted not simply through the opening words 'In the beginning God . . .' but also through the *inclusio* that exists between the 'mythical' beginnings sketched in this first biblical book (Genesis) and the 'apocalyptic' endings detailed in its final book (Revelation).

In contrast to an awe-inspiring God, mankind is created out of the dust of the Earth (which is itself created matter). And so mankind, unlike God, is one who has a beginning and an end.

Man is mortal, with a character of dependence and limited knowledge. Mankind is insignificant beside God.

And yet, secondly, humanity has always persisted in trying to usurp the place of God in its life. Genesis 2–3 clearly illustrates and decries humanity's aspiration to become like God. This distortion in mankind was first exposed through the lure and deception of the serpent: its suggestion that men and women could become like God. The serpent's intent was 'to place before [Eve] the possibility of being more than she is and more than God intended her to be . . . [For] deification is a fantasy difficult to repress and a temptation hard to reject' (so Hamilton 1990:190).

Bonhoeffer observed (1959:68) that: 'When man proceeds against the concrete Word of God with the weapon of a principle, with an idea of God, he is in the right from the first, he becomes God's master, he has left the path of obedience, he has withdrawn from God's addressing him.' And this is what has happened in fallen Man: in insisting on his own way, he has become 'a creator, a source of life . . . He is the lord of this world, but now of course the solitary lord and despot of the mute, violated, silenced, dead world of his ego' (*ibid.*:92).

Ratzinger (1990:87) saw that 'at the very heart of sin there lies the human being's denial of his creatureliness . . . [and the fact that he] 'himself wants to be God.' Hamilton (1990:190) commented: 'Whenever one makes his own will crucial and God's revealed will irrelevant, whenever autonomy displaces submission and obedience in a person, that finite individual attempts to rise above the limitations imposed on him by his creator.'

So, mankind is always (and wrongly) seeking to become like God—not in terms of God-like character (which we would want to affirm) but in terms of power and position.

Clearly related to this is a third negativity of fallen humanity, which is that people are always striving to become autonomous beings. The narrator of Genesis 'finds in man's attempt to overstep the bounds of his creaturely dependence upon God, in man's grasping at autonomy, the root of all evil and friction in the world' (so Davidson 1973:44).

Although God made man with all that was needed, man wanted more for himself (Tennant 1903:15). The serpent's temptation ('*is* it true that God has forbidden . . .?' [Ge. 3:1]) 'insinuates that God has been unnecessarily authoritarian' (Davidson 1973:44). It was 'an appeal to that human arrogance which will accept no limitations, which insists on knowing everything' (*ibid.*:40).

The insinuation was also that there was a 'possibility of an extension of human existence beyond the limits set for it by God at creation, an increase of life not only in the sense of pure intellectual enrichment but also of familiarity with, and power over, mysteries that lie beyond man' (Von Rad 1972:89).

Almost in reaction, then, it seems, mankind strove for independence and autonomy and the gaining of knowledge. Westermann noted that 'humanity is created with a strong desire to know, and to enhance its existence through knowledge' (1987:23). By wanting to appropriate that knowledge, further, mankind was 'encroaching upon [the] divine prerogative, and . . . making himself independent of and equal to God' (Tennant 1903:13).

Which overlaps with our previous observation about fallen Man: in its striving for knowledge, mankind was in actual fact seeking for itself that which is only attributable to God. In its quest for autonomy, humanity was striving to be like God: it was grasping after sovereignty.

A fourth aspect of fallen Man is its individual as opposed to corporate identity. Made in the image of God, mankind was created to be a corporate or communal person. Genesis narrates (1:26) that mankind was made in '*our* image, in *our* likeness . . .' (not *my* likeness) and (3:22) that 'man has now become like one of *us* . . .'

Standing in the place of God, however, humanity becomes a mere image of its own isolated self. Man is essentially a community being, and so the concept of man as individual self defies Man's createdness.

A fifth (and last listed here, but by no means the last) feature of sinful Man is that it suffers the consequences of sin meted out in the Garden: a sudden awareness (knowledge) of the extremes of Good and Evil (and all that this might involve); a realisation of human nakedness and hiding from God (3:7); increased pain at childbirth (3:16); intensified effort involved in sustaining life (3:17–19); an ultimate return to dust (3:19); a new name for 'Eve', relating her to 'all the living' instead of (as 'woman') to her husband, Adam, by God's design; being driven out of Eden with its beauty, self-sufficiency, promise of eternal life and, ultimately, presence of God (3:24).

Clearly Genesis 2–3 is the place to look in considering the origins of sin in the world, and in humanity.

The Nature of Sin

So, one of the striking features of these early chapters of Genesis is what it shows about sin beyond just moral wrong. This is despite ideas of sin as 'moral imperfection' (Tennant in Powell 1934:93) and original sin having been described as 'instinctive tendencies waiting to be moralised' (*ibid.*).

Working backwards over the above observations about humanity and the origin of sin, however, sin is clearly about these things instead: being outside of God's presence; being cut off from the promise of eternal life; attraction to beauty, wisdom and intellect rather than to the Lord Himself; being part of a general, 'living' humanity rather than a people of God's own workmanship, the seed of Adam; the consequences of a hard life; a lusting after Good and paranoia about Evil; individualism, as opposed to being a community being; autonomy and control; usurping God's position with self; losing a sense of insignificance beside the Almighty LORD and God of Creation.

In summary, sin is about the breaking of a once good relationship with God. It is the distortion of the image of God in what was meant to be His image. Mankind's error was not just to eat the apple; it was to disobey God and exonerate self in His place. Sin, therefore, is an inherently ontological concept, and praxis or 'moral' behaviour is a mere symptom of it.

Sin is not, in other words, so much about an act, as about an absence of relationship with God. It is about a lost relationship not a loose morality, and wrong deeds are just symptomatic of a broken relationship.

Von Rad (1972:50) supports this, seeing Man's fall in terms of 'his actual separation from God . . . (and not, for example, as a plunge into moral evil, into the subhuman!).' Jenkins (1969:25), similarly, observed that a 'proper interpretation of the Biblical approach would seem to be that being in a wrong relationship with God is equivalent to being a sinner and vice versa.' Candlish (1958:84) put it like this: 'The essence of the sin was that these desires were not kept in check by regard to the word of God; and thus the real cause of the Fall was unbelief and insubordination; unbelief, in not giving credit to God's testimony warning them of death; and insubordination, in not submitting to the will of God.'

It is too simplistic to blame sinfulness on an event (or on events) of disobedience. Even Bertrand Russell (in Greeves 1956:5) recognised this, writing: 'The sense of sin has been one of the dominant psychological facts in history, and is still at the present day of great importance in the mental life of a large proportion of mankind . . . [however] the *concept* of "sin" is obscure, especially if we attempt to interpret it in non-theological terms.'

Russell, despite his atheistic views, would be suggesting with us that sin is a fundamentally theological concept, rather than a moral one.

A merely moral view of sin—seeing it as a mere 'stepping-aside from the true line of upward progress' (so Williams 1927:514) or even as a 'fall from a high level of moral and intellectual endowment' (*ibid.*)—would leave us with two problems.

The first is that it does not explain mankind's general ignorance of its own evil (especially to people of high moral integrity). Sin as moral wrongdoing does not explain sin as an unconscious state, which it often is. This state is indicated by Greeves (1956:14) for example, writing: 'In the most literal sense we are ignorant of sin; and that is because at the centre, or root, of sin itself is ignorance of more than one kind . . . an ignorance of self and [more significantly an] ignorance of God.' (This is contra Tennant's insistence that sin is 'an activity of the will, expressed in thought, word or deed, contrary to the individual's conscience, to *his* notion of what is good and right, *his* knowledge of the moral law and the will of God' [*Cambridge lectures: 1931–2*, in Greeves *ibid.*:15].)

To an extent, this division between moral and relational views of sin and reality can be traced to Descartes and Locke, in Enlightenment thinking. For them, thought was coextensive with consciousness (Greeves 1956:21); all that we think about and do is all that we are—it is our total reality. But no explanation was given for the subconscious in one's life. The Enlightenment as a whole reflected—although it did not recognise—what Augustine referred to as 'the abysmal depths of personality' (in Greeves *ibid.*:22) and the fact that 'a man comprises something which not even the spirit of the man, which is in him, knows' (*ibid.*).

Clearly one is not always conscious of sin and neither is sin always possible to 'manage' (so, for example, Paul's well known dilemma: 'I do not do the good I want to do, but the evil I do not want to do—this I keep on doing . . . What a wretched man I am! [Ro. 7:19,24]).

This subconscious element of the doing of sin would suggest sin to be far more fundamental a concept within mankind than mere wrong action. It would suggest it to be a state of wrong-being (in relation to God, and others) far more than a simple fact of doing wrong.

The second problem follows on from this: a merely moralistic view of sin leaves us with a distorted perception that moral/intellectual failure is really more devastating than being in a state of ignorance about, and wrong-relationship with God. From a human point of view we understandably deride moral wrongdoing. However, very little condemnation occurs in the event of offence and wrong perpetrated against God Himself.

The depth of sin against God is not often considered—certainly not on a global, public scale, though of course it is very well attested to, especially in Old Testament writings. Malachi, for example, records the grievance of disobedience against the 'Lord Almighty' (2:2) with these words of His: 'If you do not listen, and if you do not set your heart to honour my name ... I will send a curse upon you, and I will curse your blessings ... I will rebuke your descendants; I will spread on your faces the offal from your festival sacrifices, and you will be carried off with it.'

In view of mankind's ignorance of sin, and the severe offence that sin is against God, salvation and the gospel should be understood afresh as inherently relational, rather than merely cultural or moralistic. Mission should be an expression and celebration of God's outstanding grace in inviting totally undeserving humanity back into a living relationship with Himself.

The 'Problem' of Subjectivity

A third and final aspect of Christian thought which may be of considerable significance in stressing the importance of ontology is the issue of subjectivity. A charge of subjectivism may be levelled against our stress on the being of God and a relationship with Him, as something that is intangible or value-based.

However, two preliminary responses to that charge do need to be considered.

The Need for Control

First, subjectivity does not have to be an uncontrolled thing. Bosch (1991:360) observed that subjectivity, *per se*, is not a problem so much as '*uncontrolled* subjectivity'. The shrewd opinion of Stanley Fish (1980:49) has already been discussed: that 'controlled subjectivity' (e.g. meaning determined in relation to God) is to be favoured over against 'an objectivity that is finally an illusion' (e.g. textual literalism and derived textual mandate).

Our question, then, should be how to determine and ensure control over subjective elements.

Valid controls noted already could, for example, include the stable text—the bible itself (so Thiselton 1992:517)—and faithful exegesis of it, though Fish would suggest that without the reader there is no stable text (in Thiselton *ibid*.:69–70). So another control, then, is the actual reader 'who objectifies the text ... and thus controls it' (Fowler 1985:14). Fish has also suggested the control of the 'critical community' or the reading community (in Fowler [*op. cit.*]). Other controls would include the publicness of the Christian faith: church doctrine, with its symbols and story, and of course the consensus of other believers.

However, most of these controls are 'from below'. They are controls that we ourselves have imposed, or determined to be adequate, and yet they may still be totally irrelevant because we do not know (humanly) what control is needed—and we do not even have the power to control what needs controlling anyway.

Unless revealed to us from beyond ourselves—hence the ultimate control of the 'original author' Himself Who has been recognised: the Holy Spirit, sent to us by the risen Christ, to teach and to guide!

The Transitory Worth of Empiricism

A second preliminary response to the problem of subjectivity is also worth considering.

Rationalism and our 'modern' demand for objectivity (or even a concern for a control over subjectivity) is, arguably, little more than an Enlightenment concern with reason and its quest for empiricism (Enlightenment was, after all, 'the age which venerated reason and science as man's highest faculty' [*op. cit.*]). John Locke's attempt to establish the objective nature of the Christian faith (in *The Reasonableness of Christianity*), for example, was simply an Enlightenment response to Enlightenment's own demand for plausibility. Even Thiemann's theological response to classical foundationalism is itself just an attempt to rationalise subjectivity in epistemology (so Plantinga 1983:48).

This structure of rationality has dominated our thought for the last two hundred years. Apcyzynski (1977:10) noted: 'Western man has laboured under a conception of knowledge that has demanded complete and total objectivity.' This structure of rationalism may, however, just be an illusion, after all (so Newbigin 1986:41). Lack of proof that a person's reading of the text is rational (i.e. absence of proof of a potentially illusory structure of thought) is therefore not problematic.

Polanyi's work has successfully shown that the distinction between what is fact, in an empirical sense, and what is value, is not a simplistic matter. There appears to be a 'fundamental logical difficulty ... [in] holding to an ideal of complete objectivity' (1983:10). Polanyi recognised that 'there are no strict rules for whether we should accept or reject an apparent coherence as a natural fact [and that there] is always a residue of personal judgment involved in deciding whether to accept any particular piece of evidence' (1962:311). One of his conclusions is a striking observation: 'Strictly speaking all empirical science is inexact' (*ibid.*).

Karl Popper (with a reputation of being 'the greatest philosopher of science this century, and, indeed, of all time' [so O'Hear 1995:45]), like Polanyi, represents a post-critical mode of thought in which the inseparability of fact and value has been recognised (in contrast to Enlightenment's narrow demand for hard, tangible fact). He has argued that the 'rejection of the false' is the only thing that scientists can do with 'complete logical certainty' (so Sir Peter Medawar, writing on Popper's methodology in O'Hear *ibid.*:44). Because of this, 'all empirical statements are based on theories that we project on the world in the light of our expectations and categorisations' (*ibid.*:43). Although, in science, attempts are made to explain and systematise the process of testing, 'even there it is our interpretation of our results that determines whether we reject a theory or not' (*ibid.*:44).

This is not to deny that God is a God of order and that He does things for a purpose—it is just allowing that in our fallen state, and as mere created man, we may not ever understand His ways ('for my ways are higher than your ways,' says the LORD [Is. 55:9]; and 'the foolishness of God is wiser than man's wisdom' [1Co. 1:25]).

And so, more is required than just to establish outward 'reasonableness' and tangibility. What Polanyi referred to as 'personal judgment' (*op. cit.*) in interpretation, others have referred to in different ways before him. Kierkegaard, for example, referred to a '"the leap of faith" . . . "heuristic step"' (in Torrance 1971:177) and Heidegger talked of a '"leap of thought" . . . beyond all causal and logical relation' (*ibid.*). Schuyler Brown (1988:232) wrote of the 'mysterious interaction' which occurs between reader and the text; and Iser (as already noted) recognised the need for an 'actualization' (1978:171–176) of meaning in the reader.

To demand 'objectivity' in a hard, this-worldly sense, then, is to overlook Polanyi's proposition that 'we can know more than we can tell' (1983:4): that there may be more to truth than we can necessarily grasp a hold of, and that subjectivity may actually be a necessary part of understanding an intangible whole.

As Jesus said, in testifying to truth: 'My kingdom is not of this world' (Jn. 18:36–38).

Not Subjectivity but Ultimate Object

In view of the above, a third proposition needs to be made: that neither subjectivity—nor even an absent or inadequate control over the subjective—should be seen as problematic. For objectivity may still reasonably exist despite or behind the subjective (in much the same way as meaning exists behind a symbol). An empirical statement is only necessarily true 'to the extent to which it reveals an aspect of reality, a reality largely hidden to us, and *existing therefore independently of our knowing it*' (Polanyi 1962:311).

It is the viability of the control of the ultimate Object that is being proposed here.

Postmodernity, admittedly, seeks to prevent the totalising control of any one objective regime (Lyotard 1984:81-82); it is reacting against the concept of a restrictive, false and (thus) terrorising (*op. cit.*) objectivity. And yet the 'objective' being proposed here is a reality that has become physically and tangibly known to mankind in the historical person of Jesus Christ (and, more, through the Holy Spirit who is present among believing people). This reality and ultimate object, therefore, is not a system or ideology, but a person. There is, in this instance, no chance of this objectivity being 'finally an illusion' (Fish *op. cit.*). In addition to this, the person in focus, here, is God; and because God is love, Lyotard's fear of one, controlling 'terror' will not be a negative realisation.

To restate all this in another way, the absence of an empirical statement does not mean an absence of the reality being proposed here of the objective Other.

Walker makes an interesting observation in discussion of the phenomenon of the miraculous: 'Without a belief . . . in the incarnation and resurrection of our Lord—not to mention a God who creates the cosmos *ex nihilo*—Christianity has no objective foundations beyond experience and subjectivism' (1993b:123). With a belief in God, however, experience and subjectivism is not a threat. Whilst it might seem intangible to root one's faith in mere belief, the Christian faith is rooted in history, in (ultimately) the Christ event.

The otherness of cosmic order in relation to God as Object is, thus (for the Christian), a paradigm of objective truth and reality rather than a subjective one.

This is the only way in which an authentic theology of mission can be established: by working from the ultimate object upon which a formerly considered 'subjective' Christian epistemology is derived. By prioritising a living relationship with God, the concept, shape and identity of the more 'subjective' aspects of Christian life can be rightly determined and acted upon.

Summary and Assessment—Identity of the Ultimate Object

It has been suggested that the ultimate authority in any form of knowing (especially in terms of biblical truth), the One who draws people out from a position of sin and broken relationship with God, and the objective truth which we seek to articulate, is the full Being of God as Person, Himself. The thought of various people and positions (Schleiermacher, postliberalism, Wright and Polanyi, Walker and Zizioulas) have been described in an attempt to show how each represents different expressions of this reality (e.g. through the narrative of the Christian Story or its symbols, tradition, liturgy and/or the eucharist and the like).

This objective truth (the person and Being of God) is best communicated through the grand narrative of Christianity because a telling of the story of Jesus Christ of Nazareth involves an exposition of the story of the objective and ontologically free being of God, and of His love. This, in turn, cuts across Enlightenment paradigms of reason and contemporary scepticism towards the concept of universal truth and a singular story.

The concept of one overriding narrative is not commonly accepted. Although narratives may be '"useful fictions" in everyday life' in postmodern thought (Grenz 1996:46.), an overall 'incredulity toward metanarratives' as already noted in relation to Lyotard (1984:xxiv) has remained. The Enlightenment project itself appealed to narrative in (for example) the form of the scientific method (Grenz 1996:45), but postmodernity's rationale has been to be 'no longer ruled by the modern concern that all discussions lead toward consensus' (*ibid.*:48). Following Nietzsche's 'all is fiction' there has been scepticism over whether there can ever be any one correct version of history (Jameson 1991:367), hence propositions like this can exist: 'Consensus is an inadequate criterion of validation' (Lyotard 1984:61).

And yet if we are to take a part of Nietzsche, we must take the whole—for example his already mentioned proposition that 'God is dead!'—and we would not want to do that!

So, there is still value in, and place for a metanarrative.

In the same way, Lyotard's thesis concerning the justice of 'multiplicities' (*ibid.*:66) appears, simply, to have arisen from cynicism towards the idea of society ever functioning as an organic whole (*ibid.*:11). This may be an understandable reaction to imposing ideologies such as Marxism (*ibid.*). But it does not mean that one, functioning society cannot exist.

Indeed it can and does, and we anticipate it and celebrate it in the Kingdom of God.

To this end, one grand narrative should not be denied, as appears to have happened. Such a narrative would be one that would serve to unite society as a whole. For narratives 'define what has the right to be said and done in the culture in question, and as such they are a part of that culture, they are legitimated by the simple fact that they do what they do' (*ibid.*:23). One overriding narrative of truth would be validated by the existence of one valid, united society and/or culture.

Postmodernity would therefore welcome such a sociological phenomenon: one that pointed to a plausible universal narrative. Such a grand narrative would be an appropriate response to postmodernity's question (Fraser and Nicholson 1994:246): 'Where does legitimation reside?' Further, and practically: if a unified story could be presented that was both reasonable, and which affirmed the freedom and personhood aspired to by all people rather than stifling it (as did Marxism), it would almost certainly be listened to and heard, and would become effective.

And this is what Christianity does with its universal story of the ontologically free being of God: His concern for the world, and the potential for human freedom in relationship with Him. The essence of truth is not to do with the category of 'narrative', *per se*, but the worldview of ultimate reality and personhood found in Him.

The true and living God is the essence of a universally relevant meta-narrative.

Thus it is only in relation to such a worldview built around the true Being of God as ultimate objectivity that an authentic understanding and theology of Christian mission can ever be determined.

PART III

RESOLUTION & CONCLUSION:
Christian Mission

Chapter 15

Mission: the Christian Life

THE PROPOSITION OF THIS work has been that the eclipsed crisis in modern mission has its roots in pragmatism: in the doing of mission. In response it has sought to clarify an ontological alternative out of which authentic mission can be defined and better understood.

These contrasting paradigms for approaching mission came about because of, and in response to the crisis that had been perceived in contemporary mission. An eclipse had taken place wherein 'problems' and proposed solutions in mission were bringing about adaptations to the meaning and practice of mission without actually dealing with the real issues involved, thereby obscuring what authentic mission really should be.

As noted earlier, the purpose of this concluding chapter, then, is to sketch the effect that an ontological, as opposed to a pragmatic start point may have on the identity of mission.

For the purpose of clarity, popular mission has here been labelled 'modern' or 'contemporary' or 'functional' or 'pragmatic' or even 'romantic' mission, in an attempt to distinguish what 'mission(s)' has become, from the authentic Christian mission we are hoping to articulate. This is not to say that former expressions of pragmatic mission have not been 'Christian' or done by Christian people; it is just a label, again, which is being used in an attempt to draw out a broader, prior concept that may overcome the issue of crisis in modern mission.

So in order to discuss what Christian mission may look like it is important, first (and at the risk of oversimplifying what has been covered), to summarise what has been determined about ontology: the paradigm out of which we understand that concept of mission to best develop. Observations that have been made will be noted in point form, here, for the sake of clarity.

Summary of Observations about an Ontological Paradigm for Mission

Through an analysis of the problem of modernity, the absence of ontology became more and more conspicuous:

1. reason was shown to be cold and empty beside the concept of a God-originating wisdom;
2. self was shown to be the newly heralded focus of Enlightenment, in the place of God; and
3. the dearth of the individual in contrast to the embrace of community was also identified.

Further indicators of the need for, and absence of an ontological backdrop were drawn out.

Linguistically, there appeared to be a simplistic approach to standard 'mission' texts and an oversight of some or more of the following ideas:

1. Peirce's argument that language is a sign, pointing ultimately to a deeper reality;
2. de Saussure's recognition that the nature of such a sign is 'arbitrary' and that meaning is generated by profound 'relationships of difference' rather than just a simple 'linguistic network of possibility';
3. his pointing, further, beyond mere written language which has (amongst other things) been 'robbed of its phonetic component';
4. Derrida, in contrast, but similar to Peirce above, pointing to the reality and location of meaning beyond the 'mere' or 'empty' symbol of the written word;
5. Ebeling's directive to look beyond any particular words to 'the word itself' and to its meaning as determined by the context;
6. Wittgenstein's observation about the 'language-game' that happens in the process of communication, whereby meaning is more than just about piecing together 'vocabulary-stock' or 'surface-grammar' but about the way in which those words are being used;
7. Gadamer's recognition that meaning is alive: that it 'encounters us ... addresses us and is concerned with us'—and his proposition of an ontological system of hermeneutics;

8. Barr's critique concerning the 'unsound method of using linguistic evidence in theological thinking'—which validates this very hermeneutical investigation—and his recognition of the importance of more than mere translation in biblical studies;

9. Ricoeur's warning about the need for 'suspicion' when one determines meaning, and the need to 'destroy the idols [of our own thinking] that we project into the sacred word.'

Hermeneutically, the need to recognise the real presence of God and to be in a living relationship with Him at every position on the hermeneutical spectrum (no matter what one's particular hermeneutical approach to Scripture may be) was illustrated.

In an attempt to unpack the essence of this ontological paradigm, the thinking of various scholars or theological positions was explored. Through Schleiermacher, first, the following was stressed:

1. the importance of the ontological: of feeling, of reality and existence and being (of authenticity, in a way: genuine personhood, not mere outward aping of a system—even a religious one);

2. that being in relation to God is of critical importance:

    (a) to just 'be' in and of one's own self leads one to a nihilistic position of absolute self (yes, people may have 'found themselves' through 'self-realisation' along the way: but it leaves them with only themselves!);

    (b) important, rather, is to find 'oneself' in and through a relationship with God (i.e. for self to be determined in relation to who God is);

3. to determine self in relation to God is a clear acknowledgement of one's absolute dependence on God for all that one needs to know in life, and to know of Him;

4. God has made it possible for us to know Him through (e.g.) revelation, redemption and inspiration;

5. our views of things Christian should, thus, derive not from our own formulations of who God may be, but from what God has revealed of Himself (through Judaism, Jesus Christ, and the testimony of the Holy Spirit);

6. thus, too, evangelism is not just about converting others to our way of thinking but rather to God, in person (i.e. our goal should be to make disciples of Jesus Christ, not of ourselves);

7. the church then, also (in Schleiermacher's view), is a body of people rightly related to God and to each other:

    (a) it is of course not just about the buildings,

    (b) but then it is also not just about the people,

    (c) it is about the faith of those people: it is about the faith and focus of the community of God's people who are in a right and living relationship with Him, and with each other (because of their focus on Him);

8. because of the priority of Being over Doing, right action will only come from the person of God Himself;

9. being in a right relationship with God will effect a diversity of equally valid activities in different people, in different situations, throughout the world.

Through postliberalism the following has been highlighted:

1. the importance of recapturing the biblical story and the world of the biblical narrative (the relevance of this for ourselves being the re-orientation of thinking from this-worldliness and 'secular' Christianity—which is such a pervasive part of our churches—to faith that is centred in the person and purposes of God);

2. the priority, then, of Scripture and the Kingdom of God;

3. the importance, too, of doctrinal teaching in recapturing this 'biblical world';

4. that, ultimately, this 'biblical world' should be captured through allowing and recognising God, made known to us in Jesus Christ, to be who He is:

    (a) not subject to any higher authority (such as, even, Scripture or doctrines themselves),

    (b) but absolute, as indicated and attested to by the 'norms' of the Christian faith;

5. we do not need 'proof' of God—because these 'norms' point to the reality of God who *is*—in and of Himself.

In all these ways, this theological programme has created the space, beyond denominational diversity and religious particularities, within which to articulate and to know just who God is—as He has made Himself known—and what it means and involves to be known by Him.

On the question of 'knowing', and how we can know truth and (for that matter) God Himself (who *is* truth), Wright's contribution has been significant. He has stressed:

1. the relational dynamic of knowledge, and Christian theology in particular;
2. how it involves a dialogue

    (a) between the knower (us),

    (b) and the thing known (God);

3. the point at issue—or the focus of our knowing—is not our reason (as we do the critiquing/searching);
4. rather, it is the subject of any knowing or enquiry on our part: God, who allows Himself to be known, and who opens Himself up to critique;
5. thus knowledge of God is never a merely cerebral venture—never independent of either us, or God;
6. further, it is about God in person and not merely about our formulations of who He is;
7. and our need is for more than any mere tradition of the faith: what is needed is a relationship with God;
8. knowledge, information and understanding of God may be conveyed through story and symbol (as has been done consistently in Judeo-Christian history) which control a subjectivity of knowing, and which point ultimately to the inner reality of who God is.

Michael Polanyi has also added invaluable support to our perception of the importance of ontology by stressing the following (in very brief overview) as regards how we know truth and God:

1. that a tacit (relational) dimension is integral to all forms of knowing;
2. that all knowing is guided by a hidden reality that exists independently of our knowledge of it;
3. that this reality is the true and living God;

4. that any right praxis—any right knowing—must, therefore, emanate from God;

5. and that for this to be effective, one needs to be in a right relationship with Him.

As noted already, this is all sounding so familiar. The reason is that we are picking up echoes of a simple orthodox viewpoint, which is why Anglo- and then Greek-orthodoxy have also been considered briefly: in order to hear a few of their contributions and insights.

Walker, firstly, representing Anglo-orthodoxy, has drawn attention to the following:

1. our Christian faith is not a private matter but something that God has revealed to all people, publically;

2. we need, therefore, to bring Christianity back into the public sphere;

3. the established church is important: united, not divided, but exclusive of non-Christian confessions;

4. Christianity is about a person: the person of God, made known in Christ, and with us by the Spirit;

5. to know Jesus of history is to know the author of history;

6. by knowing Him, His story becomes our own;

7. the 'story' is remembered through, for example:

    (a) liturgy (that 'well worn usage and practice of being in the presence of God'—or 're-enactment'—of the story [*op. cit.*]), which guards against emotionalism and distortion, experience being perceived as more valuable than doctrine, and novelty being more significant than tradition (all with a 'restless liturgy of its own' [*op. cit.*])

    (b) the eucharist (which, in Pannenberg's words 're-enacts the reality that constitutes the foundation of the church' [*op. cit.*]).

Through all this, concentration is seen to be on the personhood of God. Thus we value Zizioulas, representing another (Greek) stream of orthodoxy, for his significant perspective:

1. that personhood is about 'freedom' and not 'necessity';

2. in particular that:

(a) God has chosen to exist (which is paralleled in our own Christian experience by the choice that we ourselves have been given to be 'born again—born from above'); and that

(b) God's life is eternal not finite (which is again paralleled in our Christian experience—this time by the hope we have of a physical resurrection, 'made certain' through Christ's own resurrection, and His teaching, that He will also raise us up on the 'last day');

3. that personhood is about love—the love by which the Father willed Himself into being, and by which we ourselves are to live, in love with God, and with each other;

4. stressing the importance, in other words, of ecclesial relationships of love between:

    (a) ourselves and God, and

    (b) ourselves and other believers;

5. that personhood is also about the real presence of God: portrayed through the eucharist, on a public scale, but effected personally through the indwelling of the Holy Spirit.

Gleanings from a few other aspects of the Christian life have added to our insights (examples of this ontological reality ingrain all facets of Christianity, but these are just a few):

1. Authority, first, is:

    (a) not just textual

    (b) but relational

    (c) and sourced in

    - the Person who brought Scripture into being (who authored it in the first place), and
    - the One who was 'handed over' to us (in terms of testimony that was given to Him, and the Spirit who has been given to those who have believed in Him).

2. Sin, next, is:

    (a) not just about moralism

(b) but about a broken relationship: self-centredness, individualism, ignorance of own evil and the need for God to reveal to us just who He is

(c) (moralism being a mere symptom of a deeper reality).

3. Subjectivity, too:

(a) should not be seen as problematic

(b) to the extent to which the true and living God is not 'something' subjective but the ultimate Object of the cosmos.

These well said words (Volf 1996:50,51,52) capture the essence of the above summary:

> There is a reality that is more important than the culture to which we belong. It is God and the new world that God is creating, a world in which people from every nation and every tribe, with their cultural goods, will gather around the triune God, a world in which every tear will be wiped away and 'pain will be no more' (Revelation 21:3). Christians take a distance from their own culture because they give the ultimate allegiance to God and God's promised future . . . [This] *creates space in us to receive the other* . . . [and] *entails a judgement against evil in every culture.*

In other words, beyond culture (whether personal, ethnic cultures, or even the culture of mission or ecclesiology) is God (not just a concept but the very reality of God, whom people can 'gather around') and the kingdom of God (the 'new world that God is creating').

Only in reference to Him is 'space' created in which we can judge the evil and error that may exist in any of our own cultures, whether ethnic or, as in our own case, ecclesial—such as modernity's culture of mission.

Developing out of a relationship with God, and from the very person of God Himself, rather than out of human ideas, Christian mission may come to be regarded as 'mission' which has undergone the rebirth talked about in preamble to John's Gospel (1:12): '. . . born not of natural descent, nor of human decision or a husband's will, but born of God.'

Christian Mission

On the basis of this expansive survey of what an 'ontological' as opposed to a 'pragmatic' foundation to mission may entail, then, it is possible to start outlining (both negatively and positively) what should not, and what should and can be said about Christian mission.

Negatively:

1. 'Mission' is a non-concept outside of an active and a living relationship with God (the true and living God, as revealed in Judeo-Christian history).
2. To even say 'mission' (even more so: 'missions') is to speak a fallacious, human construct, unless we are articulating an aspect of the revealed truth concerning who God is, and who we are and what the world is or should be in relation to Him.
3. Simply establishing a 'missional' action (in terms of instituting any programme of evangelism, church work or social care—however well intentioned this may be) is not authentic 'mission' but involvement in a man-made programme of church or ecclesial and/or social development, or propagation of an ideal.
4. As such, mission is not about the 'idol' of our pre-understanding which we serve and worship and impose on the biblical text.
5. Nor is mission just a gut/guilt me-centred activity or response to any of the traditional 'Great Commission' texts which tend to motivate Christians into all sorts of 'ministries' without being balanced against a host of other texts that might suggest the appropriateness of a different course of action.

Positively:

1. What is required, then, for Christian 'mission' to be authentic, is to have first considered and to have been awed by the depth of the greatness of who the true and living God really is, and to have been drawn into a genuine relationship with Him.

2. That relationship involves having been encountered by God: addressed by Him—the reality behind the symbol of language and sign. It involves knowing God in the way He has revealed Himself to humanity, as attested to in Scripture.

3. It involves total dependence on, and response to Him who has called us into relationship and belonging in His family. It is a matter of being 'hidden with Christ in God' (Co. 3:3) and of being a living part of the church which is 'his body, the fullness of him who fills everything in every way' (Ep. 1:23) for the purpose and 'praise of his glory' (Ep. 1:14).

4. Being alive in Christ, then, mission will be shaped by who He is, rather than by our own programmes and ambitions.

5. Being right with God, Christian mission involves normal Christian life and a whole number of different but right-shaped 'doings' that will flow out of that right-'being'.

6. Christian mission is about God bringing people into a living relationship with Himself, rather than us extracting confessions from them, or bringing them into a Christian club.

These are just some of the positive and negative observations that can be made about mission as we come to try to understand it better. But in view of all that has been discussed—and on the assumption that we are able to use the term 'mission', still, without being impossibly distracted by the fixed pre-understandings of 'it' that we all will have had for so long—it is reasonable to attempt a brief definition or summary statement concerning the identity of mission: that *Christian mission is the dynamic of the people of God in a Godless world.*

Christian mission as nothing less than the Christian life—i.e. that which has been miraculously brought into being through God's undeserving work of grace in (re-)creating those who are now His children—is the catalyst of God's people living amongst those who do not confess His name, challenging them, by their own mere presence and lives in the world, with the reality and the presence of the true and living God.

As such, people of God in the fallen world will (or should) be distinctive wherever they go.

For God Himself will be the essence of those interactions. They will be about an encounter between God and those whose hearts are either for Him, or against Him.

Christian people will be a fragrance of God in the world because they are born of God and because they know God, and are known by Him: a fragrance of life for some, and for others the stench of death. The significance and gravity of this suggestion is clear from Paul's discussion in the passage referred to here (2Co. 2:12-3:18). He views these 'fragrance givers' as ministers, and asks: 'Who is equal to such a task?' Clearly none is! If a missional action and work is of God, and derives in God—who are we to be a part of it? Insignificant! And why do we—indeed, *can* we—'qualify' ourselves, or equip certain members of our churches for it? We cannot! But God can, and His 'equipping' is something that He enables in all Christian people. All people, not just some, can be used of God for His purposes, and all are effective to the extent to which they are found in Christ, and He in them, in a world that does not know Him.

Paul himself had such little regard for his own ministry or success in ministry (especially in comparison with the 'super apostles'!) outside of what God was doing in and through him, by His Spirit. And Paul's point is clear: that when we are weak, God is able to minister through us, and only by Him doing His work in and through us do 'our' ministries have any worth, strength or durability.

And so 'mission' is in no way a humanistic, but rather a profoundly theological concept or, more (because even to label it 'theological' may suggest it is sourced in our own critical thinking), a GOD-concept, because it is about the impact of God's own presence in the lives of His people, on other people in the world.

Various qualifying statements around the brief 'definition' of Christian mission offered above may be needed:

1. The *'people of God'* that we are talking about here would be people who confess the name of Christ, and who acknowledge Him, and who are in a true and living relationship with Him and the Father through Him, and who are recipient of God the Holy Spirit in their lives: re-birthed and recreated by Him and, thus, reflective of Him, in who they are.

2. The *'God'* that we have mentioned is, as articulated in Part II, the

only one, true and living God; creator of all things. He is the One from whom we have turned in, towards ourselves; the One who has sought to make Himself known to fallen man in and through the history of salvation. He is revealed fully in Jesus Christ, sufficiently and accurately attested to in Scripture, and totally present with His people in the world, through His Holy Spirit, as proclaimed by traditional church creeds.

3. Finally, *'Godless world'* is a specific reference to the world which is in rebellion against this same true and living God that we are referring to, in the way that Jesus talked of it in John's Gospel (Jn. 17:14, for example: 'I have given them your word and the world has hated them, for they are not of the world any more than I am of the world'). It is not necessarily about morally or financially destitute people (though these conditions do often follow those who are 'of the world'), but people whose focus is on self as opposed to God: those who are ignorant about God, and living apart from Him. In other words, a 'Godless world' would include all who do not confess the name of Jesus Christ as cosmic and eternal Lord—but also all that is, and who are in rebellion against Him. We are not overlooking the fact that many 'gods' are worshipped in the world, and in the minds of its people. Distracting and dangerous is any form of deism—even convincing 'forms' of Christianity and religion—other than that which directly emanates from the true and living God, presenced in the world in Jesus Christ, and Who is with all who believe in Him and confess the name of Christ, by the Holy Spirit. So the worldview that has been revealed through the whole of Judeo-Christian history—that these 'gods' are false and that there is but One, true and living God—is of critical importance.

The focus of our thinking thus far has been that any adequate theology—or even statement—of Christian 'mission' has all-too-often been eclipsed behind any number of pragmatic ventures.

In contrast, it is hoped that the straightforward 'definition' of Christian mission that has just been offered will in its simplicity serve to articulate the profound and overriding need for the real presence of God, and a grasping of Christian life which is of Him, as prior to any missiological dynamic in the world, and basic to it. Perhaps its very simplicity explains why no great theologians of 'mission' appear to exist. Historians, pragmatists, theorists of mission—yes: great men and women exist in all these fields; but not many, if any great theologians of Christian mission come to mind.

On the other hand, its profundity may equally explain the distortions, even fallacies intertwined with modern mission that have made it into a monster in many respects.

For only in knowing God, and by being remade in His image do we ourselves become authentic people; and only through a restored relationship with Him, and through being indwelt by Him can we ever reflect who He is to the world, and bear appropriate witness and testimony to Him.

Who, indeed, is equal to such a task?!

Practical Implications of an Authentic Theology of Christian Mission

Although this is the closing chapter of quite an involved, multidisciplinary study, it is clearly not the last, but just one of the first. This is not the end, but actually the beginning in many ways, because this ontological base that we have set now needs to be built on in the rest of our lives: in our homes, in our churches, out in the world as Christian people. For the implications of this simple articulation of 'mission' are profound.

Yes, Bosch's warning has been heard (*op. cit.*), that 'even the attempt to list some dimensions of mission is fraught with danger because it . . . suggests that we can define what is infinite.' If mission is of God, it is indeed an infinite thing—and to even risk defining 'mission' is to risk putting it in a box, so that it can be treated separately from the Christian life. It is also to qualify or quantify something that God did not necessarily bring about as something separate in the church: we saw throughout the bible that God 'sent', yes, but He did not establish mission(s). That is something modern man has done. And by continuing to involve ourselves in mission(s) terminology and traditions, we risk imposing this human construct as an idol onto the text, onto the living word of God, and into Christian life and culture.

Despite this we have risked—for the sake of continuity with, and respect for the broader body of the church—a definition of what we still need to call 'mission' but which we can call 'authentic mission' or 'Christian mission' (if not just 'the Christian life') from this point on.

We suggested that *Christian mission is the dynamic of the people of God in a Godless world*, which is a general enough definition to be able to hold all the proviso's and critiques that have been made up to this point. It squarely establishes 'mission' as being about God and who He is, not about us and what we do.

So to consider the practical implications of the authentic theology of Christian mission outlined here is important, though the question of how then to appropriate those implications in life is a big one. In some ways it is one that is not appropriate to address here and now in an 'academic'/theoretical sort of way. It is a devotional question: it is something that each one of us need to ask of ourselves and of the groups of Christian fellowship of which we are a part, and we need to ask it on our knees, before God. But more than that, it is something that we need to ask of the Lord: what is *He* doing? What is *He* wanting of us and our fellowships, at this time?

And yet it is still wholly appropriate to briefly explore any practical implications of an ontological approach to 'mission'.

For the sake of simplicity, these will be looked at in relation to the issue of terminology in 'mission', but also in relation to something that is arguably central to Christ's missiological purpose for all those He was leaving on earth, at His death: unity ('that all of them may be one, Father ... may they also be in us ... that they may be one as we are one ... may they be brought to complete unity to let the world know that you sent me and have loved them even as you have loved me' [Jn. 17:20–23]). It appears to be through *unity* that the world will be able to grasp that the Father has sent the Son (that 'you' have sent 'me').

'Mission' or the Christian life?

As regards 'terminology', a major implication of what has been argued concerns the question as to whether or not we should even be saying 'mission' or whether things missiological should not just be acknowledged as integral to the Christian life.

It is being proposed here that churches and theological colleges and the like should dare to not say 'mission' in order to prevent programmes and activism replacing the core of God's love and outworking God's presence in the daily routines of a 'normal' (so Burgess 2005:31) Christian life.

Yes: love for others is important (and this may involve evangelism and/or social action or both, though these in turn can all-too-easily happen without love). But true love for others is only possible because of God's first love for us, and His recreating work in us. So God Himself—and the new life that He gives us—should be our source and motivation. We need to be fuelled by an appreciation of what God has done for us, rather than driven by a passion for what we want to do for Him and for other people.

And outward-lookingness will happen: but it will be an almost imperceptible result of our devotion to God, and appreciation of who He is. It should certainly not be the whole motivation of our Christian lives (a 'passion for mission' replacing a passion for God!).

Beside God, and getting back into a right relationship with Him, and being re-created by Him, 'mission' may safely be left unsaid. Unstated! (Hence the use of inverted commas around the word 'mission' above.)

It is as we respond to the love of God working in our hearts and lives, and as we begin to live in obedience to Him, that His presence will start to be felt in the world. He alone has the ability to love the loveless, and He alone has the wisdom to deal with the complexity of situations that we find ourselves in, in life; and it is He who will affect the world, continuing to do what He clearly set out to do: communicate Himself and His love and salvific work to a fallen world.

For this reason it may arguably be more beneficial for the church to drop the term 'mission' (or 'missions') so that people are not romantically or pragmatically distracted from their worship of God and response to Him, by the worship of their own goals, instead. (Perhaps this is what Gatu had in mind, or perhaps he was speaking prophetically, when he called for a moratorium on the sending of foreign missionaries?) The church should consider shelving its narrow, specialised 'missionary' programmes and, instead of leaving it to others in foreign lands, rather encourage all its confessing Christians to themselves be dynamics of Godliness in the world that does not know Him.

If there is ever a need for 'human' agency, let the agency of the church as the people of God come into effect, rather than creating a satellite 'mission' agency to meet those needs. In this way, it would not be through humanitarian structures (for there are already plenty of these set up by secular organisations), or through sodality/modality structures

(Winter 1992:B-45–B-57) that needs would be being met, but through the church: embodying the gospel, as people of God, affected by God and living by the Holy Spirit of God.

Ultimately, then, it would be God touching the heart of the sinner and meeting need, not just arbitrary groups or people.

In this way 'Romans 10' would start to be better understood as a passage not so much about human agency ('how can they call on . . . believe in . . . hear without someone preaching to them' [10:14]) as about divine personhood and divine-human interrelationships ('"the word is near you . . . in your mouth and in your heart"' [10:8]). This interpretation would be consistent with the 'Life through the Spirit' section of Romans 8 (e.g. Paul's exhortation to 'live according to the Spirit') which is of course basic to Paul's epistle and theology, and to the gospel itself.

Our proposition has been simple: contemporary models of mission are largely read back into the biblical text. Until we learn of God, then, and until our relationship with Him is restored and nurtured, we would be better not to talk of 'mission' (because of the secular approach it so often represents) but rather to simply live as Christian people: to live authentic Christian lives instead of distracting, and possibly deceiving ourselves and others.

So terminology in mission is an issue, but it is important to explore the implications of this ontological approach to mission by looking at that which was so close to the heart of Jesus and the biblical writers: unity—not just missiologically, but ecclesiologically and in reality.

Missiological unity (in which a new depth and breadth of 'mission' is acknowledged) will be considered first, then ecclesiological unity (churches accepting each other, identifying with each other and, where relevant, working together) and finally unity in reality: ontological unity (all belonging together because of Who we belong to).

'Missiological' Unity

The distinction introduced here between 'mission' and/or the 'Christian life' may seem confusing. However, the concept posed of mission as the Christian life is something more an issue of priority and redefinition than of choice-to-be-made. Once a living relationship with God has been established (in Schleiermacher's terminology: once a right 'Being' has been entered into), a right action will result (a right 'Doing' will follow). In other words, the Christian life will always involve a dynamic response to and outworking of a living relationship with God and, in this way, will always have a 'missional' effect on the unbeliever and on the Godless world—but not simply through the agency or design of 'mission' as formerly understood.

This said, however, in some instances an outworking of one's relationship with God in the Christian life may appropriately (continue to) be effected through contemporary models of mission. In other words, having acceded to the priority of the Christian life over traditional expressions of 'mission', that life may still be appropriately outworked, and validly expressed through traditional and modern methods and agencies.

And yet space will have been created, in calling this priority, for the realisation that 'both' approaches to mission are to be of God, or not at all. Missiological praxis as an expression of the Christian life will now not just be about 'mission(s)'—but about the routines of daily life lived in a relationship with God. And 'mission(s)' activity may be recognised as a valid part of this, to the extent to which it comes out of a living relationship with God and is of Him.

The effect of recognizing even 'mission(s)' as just another aspect of the Christian ministry of Christian life, is that all who are involved in all types of 'mission' or Christian living will be pulling in the same direction, rather than competing against each other.

So, formerly diverse (even conflicting) theories of 'mission', 'mission'-programmes (or non-theories and non-programmes) and personalities involved in 'mission' or even just the Christian life should now find common ground—even if only in the common start point and motive that they share: the love of God expressed in the person of Jesus Christ. (Although this motivation for mission may already exist 'on paper', it is often not the case in practice.)

The essence of this common motivation is that each person or group of people who are involved will be attempting to serve and respond to the real person of God. Rather than working against each other, these diverse responses of faith will be complementary in that they derive from the biblical and Christ-centred, Christ-empowered worldview and life that they all share.

Forman (1957:91) expressed this well: 'All are one in hope and all will be one in time, because there is One who is above all and through all and in all who has shown us his love for all.'

Because this unity stems from a state of being, no one expression of 'mission' will be in a position to dominate, or to be raised as an example *par excellence*, for all will be authentic to the extent to which they have derived from and are appropriate to the very person of God.

If this is not so—if they cannot or do not affirm their source, meaning and theology within the paradigm of God, His working in the world and their new life in Him: if they are working in a 'missions' paradigm, rather than in a living and dynamic walk with God—any such 'mission' programme should, as shown comprehensively above, be rightly regarded as inadequate, even erroneous or fallacious.

Put differently, the success of 'mission'—or the positive effect of a Christian life—will be attributable only to God from whom any particular 'mission' (or non-'mission' but essentially 'missional') initiative will have arisen in the first place.

'Success' itself will have meaning only in relation to God, for 'numerical growth' in conversion (as shown) does not necessarily indicate success. Only God can know the inward state of a person and the relationship He may have with them, and the genuineness of an ecclesial gathering.

It also follows that productivity in 'mission' (reflected through for example high activism and the missionary enterprise) should never be a valid criteria for the assessment of the authenticity of 'mission'.

Neither should lack of productivity (or blame for such) ever be regarded negatively, as is commonly done: one competitive mission group or individual levelling criticism against another, or even Board Directors or church leaders levelling criticism at their own for inefficiency or 'lack of results' in settings of unbelief.

For the viability or effectiveness of the Christian life or 'mission' is not measurable in this way.

Perhaps the logic of a more unified understanding of mission can be shown by at least two distinctive changes in the dimensions of mission which an ontological priority makes possible. At the very least, a new breadth and depth to 'mission' is apparent.

A New Breadth to 'Mission'

Once the breadth of the being of God is acknowledged as basic to all appropriate action in the Christian life, Christian 'mission' can never again be understood simply in terms of certain particulars—either as a response to any one specific 'task'; or in the form of any one particular 'shape'; or something that is to be done by certain Christians only—but only in relation to the specific and very real presence of the living God.

No Specific Task . . .

As regards the first of these, contemporary mission has in the past been understood as the 'task' of taking the gospel into all corners of the world and converting non-believers, as discussed in Part 1.

However, 'belief' and 'Christianity' and even 'the world' are subtle terms, and it has been shown that such a definition of mission may diminish the truth and effect of the gospel, especially because of its functional approach to faith, salvation and conversion, amongst other things.

Similarly, the very grounds for an awareness of a general mission 'task' have been brought into question. For it has been suggested that a 'Great Commission' basis for 'mission' is a one-sided and narrow interpretation of Matthew 28:16–20, and that the essence of this passage is not the mandate so much as the reality and promise of the risen Lord to be ever present in the world (shown in Matthew's 'Emmanuel . . . God with us . . . to the end of the age,' which stresses ontology in contrast to functionalism).

In the same way, an authentic theology of 'mission' (in contrast to a narrow literalism and 'task'-centredness) should recognise that a specific 'task' may not necessarily or emphatically have been communicated by Christ just prior to His Ascension (or at least that this may have been a mandate given only to the 'eleven' who met Jesus on that Mount in Galilee). It should recognise, too, that this 'Commission' may have little or no perceived mandatory relevance (or any relevance, for that matter) for certain readers of the biblical text (e.g. those who hold to a reader response hermeneutic, for whom meaning does not exist unless recognised by, or actualised within the reader himself [Fish 1980:3 and Iser 1974:274–275]).

Another argument against mission as a specific task is that 'mission' as we have come to understand it is a dynamic that should just be an aspect of the lives of all believers throughout the body of the church, because of who God is, rather than because of the task we have been 'given' to do.

So Wright, for example, has been shown to talk of a 'being-in-the-world' or 'being-*for*-the-world' that is relevant for all, and not just some (1992b:133). Walker (1996:3) stresses the publicness of the Christian truth, the Christian life as integral to the Christian witness (*ibid*.:198) and public worship as integral to the missional life of the church (1992:61). Postliberalism aims to ensure the survival of the community life of the Christian religion (so Frei 1986:74) in such a way that it may 'influence the way people experience themselves and their world . . . [and so in turn] shape the entirety of life and thought' (Lindbeck 1984:33). For Zizioulas, mission involves the church 'offering herself to the world for reception' (1988b:347) and 'relat[ing] the world to God' (McPartlan 1993:289).

These dynamics should arise from little more than a commitment of faith to a reality that exists beyond oneself, rather than the pursuit of a task. The Christian life involves, or is about, not a task as such, but living in the Spirit, as children of God. This is alluded to by postliberalism's realism (as opposed to antirealism), Wright's dialogue 'between the knower and the thing known' (1992b:35), Walker's 'knowable' Jesus (1996:17) and 'free' Spirit of God (1983:106), and Zizioulas's 'Person' (1985:190) and 'living Presence' (McPartlan 1993:133).

The dynamic of God's people in a Godless world should involve the adoption of, and integration into a completely new worldview: one that is even more fundamental than Bosch's missiological paradigms, because it is prior to any definition of 'mission' as missions or related paradigm. Such a worldview exists outside of both time and culture, as illustrated by Zizioulas's recognition of the ontological freedom and being of God as the very source of human existence (1991:46, 41). Integral to such is the otherness of God, and an acknowledgement of both one's natural state of separation from that Other, as well as the means provided in Christ (as witnessed to in Judeo-Christian history) for reconciling these two mutually exclusive states of being.

Securely established in a relationship with God, Christian people should automatically become missional dynamics in a world that does not know Him. Their stress will be not fulfilling a task, nor even being a light but, rather, reflecting God's light and presence in the community.

Thus an authentic theology of 'mission' is primarily to do with the being of God and a relationship with God: God-centredness in the private and public lives of all Christian people.

Not just a mandate to go and perform a task! This would constitute a human initiative.

No Specific Shape . . .

A second aspect of a broader understanding of Christian mission is to appreciate that there may not be any one 'shape' to 'mission' as formerly held.

Practical outworkings of the Christian life, in other words, will not necessarily take the shape of formal evangelism, or social action, or cross-cultural work, or even any conscious or specific forms of praxis (although these may not, as discussed, be excluded).

Only to the extent to which one's personal identity is intrinsically sourced in God's own identity can one's life and influence ever be effective. This life, then, will impact the whole sphere of life. The power which raised Jesus from the dead is available to all of 'us who believe' (Ep. 1:19). It was effected against 'all rule and authority, power and dominion, and every title that can be given . . . in the present age' as well as in 'the age to come' (Ep. 1:21). And so the influence of the church as the body and fullness of Christ (Ep. 1:23), and the Christian life as a whole should have an equally far-reaching effect and impact.

As Walker (1984:215) put it: 'To restore the kingdom is to reclaim . . . the political, industrial and scientific infrastructures of modern societies that even mainstream Christianity has retreated from.'

In other words, this dynamic of 'mission' will exist in any and every facet of life where the dialectic between the presence and absence of God in the world is expressed by the corporate and individual lives of believers. To the extent to which sin is recognised as 'God-*lessness*' (as expressed by Schleiermacher 1989:55) or 'God-*forgetfulness*' (*ibid.*), a Christian life will be a reminder of God to those who are otherwise unaware of Him. For where 'mission' is understood in terms of the movement from being in a relationship with God outwards, to those people and places who are without God in the world, this right reality of 'mission' is profoundly different from a mere practice of 'mission(s)'.

This reinforces the above suggestions that 'mission' is not so much a task as the natural, perhaps even imperceptible consequence of a believing life.

But it is also clear that the way this will 'look' or 'appear from the outside' will vary extensively. Once the authentic essence of the Christian life is recovered, through the indwelling of God who is our life—God, who loves us, wants to know us, and who is with us eternally—different practical implications for all whose lives are recreated will come about. Practical outworkings of faith will now have originated outside of mankind, beyond mandate or tradition or text, and will vary in fundamental forms from person to person.

This is not because of individual ways of responding to an obligation but because of individual ways of responding to God, and God's own purposes being different for different people and different communities. Zizioulas (1985a:217) pointed this out, writing: 'We find it natural to speak of the community *first as a unity and then as a diversity* of ministries. But in a pneumatologically conditioned ontology the fact is that *the Holy Spirit unites only by dividing* (I Cor. 12:11).' Unity comes when, through the prompting of the Spirit, we realise and accept that He does not always lead us down the same paths in life: that He will require different things of each of us, but will also bring about ultimate unity because of the headship that is given us in Christ.

This same point was raised through Schleiermacher's realisation (1989:9) that 'a different Doing may proceed from the same Knowing in different people.' God's uniqueness will be expressed in a diversity of ways because of the uniqueness of all individual people.

Where 'mission' arises from within a purely functional paradigm, it could easily become a controlling system that stands in the place of, instead of in servitude towards the living God. It could distort or disorientate the gospel and impose incorrect obligations on Christian people.

Because of the ontological essence of Christian personhood, however, it is not possible to regard 'mission' in a purely functional, cross-cultural, trans-locational or institutionalised way. Zizioulas's work is a reminder of the freedom of uniqueness—of being truly 'me'—through a realisation that true humanness comes only through, and can exist only in relation to God's own ontological freedom (1991:45). It follows that out of these unique and dynamic *personae* of God Himself, and ourselves in a living relationship with Him, a plethora of different 'tasks' or expressions of His love in the world will emerge: a whole diversity of different things for different people, in the place of standardized 'modern mission'.

The more this is understood and outworked in the life of the church, the more we will see 'mission in crisis' coming out of its total eclipse.

No Specific Christians . . .

Exploring other implications of an ontological approach to mission, a third aspect of a broader understanding of the resultant Christian mission is that everyone is included. As an activistic and often minority expression of the church, contemporary mission has come to be regarded as something which is optional—dependent on the spirituality, characters and personal preferences of certain people only, rather than all church members. It has been viewed as something of a career.

But this should not be the case. An authentic theology of Christian mission should incorporate all Christian people, not just some. 'Mission' is not just for those who have chosen it as a career; it is not just for those who have been through Bible College, or for adults, or for the few who are unhindered by family responsibilities, ill health, physical handicap, mental or intellectual deficiency or any other such factors. All people, however young or old, healthy or unwell, articulate or not, are equally a part of 'the dynamic of the people of God in a Godless world'—in other words, the dynamic of God in a Godless world! All Christian people belong fully and equally in the church of Christ and, thus, embody Him in the world to the extent to which He is alive in them, and indwells them all. Through the breadth of the outworking of all Christian lives (as opposed to just evangelistic or 'mission' activities in only a few), a diversity and attraction will come about as all people who are in a right-standing with God become a presence and essence of God in all Godless situations. It is through God's own purity and presence that sin ('God-forgetfulness' [*op. cit.*]) is made known and salvation (or remembrance of, and submission to God) comes to be known as a thing of relevance in a world that does not acknowledge Him.

The apostle Paul put it like this (Ep. 2:8–9): 'It is by grace that you have been saved . . . not as a result of your own works, so that no one may boast. For we are God's masterpiece [not our own!] having been created in Christ Jesus to do good works previously prepared for us to walk in.' Three points may be drawn out of this passage. First, salvation is that incredible salvific, creative work that God does in each of our lives, in Christ (not what we or our churches do in the lives of those 'we' seek to save). Second, once saved, any 'works' that we ourselves might get involved in will or should be those that He has prepared for us, not ones that we have determined for ourselves. And, third, they will be works that need to be 'lived out' or 'walked in', not just done.

This is all from God, and about God; and it involves each one of us who has experienced the grace of God, living it out in a God-determined way.

John Mbiti (1986:200) once wrote in this regard: 'We must educate people away from that model of [foreign] mission, and create the picture of mission in which the whole people of God carry out mission as they live their faith in Christ . . . We should not commercialize or professionalize mission by leaving it in the hands of a few highly respected individuals.'

He recognised the need to 'conscientize the whole people of God so that everyone participates in the mission of the church' (*ibid.*:223). The church has been negligent of these crystal clear observations and propositions for too long.

From what has been argued, it should be clear that anything likely to be termed 'mission' is just an aspect of the whole of Christian Being, which is in turn sourced in Christ. It should certainly not be regarded as the task of any one particularly gifted, 'elitist' person (or people) within a church or broader denomination.

Fuller (1980:83) observed the same in describing the 'lure' of 'romantic mission', writing: 'A harmful romanticism may accompany a mission-centric view. A missionary is simply a Christian taking the message of salvation to others across cultural or sub-cultural boundaries. No special merit is won by witnessing in a foreign land. Any missionary going to another land should demonstrate his sense of responsibility and his spiritual gifts by witnessing through his own church in his own land first. Otherwise his foreign pilgrimage could be an attempt to escape the mundane in favour of what is supposed to be exotic and exciting.'

Probably because of an awareness of the same, Whitby identified a right reticence amongst churches to engage in 'recruitment among those best suited for missionary service' (in Neill 1957:203). This reticence is a right one because all Christians, in all the different spheres of life into which they are led or find themselves will, by very nature of their acknowledgement of and faith in God, be a 'missional' presence (without having ever been 'recruited' or knowingly involved in 'missionary service'!).

Carver (1979:36) put it this way: 'It cannot but be that Christians, too, bear witness when they know Jesus . . . There is no separation of the missionary impulse from a true and vital Christianity.'

One of the major reasons mission has been 'in crisis' all these years is that its primary problem has been located in the wrong place. The church's fundamental missiological problem is this: not that 70 percent of the world is non-Christian but that 30 percent of the world claims to be, but is not! Nominal Christians may say the 'right' things at times, and even try to do, or appear to be doing the 'right' things, and they may even think that they know what they believe and that they are 'sharing' their faith. But the majority of this 30 percent world-Christianity does not (arguably) know the One that it claims to believe in, in a living way—through having been born again.

Christian identity has to be grounded in the otherness of God's own identity and being. As Jesus and New Testament writers implore us, we are to live as God's children and as one of His family: born of Him, sourced in Him and abiding in Him. Those who are Christian in name only (or even in habit) are actually false statistics and (worse still) detrimental, or pseudo-witnesses to the truth of the gospel.

This is a great concern.

For all Christian people should be part of the impulse of God's presence in the world, though they can only effectively be this to the extent to which they know Him, and are known by Him.

What may appear to be an objection to this approach echoes from decades back, when Steven Neill (1959:81) observed: 'If everything is mission, nothing is mission.'

One obvious response to this objection could be to 'restrict' any hermeneutical or theological enquiry into mission that 'endangers' the existing shape and tradition of contemporary mission. So Van Engen (1996b:225) wrote: 'We must . . . be concerned with the *limits* of our missiology, so that we may prevent our missiological education from getting so broad that it becomes meaningless.'

An alternative response, though, is to understand Neill's words instructively—even prophetically—rather than negatively. His adage could be anticipating the irrelevance of 'mission' as was. Instead of protecting mission at all costs, then, we should be equipping and mobilising people for the Christian life (for the 'everything' that Neill talked about). The result of this would be not so much that 'nothing' is mission but that 'mission' is nothing (or at least a post-dated, restricting label). Authentic Christian mission would now not be about 'doing' mission in modularised forms and fashions that have become popular, so much as about living the Christian life: outworking the presence of God in the world, wherever we are.

To simply protect a tradition (in this case the tradition of mission) is not, as has been argued above, necessarily to have grasped the true identity of what it stands for, or to be protecting the authentic concept that it supposedly represents. Nor, therefore, is it necessarily instituting or perpetuating a valid tradition.

In order to address these issues of identity and authentication, our own critique of mission in this work has been focused on the foundations of traditional mission. Now, on the basis of a simple theological definition of what 'mission' is (the dynamic of the people of God in a Godless world), it has been seeking simply to unpack this and to give a framework within which it can be outworked by believing communities in the future, in multifarious and yet authentic ways. And it is clear that there is no way—building on the 'foundation' of the full Being of God and His obvious self-giving character and sacrifice of His own Son—that the scenario of 'nothing is mission' (*op. cit.*) could ever be. What is feasible, though, is that traditional 'mission' structures may be as good as negligible, if not nothing, to the extent to which they eclipse and distort what 'it' should be in the lives of all Christians.

What will follow, if everything is 'mission' and everyone is involved in it, is that the whole of Christian life will be reclaimed as authentically missional.

Bosch (1991:511) observed that mission involved the transforming of reality. However, this is only possible from the start point of the already transformed reality of the Kingdom of God (the Kingdom that does not come through 'careful observation,' but which 'is within you' [Lk. 17:20–21]).

And this involves everyone in the church.

Life in the Kingdom of God—life lived in relation to that ultimate objective being of God—is reality not just for a few select individuals, but for all Christian people. By nature of the fact that all who confess the name of Christ dwell (or should dwell) in the Kingdom of God, all should be witnesses of this alternative reality in a world that is constantly bombarded by competing worldviews. For example, in contrast to postmodernity's pastiche of media images, its spirituality of shopping mall cathedrals, developments of the technological self, cyber-reality and so on, the Kingdom of God should shine as a superior alternative reality in transforming a darkened world.

And life in the Kingdom of God should be conveyed as a dynamic of all Christian living, not just through the life of a few, zealous and thus (even in the church) marginalized Christian missionaries. Where New Testament writings endeavoured to define and redefine 'what the church was called to do in the world of their day' (Bosch *ibid.*), their concern would not have been just with an institutionalised church (which barely, if at all, existed) or an institutionalised expression of 'mission', but with the church as community of believers: everyone living out their dynamic faith in the risen Christ.

In the light of this new reality, the idols which have caused this tragic eclipse in Christian mission for so long will be dethroned: the idolatry of traditional forms of mission and the idols of missionary personnel themselves and even mission organisations. There will be hope once more for the true light of Christ to shine in those who have been reborn and who are living in Christ.

From this proposition, it will be clear that all Christian people are of integral importance and worth within this authentic 'missional' dynamic of Christianity in an unbelieving world.

A global acceptance and adoption of this perspective would radically influence how Barrett's already mentioned 'missionary statistics' are read. For instead of the perception of only one missionary for every three hundred and seventy two non-believers (a 1:372 ratio at best [based on statistics in Part 1]), there will be one Christian 'missionary' for every two non-Christian people (a 1:2 ratio) in the world.

This is a bit more realistic and makes the idea of Christian witness a whole lot more attainable and meaningful. For all Christian people do not need to up and leave their places of work, but simply befriend, care for, pray for and (hopefully) disciple at least two non-believers in those places of work or society where God has placed them. Although this is an obvious generalisation, it in essence addresses the problems of inadequate workforce (all Christians are involved), burn-out (humanly we cannot always be available to all people all the time [even Jesus avoided the crowds, and had to call priorities in His ministry, leaving people unhealed behind Him]) and superficiality (what's required is not just a brief encounter, or just taking people up to a point of confession in Christ, but being beside them in life, loving them through their ups and downs and being there for them and their families).

To this extent then, all Christian people—by very nature of what a new life in Christ involves—will be dynamically engaged in the tension between the reality of this world and that of the kingdom of God. 'Mission' is not just something functional which should be achieved in a cross-cultural setting by a very select few. It is inherently ontological, and should be an aspect of the life of all believers—all ecclesial people—as they dwell in relationship with God and live by His Spirit in a fallen world.

The Specific and Very Real Presence of the Living God

Because of this, and because 'mission' or the Christian life involves the spread of the good news about Jesus Christ in an unbelieving world, then just as God is the one who made the first move in making Himself known through the Judeo-Christian story, so He is the one through whom that gospel will continue to be spread in a darkened world.

For this was His purpose in sending His Son.

The transforming of reality discussed above does not come so much from a change of one's own personal perspectives, as from the impact of God's own being on and in the world. Christian reality derives from the relating being of God, who has come into our world as Emmanuel—God with us. And whilst all this may admittedly be expressed anthropomorphically, people will only be expressions of the love and presence of God to the extent to which God is first known to individuals and communities who are His.

Then, if certain lives, projects or programmes are not authentically sourced in the life of God, it would indeed be good for these former semblances of mission to be recognised as 'nothing' (as discussed). In other words: stop thinking about mission, and just be Christian, because all Christian living is a sensitive missiological reality in the true sense of the word and concept of mission.

Jesus' prayer recorded in John's Gospel (ch.17) stresses over and again the importance of people (whom the Father had given Him) recognising and knowing that He had come from, and had been sent by the Father. This was a recurring theme of His meditations in that chapter, and it should be the theme of ours as well: not that we are sent, or that we send ourselves or others, but that Jesus was sent by the Father, and that people should know this, for the sake of the Father's glory and for their own salvation. (For 'this is eternal life: that they may know you ... and Jesus Christ, whom you have sent' [17:3]; 'they knew with certainty that I came from you, and they believed that you sent me' [17:8]; 'you sent me into the world' [17:18].)

Jesus' stress was on the Father, and how He, Jesus, had been sent into the world by the Father for fallen Man. His desire 'that the love you had for me [Jesus] from the beginning of the world may be in them, and that I myself may be in them' (17:26).

This is the gospel: that God has presenced Himself with humanity and made it possible for us to live with Him, as His children, in love; and this is biblical mission: that Jesus, the Son—the exact representation of the being of God—has been sent into the world by the Father to make this good news known to us, and to enable it in us.

'Mission' then, as with the whole of the Christian story, is all about God, and about God making Himself known in the world.

Far be it from fallen mankind to think that he or she has the capacity to convict other sinners to turn to Christ. As Paul considers (Ro. 9:19): 'God has mercy on whom he wants to have mercy, and he hardens whom he wants to harden.' And if this is difficult for us to accept, Paul's response anticipates it, and is simple: 'Who are you, O man, to talk back to God? "Shall what is formed say to him who formed it, 'Why did you make me like this?'"'

This may still not help much, in our rationalistic age, but elsewhere we read that 'the god of this age has blinded the minds of unbelievers' (2Co. 4:4). There is a spiritual reality far larger than we are aware of, or can even comprehend, when we talk about reaching out to others with the gospel.

We flatter ourselves by thinking that 'mission' is our job, or that we have the ability to draw people to God! What is required of us, though, is to love God and to love each other. That is a much harder call than to 'go', which is why we make a new moralism (or 'spirituality') for ourselves out of 'going' and being 'sent' (it is so much easier, and more heroic in our own eyes to achieve the goals and small ambitions we set for ourselves!).

But of course even this cannot be done humanly (for 'I have the desire to do what is good, but I cannot carry it out' [Ro. 7:18]; and 'those controlled by the sinful nature cannot please God' [Ro. 8:8]). What is required of us can only be done by living according to the Spirit, and this in turn is only possible 'if the Spirit of God lives in you' (Ro. 8:9). And Paul's further warning is appropriate to the whole essence of a Christian life: 'If anyone does not have the Spirit of Christ, he does not belong to Christ' (Ro. 8:9).

To love God and to love each other is only possible because of the life He puts in us, and the ability that He creates in us.

So yes: things are required of us in our Christian lives, through the Spirit; as mentioned: to love God and each other; or to 'stand firm' in our faith; to live lives worthy of the calling we have received in Christ (Ep. 4:1); and to 'live such good lives among the unbelievers that they may not accuse us of doing wrong' (1Pe. 2:12)—'so that no-one will malign the word of God (Ti. 2:5). But these things are only possible through being 'born again' (Jn. 3:3)—being made alive again in Christ (Ro. 6:1,11; 1Co. 15:22; Ep. 2:1,5; Co. 2:13)—and dying to self forever.

The very real presence of God is core to the Christian life. But this is only possible through laying down our own selves.

Sweet 'mission': what a fine scapegoat to eclipse the real task of dying to self! How easy to talk about, hide behind and find fulfilment in labouring and even 'succeeding' in 'mission'.

The far harder task, though, is dying to 'me'!

A New Depth to 'Mission'

In considering the unification of mission efforts, we have pondered the new breadth of Christian mission that should be effected by an ontological approach to understanding it. But a new depth to mission has also been suggested.

The future of the mission agency, or society, has clearly been brought into question in all that has been thought about and suggested up to this point. The relevance of mission as a career (and of the 'career missionary') has also been seriously minimised and has even been accused of eclipsing the problem of the identity and practice of authentic mission in our age.

One way forward, or at least one logical response, would of course be to disinvest in the agency work of foreign mission and Christian services. This would, after all, free up some US$29 billion per annum which was received in 2010 for global foreign missions alone (*op. cit.*).

And yet, as noted by Bosch (1991:344) and mentioned already above, there is a natural tendency to want to appease those not prepared to 'jettison the missionary idea and ideal.' And there may still, after all, be intrinsic value in the present structures and methodology of contemporary mission. The concept and enterprises of the professional missionary may still have a positive effect, and may still accord with the concept of Christian mission as an aspect of the Christian life that is being proposed here.

But this will only be possible to the extent to which those career missionaries (and their programmes) themselves understand (and represent) the gospel in less functional terms: in terms, rather, of personhood attained in relation to the being of God, who has brought all being into existence (Zizioulas 1985a:40–41); in terms of the primary importance of their lives being a fragrance of their relationships with the living God; in terms of their lives, lived on the field, not in themselves (their 'sinful natures') but 'in the Spirit' as children of God.

So undoubtedly a deeper perception of what mission is, is required by all. And what would be involved, in seeking a deeper, not just a broader approach to mission, is that all who are currently involved in traditional forms of mission should understand and consciously work to avoid contemporary mission's romanticism and high stress on the individual self: personality, charisma, abilities and gifting, and the related limitations and/or illusory powers that become available in such positions. The work in which they engage should be in genuine accord with God's purpose for their lives—not simply their own perceptions of it—and with God's essential nature and His kingdom, and their lives lived (born again, from above) as His children.

More than this, it should in no way be regarded or portrayed as superior to the apparently mundane role of others in the church.

This, then, should result in a deeper integrity in service through a mission agency, and a deeper assurance on the part of missionaries not only that they are where God has put them, but that their message brings life and is true (not that it is just open to choice in a marketplace of religions). This would, in other words, authenticate and add depth to current mission.

The primary *raison d'être* of these 'professional missionaries' and their programmes would be—with other believers back 'home', and as part of the church—knowing God, and being in, and outworking a living relationship with Him. In this way the presence of God would be brought to others—true life and relationship, found only in the life of God who is life (revealed in Christ and with us by the Holy Spirit) would be brought into the world—and others, in turn, would be brought back from the world into the very real presence of God.

However, because of the breadth of the concept of 'mission' drawn out by the present work, cross-cultural mission or full-time Christian ministry will no longer be the only way to outwork a keen devotion to God in the world. Mission service will not be the only, or prime way of 'losing one's life' in order to subsequently 'find' it again. And foreign or cross-cultural mission will only be conducted in response to a clear perception of need, preferably in conjunction with a call by the local Christian people in a country or community—or at least with a very real sense of God's own call.

In this way there will be fewer people engaged in the 'task' of missions, and more Christians engaged in mission as an unobtrusive aspect of the church and outworking of personal faith. This will stem from a more deep-seated realisation of the importance of one's existence as a Christian in the world, and this in turn not because of one's piety and spirituality, but through an appreciation that true humanity is a God-given thing. Lindbeck (1984:62) observed that it was through the internalisation of an external, ontological reality that true humanness or the 'humanly real' existed. Through the concept of rebirth, and the example of Christ's own incarnation, comes a realisation that to be human and to live a human life is fundamentally a divine thing.

So to this end, the mission action of any 'task' oriented missionaries will be deeper, and more keen, and will hopefully meet a more specific need, because any action of theirs will be God-sourced. Their missional impetus will derive from who God is, and from the humanity that He has recreated, rather than from any of their own impulsive efforts. The success and essence of 'mission' will be expressly refocused away from numbers, conversions, and empirical evidence of achievement. And there will be less pressure on the missionary individual: less expectation of measurable success from sending churches or countries, and less of a fatalistic attitude towards missionaries when specific, empirically measurable targets are not attained. This should in turn result in a cessation of the problem of career missionary 'casualties' returning home. And the abhorrent patronisation of 'receiving' communities by 'sending' communities should become a thing of the past, because ministry will simply be a passing on of what God has done in our own lives in recreating us, and loving others with the love that we ourselves—the unlovables—have received first.

More than this though, as stated, the depth of 'mission' will be evidenced in the effect and the number of Christian people now sensitised to the impact that their saved humanity can have. Through it, their living faith and the living Lord whom they serve should have a very real, God-communicating effect on the world of darkness in which they live, work and play, and on those who have no faith.

As mentioned, the 'good works' (Ep. 2:8–9) given us to do or 'walk in' are things that *God* prepares for us to do: they are not premeditated acts on our parts, but sourced in Him. Obedience in the Christian life is about being willing to do what *He* brings across our path: loving the people *He* brings for us to love (not the ones we necessarily choose!), and doing the work that *He* gets us involved in (perhaps even against our will!) but most of all walking the life *He* gives for us to walk.

In this sense, Christian mission is something far bigger than we can control, far deeper than we can conceive of; it is something divine, something which has already involved the Father's sending of Christ into the world, and which—if there is to be any effect in our own lives—will involve a sending that God alone will determine and govern in the way that He alone chooses and which will pale any efforts of our own into insignificance.

Ecclesiological Unity

One profound result of all that has been discussed should be a refreshed dimension of unity between Christian churches and Christian people. This is because of the ultimate Being that they represent, and whose family they are all a part of: the being of God, who is 'Our Father', and who has been made known to us in Jesus Christ and who is present with us by His Holy Spirit.

If we are honest, present ecclesial reality is marked by diversity, not unity. Volf (1996) suggested that diversity in ecclesial identity is an echo of the diversity found in ethnic identity. (Perhaps this was what McGavran was trying to articulate in his homogenous unit principle.) But this does not have to be an endpoint in the reality of church life. It is certainly not what Jesus prayed for: He prayed that they may 'be one, as we are one: I in them, and you in me. May they be brought to complete unity . . . (Jn. 17:22b–23).

All-too-often, churches are so busy finding, establishing and sustaining themselves—their own identities and interrelationships—that God is left out of the picture (except perhaps in name or in doctrine). So just as a bridging of ethnic divisions is needed, ecclesial divisions should also be bridged—and this by the One who is common to them all: the living God.

Ecclesial divisions should certainly not be retained by pampering to who we are: to our own wants and preferences in 'Christian' and 'spiritual' life. By indulging these personal, ecclesial 'tastes' of ours, religion has become an almost ethnic reality for us and has become sacred in our eyes.

Volf argued effectively against this: 'Religion must be de-ethnicized so that ethnicity can be de-sacralized' (1996:49). As the apostle Peter wrote: 'the time has come for judgment to begin with the household of God' (1Pe. 4:17). If our churches, in focusing on their common Lord and Saviour, will risk pulling down the barriers that surround them like ethnicity (whether religious, as in this example, or other) or missiological prejudices (in the example and case of the broader context under discussion in this work) then those particular, prejudiced or even cultural positions will lose their segregating hold on us.

But there is only hope of this happening once the person of God is reinstated and worshipped as core to the Christian faith, in place of the various 'sacred' ethnicities of Christian expression such as our dogmas and traditions. As with ethnic conflict on a socio-political scale, there is no future for the church or its impact on the world if it is ruptured by internal conflict. Unity can only come, and therefore must be allowed to come, through the One who is common to all Christian expressions of faith as they grow towards Him: the living God Himself.

Neill (against the practical background of his life and efforts in India) highlighted the need for church unity back in the 1950s. Addressing the question: 'Where do we go from here?' (1957:200) he suggested: 'All our thinking to-day must be ecumenical.'

But ecumenism as a mere ecclesial principle should not be intended, here, because unity cannot be gained through a simple standard, code or idea (e.g. the idea that 'world-wide witness is that very thing for which the church exists' [*ibid.*:202]). No! Principles and ideas become prescriptions, and prescriptions become laws. And laws, more than anything else, most often show us what we cannot attain humanly (so Paul's argument in his epistle to the Romans). So unity cannot come through an ideal or principle. It can only come through reality, in particular the real love of the One who died for all, and the relationships that come into being as a result of who He is: the relationships of the ecclesial body through (primarily) their relationships with its head (Zizioulas 1985b:32).

Schleiermacher understood the importance of these primary relationships and expressed them in terms of the feeling of communion and undivided Being (1989:3,5,7). Volf underlined them by writing of the 'catholicity of the church' (1998:278) and suggesting that 'the universal church is not a "unity in collectivity" so much as a "unity in identity"' (*ibid.*:106). Church members 'are not the individual pieces of a larger or smaller ecclesial puzzle who must fit into the whole without themselves having to be complete or whole . . . [Rather] churches will be catholic only if each member is catholic as well' (*ibid.*:278—the idea of 'catholicity' here stemming simply from common identity gained through relationship with God).

The church is, in other words, united not through what it does (or even what it believes) so much as through the relationships by which it is comprised, and primarily through its relationship with God.

Important to note is that this was a relationship initiated by God who loved the loveless. For it is 'while we were yet sinners, [that] Christ died for the ungodly' (Ro. 5:6,8); and prior even to this, despite being 'filled with grief over the state of mankind' (Ge. 6), that God reached down into our ignorant worlds, and made Himself known to us.

God alone should be the very real essence of any ecclesial existence, and because of who He is, there is a realistic hope and reality even now of ecclesial unity.

This is illustrated in the core doctrine of sin that has been touched on several times, above. In relation to the objective essence of God, sin has been described as a state of separation from God. More, it is about wanting to take the place of God (i.e. rebellion against God). Zizioulas (1985a:102) put it this way: 'The fall results from the claim of created man to be the ultimate point of reference in existence ([i.e.] to be God) . . . [i.e.] idolatry.' However, Christ's death on the Cross adequately confronts a person with his/her rebellion against God (through the sentence of death against mankind being implemented); and that same death of Christ on the Cross enables a relationship with God to come into being. God by Himself has taken the punishment deserved by all mankind, and has opened a relationship of love, forgiveness and mercy to all who would enter into it. This is the bedrock of ecclesial life!

And so, however diverse and complex Christian spiritualities and expressions of faith are or get to be, churches have no other option (despite the extent of differences and contradictions that may exist between them) in the bigger picture, but to stand together. For true being is only possible through true communion (Zizioulas *ibid.*), and this in turn is possible only through the person and work of Jesus Christ.

In other words, relationship with God, relationships with each other, and relational priorities as determined by Kingdom values are the non-negotiables that are in focus here.

This will have far-reaching implications. So Moltmann (for example) observes: 'The great ecumenical challenge to Christian theology today is not the personhood of the people in the First World, who have become the "determining subjects" of their own lives. It is the human dignity of the people in the Third World, who have been turned into non-persons.' (1990:65). A right focusing on our divine relationship with God enables a rethinking of what human, ecclesial relationships should involve. Indeed, a right 'Christopraxis', or 'doing of God's will in which knowing Jesus as the Lord really becomes whole and entire' (*ibid.*:43), will inevitably lead 'the community of Christ to the poor, the sick, to "surplus people" and to the oppressed . . . Christ's community belongs for Christ's sake to the fellowship of "the least" of his brothers and sisters' (*ibid.*).

Clearly, then, ecclesial unity is and/or should be an integral aspect of our Christian life. If this unity is not being respected or outworked, 'mission' will almost certainly be inauthentic.

Contemporary mission is almost always denomination-based and (thus, sadly) almost separatist by definition (except of course where the likes of Stephen Neill and many others have worked for ecclesial unity). In contrast, a simple living of the Christian life would bring into effect a crossing of boundaries and ecclesial unity because its concern would not be for any one church body or organisation. Its focus would be the reality of a restored relationship with God coming into being. Informed by the Spirit, it would have a source of wisdom regarding appropriate grassroots relationships and activities across church boundaries.

In this way, it would also more effectively convey personhood and true humanity to those who do not know Him.

God-consciousness and a living relationship with God would reform and unite individuals and church communities because of the whole and the One that God is, in and of Himself, and would enable and bring into effect the common goal of being the true people of God, gathered around the person of God and responding to Him in a world that is ignorant of Him.

Ontological Unity—True Mission

So missiological unity and ecclesial unity are both direct effects that an ontological approach to Christian mission should bring about. But this is because of the ontological unity that missional efforts and ecclesial expressions both share. Already discussed in relation to those paradigms of mission and the church, ontological unity is worth considering briefly here alone, in closing, as this is the core of what has been established as fundamental to the Christian life and outworking of it in the dynamic of Christian mission.

If sin has been suggested to be the state of being separated from God and focused in on self, then salvation in a person's experience is on the one hand momentary (in the recognition of Christ as the way back to God and a commitment to a new way of life through Him) and on the other hand a process. This process will be about getting accustomed to a new worldview—a new reality. It will entail being transformed and being made new—putting off the 'old', putting on the 'new', and being found 'in Christ'—which will in turn demand a continual re-focusing on God and turning from self. Integral to this will be the sanctifying work of the Holy Spirit.

Through stress on the need for a relationship with God, and a basic living out of the Christian life as integral to the meaning of 'mission', a focus has been advocated that is otherworldly and not primarily to do with methodology or with action. Through focusing on the being of God, human effort is shown to be worthless unless genuinely rooted in an authentic relationship with Him: deriving from Him, and done in response to what He Himself has prepared for us to do.

And so, 'mission' is not about human strategies or methodologies of mission agency, society or Christian group or career or initiative: it is about God, and about His nature of love that alone can transform society and individuals as they come to be what He intended them to be. It is about God, and how God in us can and does (often even without us knowing it) affect the world that we all live in as Christian people.

Through the transformed worldview that Christians have as the people of God (people whose identity depends on the presence of God and a restored relationship with Him, and who have a focus of future fulfilment of this identity in the eschaton) the whole of Christian life should be regarded as 'mission'.

The Christian life will be 'mission' by the very nature of how it contrasts with secular life. As a result, all Christians will be direct and immediate participants in Christian mission: 'Christ's ambassadors, as though God were making his appeal through us' (2Co. 5:20a). All Christians are people of God in a Godless world and, as such, they represent the truths and revelations of the Creator of their world. They embody the timeless reality of God in a society and world which should be His, but which is fragmented by the intrusions and distortions of fallen man. Christian people will, thus, point other people to the living God through their very lives, and like Paul will 'implore [them] on Christ's behalf: Be reconciled to God' (2Co. 5:20b).

As Volf observed, it is only through a true recognition of identity that one's practical contribution to the world can become one of relevance (1996:18). This is certainly the case where 'identity' is sourced in our new beings, re-created through rebirth as children of the true and living God into His eternal family. Of course this is not an ideological, individual identity, for it is through God's historic Judeo-Christian revelation of Himself, and through an essential rebirth, transformation and outworking of a relationship with God that this inherently ontological dimension of 'identity' is realised. 'To claim the comfort of the Crucified while rejecting his way is to advocate not only cheap grace but a deceitful ideology' (*ibid.*:24).

So, the validity of our being in the world is directly proportional to the extent to which the living God dominates our worldview, and to which we 'live in' Him, and He in us. If God is the integral source of a person's corporate and individual identity and way of life, then authentic

Christian mission will happen in that person's experience, although often only imperceptibly.

Needless to say, this dynamic will not be realised through our own mental or spiritual efforts but only through an appreciation and out-working of God as source of our very being, and related behaviour and actions.

It is only through an ortho-ontics (a right-being) that an ortho-praxis (a right-doing) and, thus, an ortho-doxy (a right teaching or tradition) can emerge. A right theology and practice of Christian mission, in other words, has to start on our knees, before God—it can only come out of a living relationship with Him.

Through a realisation of this ontological foundation of reality, then, all Christians should be recognised as 'missionaries', not just potential ones. Their involvement in Christian mission will be realised to the extent to which the reality of God is foundational to their ethical, moral, physical, domestic, social, political, ecclesial and all other facets of human existence.

For 'mission' is simply an aspect of the normality of a 'born again' Christian life.

So, family life and possessions (for example) should not necessarily be 'sacrificed' to a romantic, functional form of mission as 'mission(s)', but rather made available to a living Lord. This is a far more profound and difficult exercise: in respecting the order of creation, to express one's relationship with God through the bearing of responsibilities to family and others in the community. This embodies, and should (amongst other things) therefore be recognised and taught as authentic Christian mission in the church.

Only through the reality of God being honoured and affirmed in the lives of believers can those without God ever be made aware of their inadequate one-dimensional perception of 'reality' (at least in terms of human involvement).

The implications of this proposed ontological priority at the heart of authentic Christian mission, then, will be infinitely diverse, but will be determined in little more than the lives of individual believers and their worshipping communities. For inherent in these is the wholly revolutionary and dynamic presence of the full being of God: sourcing and sustaining all Christian identity in an otherwise Godless, God-forgetting world.

In relation to the diversity, creativity and sheer otherness of the Triune God in relationship, Christian mission as quite simply the Christian life may be inconspicuous, and yet far greater than anything this world could ever dream of.

Bibliography

Ad Gentes Divinitus. *Documents of Vatican II*. In Flannery, A (ed.) 1992. *Vatican Council II: The conciliar and post conciliar documents*. Vol. 1. Ireland and Australia: Dominican Publications and E. J. Dwyer.
Almond, P 1978. Karl Barth and anthropocentric theology. *Scottish Journal of Theology*. 31,5. 435–47.
Anderson, G 1974. A moratorium on missions? *Christian Century*. January 16. http://www.religion-online.org/showarticle.asp?title=1574. Accessed 04 April 2011.
Anderson, J 2000. World Missionary Conference (Edinburgh 1910). In Moreau, A S (ed.) 2000. *Evangelical dictionary of world missions*. Grand Rapids: Baker.
Apcyzynski, J 1977. *Doers of the Word*. Missoula: Scholars Press.
Barker, E (ed.) 1993. *Of gods and men*. Georgia: Mercer University Press.
Barr, J 1961. *The semantics of biblical language*. Oxford: Oxford University Press.
Barr, J 1980. Childs' introduction to the Old Testament as Scripture. *Journal of the Study of the Old Testament*. 16. 12–23.
Barrett, D 1994. Annual statistical table of global mission: 1994. *International Bulletin of Missionary Research*.18,1 January. 24–25.
Barrett, D 1995. 'Count the worshippers!' The new science of missiometrics. *International Bulletin of Missionary Research*.19,4 October. 154–60.
Barrett, D 1997. Annual statistical table of global mission: 1997. *International Bulletin of Missionary Research*. 21,1 January. 24–25.
Bebbington, D 1989. *Evangelicalism in modern Britain*. London: Unwin Hyman.
Bellah, R et al.1985. *Habits of the heart*. Berkeley, Los Angeles and London: University of California Press.
Bergendoff, C (ed.) 1958. *Luther's works*. Vol. 40. Philadelphia: Muhlenberg Press.
Biggar, N (ed.) 1988. *Reckoning with Barth*. London and Oxford: Mowbray.
Boer, H 1961. *Pentecost and missions*. London: Lutterworth Press.
Bonhoeffer, D 1959. *Creation and Fall*. Transl. Fletcher, J. London: SCM Press.
Bosch, D 1980. *Witness to the world*. London: Marshall, Morgan & Scott.
Bosch, D 1991. *Transforming mission*. New York: Orbis Books.
Braaten, C 1985. *The apostolic imperative*. Minneapolis: Augsburg Publishing House.
Bromiley, G 1983. The Church Fathers and Holy Scripture. In Carson, D and Woodbridge, J 1983. *Scripture and truth*. Leicester: IVP. 225–43.
Brown, C 1990. *Christianity and Western thought*. Vol. 1. Leicester: Apollos/IVP.
Brown, S 1988. Reader Response: Demythologizing the text. *New Testament Studies*. 34. 232–37.
Brownson, J 1996. Speaking the truth in love: Elements of a missional hermeneutic. In Hunsberger, G and Van Gelder, C (eds.) 1996. *The church between gospel and culture*. Grand Rapids: Eerdmans. 228–59.

Brueggemann, D 1989. Brevard Childs' Canon Criticism: An example of post-critical naiveté. *Journal of the Evangelical Theological Society.* 32. 311–26.
Brueggemann, W 1993. Against the stream: Brevard Childs's biblical theology. *Theology Today.* 50. 279–84.
Burgess, M 2005. Dimensions of the faith: A shaping of evangelicalism. *Evangelical Review of Theology.* 29,1 January. 16–31.
Calvin, J 1960. *Institutes of the Christian religion.* Ed. McNeil, J. Philadelphia: The Westminster Press.
Campbell, C 1986. Response to Colin Gunton. *Theology Today.* 43,3 October. 331–333.
Camps, A 1996. My pilgrimage in mission. *International Bulletin of Missionary Research.* 20,1 January. 33–36.
Candlish, D 1958. *The biblical doctrine of sin.* Edinburgh: T&T Clark.
Carey, W 1792. *An enquiry into the obligations of Christians to use means for the conversion of the heathens.* (1942 facsimile edition of the original by London: Baptist Missionary Society). London: Ann Ireland.
Carson, D and Woodbridge, J 1983. *Scripture and truth.* Leicester: IVP
Carver, W 1979. 'The missionary idea in the bible' from *Missions in the plan of the ages.* In DuBose, F (ed.) 1979. *Classics of Christian missions.* Nashville: Broadman Press. 29–36.
Cassirer, E 1979. *The philosophy of the Enlightenment.* Transl. Koelin, F and Pettegrove, J. Princeton: Princeton University Press.
Castro, E 1973. Bangkok: The new opportunity. *International Review of Mission.* 62,246 April. 136–43.
Chaney, C 1976. *The birth of missions in America.* Pasadena: William Carey Library.
Childs, B 1964. Interpretation in faith. *Interpretation.* 18,4. 432–49.
Childs, B 1980. Response to reviewers of *Introduction to the Old Testament as Scripture.* *Journal of the Study of the Old Testament.* 16. 52–56.
Childs, B 1984. *The New Testament as canon: An introduction.* London: SCM Press.
Clements, K 1986. Bonhoeffer, Barmen and Anglo-Saxon individualism. *Journal of Theology for South Africa.* 54 March. 15–24.
Clements, K 1987. *Friedrich Schleiermacher: Pioneer of modern theology.* Suffolk: Collins.
Clendenin, D 1990. A conscious perplexity: Barth's interpretation of Schleiermacher. *Westminster Theological Journal.* 52. 281–301.
Clouse, R 2000. The Crusades. In Moreau, A S (ed.) 2000. *Evangelical dictionary of world missions.* Grand Rapids: Baker. 248–49.
Conn, H 1983. The missionary task of theology: A love/hate relationship. *Westminster Theological Journal.* 45. 1–21.
Cotterell, F P 1990. *Mission and meaninglessness.* London: SPCK.
Cotterell, F P 1997. Linguistics, meaning, semantics, and discourse analysis. In Van Gemeren, W (ed.) 1997. *New international dictionary of Old Testament theology and exegesis.* Vol. 1. Carlisle: Paternoster Press. 134–160.
Cotterell, F P and Turner, M 1989. *Linguistics and biblical interpretation.* London: SPCK.
Coupland, D 1994. *Life after God.* London: Simon and Schuster.
D'Costa, G 1996. The end of 'Theology' and 'Religious Studies'. *Theology.* XCIX,791. 338–352.
Davidson, R 1973. *Genesis 1–11.* Cambridge: Cambridge University Press.
Descartes, R 1912. *A discourse on method, etc..* Transl. Veitch, J. London: J.M. Dent and Sons.

Dodd, C 1944. *The authority of the bible*. London: Nisbet and Co.
Donnelly, J (ed.) 1972. *Logical analysis and contemporary theism*. New York: Fordham University Press.
Dostoevsky, F 1976. *The Brothers Karamazov*. Transl. Garnett, C. Rev. and ed. Matlaw, R. New York: Norton.
Dressler, W (ed.) 1987. *Current trends in text linguistics*. Berlin and New York: Walter de Gruyter.
Drury, J 1991. Christian individualism. *Theology*. 94,757 Jan/Feb. 332-337.
DuBose, F (ed.) 1979. *Classics of Christian missions*. Nashville: Broadman Press.
Dunn, J 1987. *The living Word*. London: SCM Press.
Ebeling, G 1961. *The nature of faith*. London and Glasgow: Collins.
Engle, J and Dyreness, W 2000. *Changing the mind of missions*. Downers Grove: IVP.
Escobar, S 2003. *A time for mission*. Leicester: IVP.
Etzioni, A 1995. *The spirit of community*. Hammersmith: Fontana Press.
Feuerbach, L 1957. *The essence of Christianity*. Transl. Eliot, G. New York: Harper.
Fish, S 1980. *Is there a text in this class?* London: Harvard University Press.
Flannery, A (ed.) 1992. *Vatican Council II: The conciliar and post conciliar documents*. Vol. 1. Ireland and Australia: Dominican Publications and E.J. Dwyer.
Ford, D (ed.) 1997. *The modern theologians*. Oxford: Blackwell.
Forman, C 1957. *A faith for the nations*. Philadelphia: The Westminster Press.
Fowl, S 1984. The canonical approach of Brevard Childs. *The Expository Times*. 96. 173-176.
Fowler, R 1985. Who is 'The Reader' in Reader Response Criticism? *Semeia*. 31. 5-23.
Fraser, N and Nicholson, L 1994. Social Criticism without philosophy: An encounter between feminism and postmodernism. In Seidman, S (ed.) 1994. *The postmodern turn*. Cambridge: Cambridge University Press. 242-261.
Frei, H 1974. *The eclipse of the biblical narrative*. New Haven: Yale University Press.
Frei, H 1986. The 'literal reading' of the biblical narrative in the Christian tradition: Does it stretch or will it break? In McConnell, F (ed.) 1986. *The bible and the narrative tradition*. New York and Oxford: Oxford University Press. 36-77.
Frei, H 1987. Response to 'Narrative Theology: An Evangelical Appraisal.' *Trinity Journal*. 8,1 Spring. 21-24.
Fuller Theological Seminary, 1996. *Fuller Theological Seminary Catalog for 1996-1997*. Pasadena: Fuller.
Fuller Theological Seminary, 2010a. *Mission beyond the Mission*. http://www.fuller.edu/about-fuller/mission-and-history/mission-beyond-the-mission.aspx. Accessed 25 November 2010.
Fuller Theological Seminary, 2010b. *Documents*. http://documents.fuller.edu/registrar/catalogs/Fall_2009/01_Introduction_To_Fuller/2_The_History_of_Fuller.asp. Accessed 01 December 2010
Fuller, W H 1980. *Mission-church dynamics*. Pasadena: William Carey Library.
Gadamer, H-G 1975. *Truth and method*. London: Sheed and Ward.
Gerrish, B 1987. Nature and the theater of redemption: Schleiermacher on Christian dogmatics and the creation story. *Ex Auditu*. 120-136.
Gill, J 1972. The tacit structure of religious knowing. In Donnelly, J (ed.) 1972. *Logical analysis and contemporary theism*. New York: Fordham University Press. 246-275.
Gill, J 1978. Reasons of the heart: A Polanyian reflection. *Religious Studies*. 14. 143-157.

Godfrey, W 1983. Biblical authority in the sixteenth and seventeenth centuries: A question of transition. In Carson, D and Woodbridge, J 1983. *Scripture and truth*. Leicester: IVP. 199-220.
Gonzalez, J 1985. *The story of Christianity. Vol. 2*. New York: HarperCollins.
Greeves, F 1956. *The meaning of sin*. London: The Epworth Press.
Grenz, S 1996. *A primer on postmodernism*. Grand Rapids: Eerdmans.
Gundry, R 1982. *Matthew*. Grand Rapids: Eerdmans.
Gunton, C 1980. The truth of christology. In Torrance, T F (ed.) 1980. *Belief in science and in Christian life*. Edinburgh: The Handsel Press. 91-107.
Gunton, C 1986. Barth, the Trinity and human freedom. *Theology Today*. 43,3 October. 316-330.
Gunton, C 1988. No other foundation: One Englishman's reading of *Church Dogmatics* Chapter V. In Biggar, N (ed.) 1988. *Reckoning with Barth*. London and Oxford: Mowbray. 61-79.
Hamilton, V 1990. *Genesis 1-17*. Grand Rapids: Eerdmans, 1990.
Hamm, P 1972. Creative tension in Mennonite Brethren Church-mission relations. *Direction*. 1,2. April. 47-57. http://www.directionjournal.org/article/?15#1. Accessed 25 November 2010.
Hampson, N 1968. *The Enlightenment*. Harmondsworth: Penguin.
Hare, D 1993. *Matthew*. Louisville: John Knox Press.
Harrison, E 1984. Is the Great Commission God's command? In McGavran, D 1984. *Momentous decisions in missions today*. Grand Rapids: Baker Book House. 75-83.
Hastings, A (ed.) 1991. *Modern Catholicism*. London: SPCK.
Hastings, A 1996. The diversities of mission. *Missionalia*. 24,1 April. 3-16.
Hauerwas, S 1984. *The peaceable kingdom*. London: SCM Press.
Hayes, S 2002. Southern African missiology: A missiological dialogue with Willem Saayman. *Missionalia*. 30,1 April. 109-121.
Hendrix, O 1966. Too many missions? *Evangelical Missionary Quarterly*. 2,4 Summer. 227-230.
Henry, C 1966a. Good News for a world in need. *Christianity Today*. 11,1 October 14. 34.
Henry, C 1966b. Editor's note. *Christianity Today*. 11,2 October 28. 2.
Henry, C 1996c. The Good, Glad News. *Christianity Today*. 11,2 October 28. 3.
Henry, C and Mooneyham, W (eds.) 1967. *One race one gospel one task*. Vols. 1&2. Minneapolis: World Wide Publications.
Hensley, J 1996. Are postliberals necessarily antirealists? Re-examining the metaphysics of Lindbeck's postliberal theology. In Phillips, T and Okholm, D (eds.) 1996. *The nature of confession*. Illinois: IVP. 69-80
Hill, C 1965. *The intellectual origins of the English Revolution*. Oxford: Clarendon Press.
Hirsch, E D 1967. *Validity in interpretation*. New Haven and London: Yale University Press.
Hirsch, E D 1976. *The aims of interpretation*. Chicago: University of Chicago Press.
Howell, B 2009. Mission to nowhere: Putting short-term missions into context. *International Bulletin of Missionary Research*. 34,4 October. 206-211.
Hubbard, B 1974. *The Matthean redaction of a primitive apostolic commissioning: An exegesis of Matthew 28:16-20*. Montana: SBL.
Hulme, P and Jordanova, L (eds.) 1990. *The Enlightenment and its shadows*. London and New York: Routledge.
Hunsberger, G and Van Gelder, C (eds.) 1996. *The church between gospel and culture*. Grand Rapids: Eerdmans.

Im Hof, U 1994. *The Enlightenment*. Transl. Yuill, W. Oxford: Blackwell.
Iser, W 1974. *The implied reader*. Baltimore and London: The John Hopkins University Press.
Iser, W 1978. *The act of reading*. Baltimore and London: The John Hopkins University Press.
Jameson, F 1991. *Postmodernism, or, the cultural logic of late capitalism*. London: Verso.
Jenkins, D 1969. Responsibility, freedom and the Fall. In Kemp, E (ed.) 1969. *Man fallen and free*. London: Hodder and Stoughton. 13-32.
Johnson, E 1990. *Expository hermeneutics: An introduction*. Grand Rapids: Zondervan.
Johnson, T, Barrett, D and Crossing, P 2010. Christianity 2010: A view from the new atlas of global Christianity. *International Bulletin of Missionary Research*. 34,1 January. 29-36.
Kant, I 1933. *Critique of pure reason*. Transl. Smith, N. London: Macmillan Education.
Kemp, E (ed.) 1969. *Man fallen and free*. London: Hodder and Stoughton.
Koll, K 2010. Taking wolves among lambs: Some thoughts on training for short-term mission facilitation. *International Bulletin of Missionary Research*. 34,2 April. 93-96.
Köstenberger, A and O'Brien, P 2001. *Salvation to the ends of the earth: A biblical theology of mission*. Leicester: IVP.
Lasor, W 1986. The sensus plenior of biblical interpretation. In McKim, D (ed.) 1986. *A guide to contemporary hermeneutics*. Grand Rapids: Eerdmans. 47-64.
Lausanne Covenant, 2010. http://www.lausanne.org/covenant. Accessed 21 December 2010.
Lindbeck, G 1984. *The nature of doctrine*. London: SPCK.
Liston, G 2010. Asking the big questions: A statistical analysis of three missiological journals. *International Bulletin of Missionary Research*. 34,4 October. 215-221.
Longacre, R 1983. *The grammar of discourse*. London and New York: Plenum.
Longacre, R and Levinsohn, S 1978. Field analysis of discourse. In Dressler, W. (ed.) 1987. *Current trends in text linguistics*. Berlin and New York: Walter de Gruyter.
Lukes, S 1973. *Individualism*. Oxford: Basil Blackwell.
Luther, M 1958. Infiltrating and clandestine preachers. In Bergendoff, C (ed.) 1958. *Luther's works*. Vol. 40. Philadelphia: Muhlenberg Press. 383-394.
Lyotard, J-F 1984. *The postmodern condition: A report on knowledge*. Transl. Bennington, G and Massumi, B. Manchester: Manchester University Press.
Mackintosh, H 1964. *Types of modern theology: Schleiermacher to Barth*. London: Fontana.
Madges, W 1996. Faith, knowledge and feeling: Towards an understanding of Kuhn's appraisal of Schleiermacher. *The Heythrop Journal*. 37,1 January. 47-60.
Maier, G 1977. *The end of the historical-critical method*. Transl. Leuerenz, E and Norden, R 1974. St Louis: Concordia.
Mantello, F and Rigg, A 1996. *Medieval Latin: An introduction and bibliographical guide*. Catholic University of America Press.
Marsden, G 1987. *Reforming fundamentalism*. Grand Rapids: Eerdmans.
Martin, D and Mullen, P 1984. *Strange gifts?* Oxford: Blackwell.
Massey, J 1976. Feuerbach and religious individualism. *The Journal of Religion*. 56,4 October. 366-381.
Mbiti, J 1986. *Bible and theology in African Christianity*. Nairobi: Oxford University Press.
McBrien, R 1991. The church (*Lumen Gentium*). In Hastings, A (ed.) 1991. *Modern Catholicism*. London: SPCK. 84-95.

McConnell, F (ed.) 1986. *The bible and the narrative tradition*. New York and Oxford: Oxford University Press.
McDonald, E 1996. *Alpha: New life or new lifestyle?* Cambridge: St Matthew Publications.
McGavran, D (ed.) 1972. *Crucial issues in missions tomorrow*. Chicago: Moody Press.
McGavran, D 1970. *Understanding church growth*. Grand Rapids: Eerdmans.
McGavran, D 1972a. Salvation today. *Church Growth Bulletin*. September.
McGavran, D 1972b. Crisis of identity for some missionary societies. In McGavran, D (ed.) 1972. *Crucial issues in missions tomorrow*. Chicago: Moody Press. 188-201.
McGavran, D 1984. *Momentous decisions in missions today*. Grand Rapids: Baker Book House.
McGavran, D 1986. My pilgrimage in mission. *International Bulletin of Missionary Research*. 10,2 April. 53-58.
McGinn, B, Meyendorff, J and Leclercq, J (eds.) 1985. *Christian spirituality: Origins to the twelfth century*. New York: Crossroad.
McGrath, A 1996. An evangelical evaluation of postliberalism. In Phillips, T and Okholm, D (eds.) 1996. *The nature of confession*. Illinois: IVP. 23-44.
McKim, D (ed.) 1986. *A guide to contemporary hermeneutics*. Grand Rapids: Eerdmans.
McPartlan, P 1993. *The eucharist makes the church*. Edinburgh: T&T Clark.
Meier, J 1977. Two disputed questions in Matt 28:16-20. *Journal of Biblical Literature*. 96,1. 407-424.
Miller, J 1987. *Ideology and Enlightenment*. New York: Garland Publishing.
Moltmann, J 1967. *Theology of hope*. London: SCM Press.
Moltmann, J 1974. *The crucified God*. London: SCM Press.
Moltmann, J 1977. *The church in the power of the Spirit*. London: SCM Press.
Moltmann, J 1981. *The Trinity and the Kingdom of God*. London: SCM Press.
Moltmann, J 1990. *The way of Jesus Christ*. London: SCM Press.
Moreau, A S (ed.) 2000. *Evangelical dictionary of world missions*. Grand Rapids: Baker.
Moreau, A S 2000a. Mission and missions. In Moreau, A S (ed.) 2000. *Evangelical dictionary of world missions*. Grand Rapids: Baker. 636-638.
Morris, L 1992. *The gospel according to Matthew*, Leicester: IVP.
Mouw, R 1982. Individualism and Christian faith. *Theology Today*. 38,4 January. 450-457.
Mudge, S (ed.) 1981. *Essays on biblical interpretation*. London: SPCK.
Mudge, S 1981. Paul Ricoeur on biblical interpretation. In Mudge, S (ed.) 1981. *Essays on biblical interpretation*. London: SPCK. 1-40.
Murray, I 1971. *The Puritan hope*. London: The Banner of Truth Trust.
Neill, S 1957. *The unfinished task*. London: Lutterworth Press.
Neill, S 1959. *Creative tension*. Edinburgh: T&T Clark.
Neill, S 1966. *Colonialism and Christian missions*. London: Lutterworth Press.
Newbigin, L 1979. Context and conversion. *International Review of Mission*. 68,271. 301-312.
Newbigin, L 1983. *The open secret*. Grand Rapids: Eerdmans.
Newbigin, L 1986. *Foolishness to the Greeks*. London: SPCK.
Newbigin, L 1991. *Truth to tell*. London: SPCK.
Newbigin, L 1992. *The gospel in a pluralist society*. London: SPCK.
Nicholls, B 1993. The theology of William Carey. *Evangelical Review of Theology*.17,3 July. 369-380.

Niringiye, D 1996. The nature and character of God's mission. *Evangelical Missionary Quarterly.* 32,1 January. 60–68.
Noll, M 1996. The challenges of contemporary history, the dilemmas of modern history, and missiology to the rescue. *Missiology.* 24,1 January. 47–64.
Noll, M and Bebbington, D (eds.) 1994. *Evangelicalism.* New York and Oxford: Oxford University Press.
O'Hear, A 1985. Popper and the philosophy of science. *New Scientist.* 22 August. 43–45.
O'Neil, O 1990. Enlightenment as autonomy: Kant's vindication of reason. In Hulme, P and Jordanova, L (eds.) 1990. *The Enlightenment and its shadows.* London: Routledge. 184–199
Ochs, P 1997. Judaism and Christian theology. In Ford, D (ed.) 1997. *The modern theologians.* Oxford: Blackwell. 607–625.
Ogden, S 1996. *Doing theology today.* Pennsylvania: Trinity Press International.
Outram, D 1995. *The Enlightenment.* Cambridge: Cambridge University Press.
Paché, R 1969. *The inspiration and authority of Scripture.* Chicago: Moody Press.
Pannenberg, W 1983. *Christian spirituality and sacramental community.* London: Darton, Longman and Todd.
Payne, E 1993. Carey's 'Enquiry'. *Evangelical Review of Theology.* 17,3 July. 309–315.
Peskett, H 1996. God's missionary railway according to Stott and Wagner. *Evangelical Missionary Quarterly.* 32,4 October. 480–484.
Phillips, T and Okholm, D (eds.) 1996. *The nature of confession.* Illinois: IVP.
Placher, W 1987. Paul Ricoeur and postliberal theology: A conflict of interpretations? *Modern Theology.* 4,1 October. 35–52.
Plantinga, A 1983. Reason and belief in God. In Plantinga, A and Wolterstorff, N (eds.) 1983. *Faith and rationality.* Indiana: University of Notre Dame Press. 16–93.
Plantinga, A and Wolterstorff, N (eds.) 1983. *Faith and rationality.* Indiana: University of Notre Dame Press.
Polanyi, M 1958. *Personal knowledge.* London: Routledge.
Polanyi, M 1960. *Knowing and being.* London: Routledge and Kegan Paul.
Polanyi, M 1962. *Personal knowledge.* London: Routledge and Kegan Paul.
Polanyi, M 1983. *The tacit dimension.* Gloucester, Mass.: Peter Smith.
Pomerville, P 1985. *The third force in missions.* Massachusetts: Hendrickson Publishers.
Pope, S 1991. Expressive individualism and true self-love: A Thomistic perspective. *The Journal of Religion.* 71,3 July. 384–399.
Powell, H 1934. *The fall of man.* London: SPCK.
Presler, T 2010. Mission is ministry in the dimension of difference: A definition for the twenty-first century. *International Bulletin of Missionary Research.* 34,4 October. 195–204.
Puddefoot, J 1980. Indwelling: Formal and non-formal element in faith and life. In Torrance, T F (ed.) 1980. *Belief in science and in Christian life.* Edinburgh: The Handsel Press. 28–48.
Ramsey, M 1962. *The authority of the bible.* London: Thomas Nelson and Sons.
Ratzinger, J 1990. *In the beginning . . .* Transl. Ramsey, B. Indiana: OSV Publishing Division.
Ricoeur, P 1981. *Hermeneutics and the human sciences.* Cambridge: Cambridge University Press.
Rogers, J and McKim, D 1979. *The authority and interpretation of the bible.* San Francisco: Harper & Row.

Roy, L 1997. Consciousness according to Schleiermacher. *The Journal of Religion.* 77,2 April. 217–232.
Saayman, W 1994. Christian mission in South Africa: A historical reflection. *International Review of Mission.* 83,328. 11–19.
Saayman, W 1996. A South African perspective on *Transforming Mission.* In Saayman, W and Kritzinger, K (eds.) 1996. *Mission in bold humility.* Maryknoll: Orbis Books. 40–52.
Saayman, W and Kritzinger, K (eds.) 1996. *Mission in bold humility.* Maryknoll: Orbis Books.
Sanders, J 1987. *From sacred story to sacred text.* Philadelphia: Fortress Press.
Schleiermacher, F 1966. *Brief outline on the study of theology.* Transl. Tice, T. Atlanta: John Knox Press.
Schleiermacher, F 1989. *The Christian faith.* Edinburgh: T&T Clark.
Schneider, J 1967. The authority for evangelism. In Henry, C and Mooneyham, W (eds.) 1967. *One race one gospel one task.* Vol. 2. Minneapolis: World Wide Publications. 1–10.
Schwöbel, C and Gunton, C (eds.) 1991. *Persons, divine and human.* Edinburgh: T&T Clark.
Scott, D 1985. *Everyman Revived: The common sense of Michael Polanyi.* Grand Rapids: Eerdmans.
Seidman, S (ed.) 1994. *The postmodern turn.* Cambridge: Cambridge University Press.
Senior, D and Stuhlmueller, C 1983. *The biblical foundations for mission.* London: SCM Press.
Smail, T, Walker, A and Wright, N 1993. *Charismatic renewal,* London: SPCK.
Smith, C 1993. The legacy of William Carey. *Evangelical Review of Theology.* 17,3 July. 293–308.
Stamoolis, J 2000. History of missions. In Moreau, A S (ed.) 2000. *Evangelical dictionary of world missions.* Grand Rapids: Baker. 439–446.
Stanley, B 1990. *The bible and the flag.* Leicester: Apollos.
Stanley, B 2009. *The World Missionary Conference, Edinburgh 1910.* Grand Rapids: Eerdmans.
Stuhlmacher, P 1977. *Historical-Criticism and theological interpretation of Scripture.* London: SPCK.
Sykes, S 1984. *The identity of Christianity.* London: SPCK.
Tennant, F 1903. *The sources of the doctrines of the Fall and original sin.* Cambridge: Cambridge University Press.
Thiemann, R 1985. *Revelation and theology.* Indiana: University of Notre Dame Press.
Thiselton, A 1980. *The two horizons.* Exeter: Paternoster Press.
Thiselton, A 1992. *New horizons in hermeneutics.* London: Harper Collins.
Thomas, N (ed.) 1995. *Readings in world mission.* London: SPCK.
Topping, R 1991. The anti-foundationalist challenge to evangelical apologetics. *The Evangelical Quarterly.* 63,1. 45–60.
Torrance, A 1996. *Persons in communion.* Edinburgh: T&T Clark.
Torrance, T F (ed.) 1980. *Belief in science and in Christian life.* Edinburgh: The Handsel Press.
Torrance, T F 1971. *God and rationality.* London: Oxford University Press.
Treier, D 2008. *Introducing theological interpretation of Scripture.* Grand Rapids: Baker Academic.

Tucker, R 2004. *From Jerusalem to Irian Jaya: a biographical history of Christian missions*. Grand Rapids: Zondervan.
Van den Berg, J 1956. *Constrained by Jesus' love: An enquiry into the motives of the missionary awakening in Great Britain in the period between 1698 and 1815*. Kampen: Kok.
Van Engen, C 1981. *The growth of the true church*. Amsterdam: Rodopi.
Van Engen, C 1993. The relation of bible and mission in mission theology. In Van Engen, C, Gilliland, D and Pierson, P (eds.) 1993. *The good news of the Kingdom*. Maryknoll: Orbis Books. 27–36.
Van Engen, C 1996a. *Mission on the way*. Grand Rapids: Baker Book House.
Van Engen, C 1996b. Specialization/integration in mission education. In Woodberry, J, Van Engen, C and Elliston, E (eds.) 1996. *Missiological education for the twenty-first century*. Maryknoll: Orbis Books. 208–231.
Van Engen, C, Gilliland, D and Pierson, P (eds.) 1993. *The good news of the Kingdom*. Maryknoll: Orbis Books.
Van Gemeren, W (ed.) 1997. *New international dictionary of Old Testament theology and exegesis*. Vol. 1. Carlisle: Paternoster Press.
Verkuyl, J 1978. *Contemporary missiology: An introduction*. Transl. and ed. Cooper, D. Grand Rapids: Eerdmans.
Volf, M 1996. *Exclusion and embrace*. Nashville: Abingdon Press.
Volf, M 1998. *After our likeness*. Grand Rapids: Eerdmans.
Von Rad, G 1972. *Genesis*. London: SCM Press.
Wagner, C P (ed.) 1972. *Church/mission tensions today*. Chicago: Moody Press.
Wagner, C P 1971. *Frontiers in missionary strategy*. Chicago: Moody Press.
Wagner, C P 1972. Mission and church in four worlds. In Wagner, C P (ed.) 1972. *Church/mission tensions today*. Chicago: Moody Press. 215–232.
Wagner, C P 1979. *Our kind of people*. Atlanta: John Knox Press.
Wagner, C P 1981. *Church growth and the whole gospel*. San Francisco: Harper and Row.
Wagner, C P 1989. Territorial spirits and world missions. *Evangelical Missionary Quarterly*. 25,3 July. 278–288.
Walker, A (ed.) 1988. *Different gospels*. London: Hodder and Stoughton.
Walker, A 1984. The theology of the 'Restoration' house churches. In Martin, D and Mullen, P 1984. *Strange gifts?* Oxford: Blackwell. 208–216.
Walker, A 1990. Under the Russian cross: A research note on C.S. Lewis and the Eastern Orthodox Church. In Walker, A and Patrick, J (eds.) 1990. *A Christian for all Christians*, London: Hodder and Stoughton. 63–67
Walker, A 1992. Pluralism and the privatization of religion. In Willmer, H (ed.) 1992. *20/20 visions*. London: SPCK. 46–64.
Walker, A 1993a. Pentecostal Power: The 'Charismatic Renewal Movement' and the politics of pentecostal experience. In Barker, E (ed.) 1993. *Of gods and men*. Georgia: Mercer University Press. 89–108.
Walker, A 1993b. Miracles, strange phenomena, and holiness. In Smail, T, Walker, A and Wright, N 1993. *Charismatic renewal*, London: SPCK. 123–130.
Walker, A 1996. *Telling the story*. London: SPCK.
Walker, A and Patrick, J (eds.) 1990. *A Christian for All Christians*, London: Hodder and Stoughton.
Walls, A 1996. *The missionary movement in Christian history*. Maryknoll and Edinburgh: Orbis Books and T&T Clark.

Warneck, G 1979. 'The age of pietism' from *Outline of a history of Protestant missions from the Reformation to the present time*. In DuBose, F (ed.) 1979. *Classics of Christian missions*. Nashville: Broadman Press. 74–93.
Weightman, C 1994. *Theology in a Polanyian universe*. New York: Peter Lang Publishing.
Wells, D 1992. *No place for truth, or whatever happened to evangelical theology*. Grand Rapids: Eerdmans.
Westermann, C 1987. *Genesis*. Transl. Green, D. Edinburgh: T&T Clark.
Williams, N 1927. *The ideas of the Fall and of original sin*. London: Longmans, Green and Co.
Williams, R 1989. Book review: Being as communion. *Scottish Journal of Theology*. 42. 101–105.
Willmer, H (ed.) 1992. *20/20 visions*. London: SPCK.
Wink, W 1973. *The bible in human transformation*. Philadelphia: Fortress Press.
Winter, R 1992. The two structures of God's redemptive mission. In Winter, R and Hawthorne, S (eds.) 1992. *Perspectives on the world Christian movement*. California: William Carey Library. B-45–B-57.
Winter, R and Hawthorne, S (eds.) 1992. *Perspectives on the world Christian movement*. California: William Carey Library.
Wolterstorff, N 1976. *Within the bounds of reason alone*. Grand Rapids: Eerdmans.
Woodberry, J, Van Engen, C and Elliston, E (eds.) 1996. *Missiological education for the twenty-first century*. Maryknoll: Orbis Books.
Wright, N T 1986. 'Constraints' and Jesus of history. *Scottish Journal of Theology*. 39,2 July. 189–210.
Wright, N T 1991. *The climax of the covenant*. Edinburgh: T&T Clark.
Wright, N T 1992a. Romans and the theology of Paul. *Society of Biblical Literature: 1992 Seminar Papers*. Atlanta: Scholars Press. 184–213.
Wright, N T 1992b. *The New Testament and the people of God*. London: SPCK.
Wright, N T 1992c. *Who is Jesus?* London: SPCK.
Wright, N T 1996. *Jesus and the victory of God*. London: SPCK.
Yarnold, E and Chadwick, H 1977. *Truth and authority: A commentary of the agreed statement of the Anglican-Roman Catholic International Commission, Authority in the Church, Venice 1976*. London: SPCK and The Catholic Truth Society.
Yates, T 1994. *Christian mission in the twentieth century*. Cambridge: Cambridge University Press.
Zeis, J 1990. A critique of Plantinga's theological foundationalism. *International Journal for Philosophy and Religion*. 28. 173–189.
Zizioulas, J 1985a. *Being as communion*. Crestwood: St Vladimir's Seminary Press.
Zizioulas, J 1985b. The early Christian community. In McGinn, B, Meyendorff, J and Leclercq, J (eds.) 1985. *Christian spirituality: Origins to the twelfth century*. New York: Crossroad. 23–43.
Zizioulas, J 1985c. The theological problem of 'Reception'. *One In Christ*. 21,3. 187–193.
Zizioulas, J 1988a. The mystery of the church in Orthodox tradition. *One In Christ*. 24,4. 294–303.
Zizioulas, J 1988b. The nature of the unity we seek—The response of the Orthodox observer (reply to the keynote address of the Archbishop of Canterbury to the 1988 Lambeth Conference). *One In Christ*. 24,4. 342–348.
Zizioulas, J 1991. On being a person: Towards an ontology of personhood. In Schwöbel, C and Gunton, C (eds.) 1991. *Persons, divine and human*. Edinburgh: T&T Clark. 33–46.

www.ingramcontent.com/pod-product-compliance
Lightning Source LLC
Chambersburg PA
CBHW050340230426
43663CB00010B/1932